THE
MAN'S BOOK

THE
MAN'S BOOK

Thomas Fink

WEIDENFELD
& NICOLSON

LONDON

First published in Great Britain in 2006
by Weidenfeld & Nicolson

1 3 5 7 9 10 8 6 4 2

A CIP catalogue record for this book is
available from the British Library.

ISBN-13 978 0 297 85163 9
ISBN-10 0 297 852163 2

Printed in Great Britain
by Butler and Tanner Ltd,
Frome and London

Weidenfeld & Nicolson

The Orion Publishing Group Ltd
Orion House
5 Upper Saint Martin's Lane
London, WC2H 9EA
www.orionbooks.co.uk

The Orion Publishing Group's policy is to use papers that are
natural, renewable and recyclable products and made from wood grown in
sustainable forests. The logging and manufacturing processes are expected to
conform to the environmental regulations of the country of origin.

In memoriam
Steven Thorn

CONTENTS

PREFACE

The Man's Book is the authoritative handbook for men's customs, habits and pursuits—a vade-mecum for modern-day manliness. It comprehensively examines the essential elements of a man's life and provides a guide to the year ahead. It is systematic in spirit, system being a masculine strength: it records unspoken customs, separates the essential from the incidental and simplifies what from the outset can seem complex. It is also up to date: it notes the latest trends, considers upcoming events and catalogues the rhythms of the year.

Sometimes system can be backed up by reason, and scattered throughout *The Man's Book* are some algorithms for life and mathematics for men. They are set apart from the main text and are marked '☢ *For geeks*'. The symbol ☢ is the international radiation sign; it serves as a warning that technical material follows. None of the material is essential, and some of it is for specialists, but it might help readers out of an occasional tight spot—every man is to some extent a boffin.

In the centre of *The Man's Book* is a 24-page almanack for the year 2007. Like all traditional almanacks—from the *Kalendar of Sheepehards* to *The Old Farmer's Almanac*—it contains a month-by-month diary of the heavens and the world. In it can be found the motions of the sun and moon, astronomical phenomena, weather statistics, holidays and inauspicious days, feasts, fasts and holy days, days of note, verse and practical advice.

At a time when the sexes are muddled and masculinity is marginalized, *The Man's Book* unabashedly celebrates being male. Blokes, chaps, men on the Clapham omnibus, rejoice: with *The Man's Book* you will find inspiration everywhere.

Thomas Fink
London, July 2006

THE
MAN'S BOOK

HEALTH

Here is a statistical portrait of the modern-day John Bull, the typical male today. Unless otherwise indicated, he is aged 16 or over.

PHYSICAL ATTRIBUTES

Height	5 ft 9.5 in	Body mass index[1]	25.3
Weight	174 lb	Left-handed	11%
Chest	42 in	Cholesterol[2]	6.2 mmol/l
Waist	37 in	Life expectancy at birth	77 yr
Hips	40.5 in	Healthy life expectancy	67 yr
Shoe size	9	Lose hair	66%
Underweight	4%	Circumcised[3]	6%
Overweight (not obese)	47%	Have a lower left testicle[4]	62%
Obese	21%	Women per 1000 men	1048

HABITS AND BELIEFS

Smoke cigarettes	26%	Number of shirts (with buttons)	16
Hand-roll their own	8%	Number of neckties	14
Smoke cigars[5]	5%	Pass their driving test	46%
Smoke a pipe	2%	Hold a car-driving licence	82%
Age at first marriage	31	Median hourly pay	£11.04
Age at any marriage	35	Wear Y-fronts	44%
Cost of engagement ring	£1,289	Have a religion	83%
Exercise per week (hr:min)[6]	1:47	Admit to racial prejudice	39%
Reading per week[6]	2:03	Weekly ethanol intake[7]	181 ml
TV, video and radio[6]	15:54	Work over 40 hours a week[8]	65%
Married, cohabiting	53%	Wear a wedding ring (married)	46%
Never married, not cohabiting	27%	Have a 1st class degree	10%

(1) Body mass index (BMI) is weight in kilograms divided by height in metres squared; 20–25 is normal. (2) 45–64-year-olds. Under 5.2 is desirable, 5.2–6.2 is borderline high risk; mmol/l = millimoles per litre. (3) 16–44-year-olds. See p. 10. (4) 27% have a lower right testicle; the rest are indistinguishable. See p. 11. (5) At least one cigar a month. (6) Full-time workers. (7) Recommended = 210 ml or 7.4 pints of beer. See p. 19. (8) Amongst fathers.

PROPORTION OF MAN

Leonardo da Vinci's well-known Vitruvian Man is based on the ancient ideal proportions of man written down by Vitruvius. According to the Roman architect and the text accompanying da Vinci's drawing, the proportions of ideal man satisfy the following criteria:

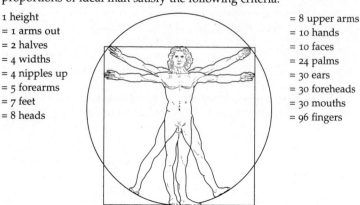

1 height	= 8 upper arms
= 1 arms out	= 10 hands
= 2 halves	= 10 faces
= 4 widths	= 24 palms
= 4 nipples up	= 30 ears
= 5 forearms	= 30 foreheads
= 7 feet	= 30 mouths
= 8 heads	= 96 fingers

where *half* = beginning of genitals to top of head; *width* = width at shoulders; *nipples up* = nipples to top of head; *forearm* = elbow to tip of hand; *head* = bottom of chin to top of head; *upper arm* = elbow to armpit; *hand* = length of hand; *face* = bottom of chin to hairline; *palm* = width of palm; *ear* = length of ear; *forehead* = eyebrows to hairline; *mouth* = bottom of chin to nose; *finger* = width of finger.

The Swiss architect and designer Le Corbusier (Charles-Edouard Jeanneret) developed the Modulor, 'a measure based on mathematics and the human scale: it is constituted of a double series of numbers, the red series and the blue'. The blue series is twice the red, and any two consecutive lengths in the same series differ by a factor of the Golden ratio (see opposite), making the series infinitely extendable.

	4	3	2	1	0	-1	-2	-3	-4	-5
Red series (in)	188	116	72.0	44.5	27.5	17.0	10.5	6.5	4.0	2.5
Blue series (in)	377	233	144	89.0	55.0	34.0	21.0	13.0	8.0	5.0

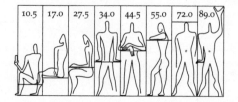

STAGES OF MAN

Man's life is sometimes broken into stages by analogy with the 12 months of the year. A medieval example, in which each month symbolizes six years, is given in the upper right-hand pages of the Almanack (pp. 73–100). If the periods are to correlate with the physical and mental stages of man, the early periods must be shorter than the later ones. One purely abstract method breaks life into periods according to the Fibonacci numbers, 1, 2, 3, 5, 8, 13, 21, 34, 55, 89, ..., where $1 + 2 = 3$, $2 + 3 = 5$, $3 + 5 = 8$, and so on. Each period corresponds to a different stage in man's life. (The stages of a woman's life, by contrast, are given by the related sequence of Lucas numbers, 1, 3, 4, 7, 11, 18, 29, 47, 76, ...) It has been suggested that one's sense of time speeds up with age such that each period seems to be of similar duration.

I	0–1	infancy		VI	8–13	adolescence
II	1–2			VII	13–21	youth
III	2–3			VIII	21–34	second youth
IV	3–5			IX	34–55	maturity
V	5–8	boyhood		X	55–89	old age

❧ *For geeks* The Fibonacci numbers above are defined by

$$F_n = F_{n-1} + F_{n-2}, \text{ where } F_1 = 1 \text{ and } F_2 = 2.$$

The Lucas numbers are similarly defined: $L_n = L_{n-1} + L_{n-2}$, but with $L_1 = 1$ and $L_2 = 3$. The ratio F_n / F_{n-1} approaches the Golden ratio $\phi = 1.61803\ldots$:

$$\tfrac{3}{2} = 1.5, \quad \tfrac{5}{3} = 1.667, \quad \tfrac{8}{5} = 1.6, \quad \tfrac{13}{8} = 1.625, \text{ and so on.}$$

The Golden ratio ϕ itself has many special properties. Its inverse is itself minus one ($1/\phi = \phi - 1$) and its square is itself plus one ($\phi^2 = \phi + 1$). From these properties its exact value can be deduced:

$$\phi = (\sqrt{5} + 1)/2 = 0.5 \times 5^{0.5} + 0.5.$$

Geometrically, it is represented by the rectangle with ratio of width to height equal to ϕ. If one removes a square from the rectangle, the resulting rectangle is again in the proportion of the Golden ratio. The series of powers $\phi^2, \phi^3, \phi^4, \phi^5, \phi^6, \ldots$ can be written

$$\phi + 1, \quad 2\phi + 1, \quad 3\phi + 2, \quad 5\phi + 3, \quad 8\phi + 5, \ldots,$$

in which the Fibonacci numbers can be observed. Furthermore,

$$\phi = \sqrt{1 + \sqrt{1 + \sqrt{1 + \ldots}}} \quad \text{and} \quad \phi = 1 + \cfrac{1}{1 + \cfrac{1}{1 + \cfrac{1}{1 + \ldots}}}.$$

BEARDS

Though not widely seen today, one of the most striking visual differences between the sexes is man's natural display of facial hair. The beard 'is the badge of a man', wrote St Clement of Alexandria. 'Whatever smoothness or softness there was in him God took from him when he fashioned the delicate Eve from his side...'

On average, facial hair grows as long as it is wide every three hours. It grows about 0.4 inches a month, or a third of a millimetre a day. A more natural unit for beard length can be borrowed from typography: the point, where 72.3 points = 1 inch (see p. 135). Beards grow 1 point (pt) per day. Different lengths of facial hair have different names.

Name	Days	Length (pt)	Notes
shadow	<1	<1	Change of shade; whiskers not noticeable.
umbra	1–2	1–2	Worn with impunity: 'I've been *very* busy.'
stubble	3–4	3–4	Ambiguous: 'Did he forget to shave?'
designer stubble	5–8	5–8	Stubble with intent; no longer negligence.
bristle	9–16	9–16	Most awkward stage of growing a beard.
beard	17+	17+	Will continue to grow at five inches a year.

There are two myths about beards which should be dispelled. The first is that the speed of growth diminishes with the length of hair. This is not possible, since the hair follicle cannot tell how long the hair has been cut: there is no communication along the hair shaft, which is dead. But the follicle does know how old the hair is, and after a fixed period the hair is expelled and a new hair emerges, which is why hair does not grow beyond a set length. The second myth is that shaved hair grows back thicker. This is only partly true, in that the first growth of a hair is the finest part, with further growth of normal thickness. Cutting off the tip makes the new end thicker, but cutting it again has no effect.

Trimming a beard not only reduces its length but also makes it thicker: the surface of an untrimmed beard is sparse, because not all hairs grow at the same rate. The hair below the neckline should always be shaved, even in the case of full beards. The only facial hair allowed in the British armed forces is the moustache, except in the Royal Navy, which permits a 'full set', that is, a moustache and beard combined. At one point, the Catholic Church allowed priests to have facial hair only on the condition that they did not trim it, this being a sign of vanity. The fashion for facial topiary during the 1990s now seems rather studied, and today the the most accepted form of facial hair is a full set not longer than 3/4 inch = 54 points = 54 days.

INSTRUCTIONS FOR SHAVING

The average man will shave his beard approximately 15,000 times in his lifetime, spending a total of 80 full days. So it is worth considering how this essential ritual is best executed. Shaving comprises three steps: (1) pre-shave; (2) shave; and (3) post-shave.

1 The most important ingredient for shaving with a razor is water. Not only should the face be wet, but the skin and whiskers should also have absorbed water. If you can't shave right after a shower, rinse your face generously with hot water a couple of minutes before shaving. Then, using a brush or your hand, lather cream onto face for at least 15 seconds.

2 Using a sharp razor, apply short strokes along the grain of growth. Don't press down—a light contact will do if the blade is sharp. Begin with the least dense areas and finish with the densest: the sides, then cheeks, neck, upper lip, lower lip and chin. Whilst shaving against the grain may cause later irritation, the best barbers finish by shaving across the grain.

3 Rinse your face with cold water to remove cream and close pores. Press small cuts with wet paper, then dry paper, or apply an alum block. A skin cream at this stage would not go amiss (though no eyebrow plucking). If using a brush, rinse it in warm water, shake out excess and stand to dry.

SHAVING BRUSHES

Shaving razors have advanced so much during the last century that nearly all standard cartridge razors are superior to the traditional double-edged safety and straight razors. What is often neglected, however, is the choice and application of shaving lubricant. The best lubricants are not available as a foam or gel, but rather as a cream or hard soap which must be whisked into a foam with the aid of a shaving brush. Cream comes in a tub, and the brush is dipped into it and whisked into a foam directly on the face; soap must be whisked partly in the pot. For those who have sensitive skin, it is wise to mix an equal part of skin lotion directly into the cream before lathering.

The best shaving brushes are made from badger hair. Badger hair is flexible, stores heat and retains water. But not all badger bristles are equal; the softest, finest-tipped hairs are found around the badger's neck, and only in winter. A brush made of these makes anything lather.

Name	*Source*	*Colour*	*Texture*	*Animal rights activist response*
Boar	various	white or dark	coarse	tepid
Dark badger	underbelly	nearly black	coarse	threatening stares
Pure badger	tail	grey	medium	hate mail
Best badger	back	light-dark-light	fine	prick car tyres
Super badger	neck	silver-tipped	very fine	tar & feather owner

INTRODUCTION

Given that two-thirds of men will suffer from hair loss at some point in their lives, it is puzzling to find the subject so full of misinformation, pseudoscience and charlatanism. In part this is explained by a limited understanding of what causes—and prevents—the spontaneous thinning of hair. The rest is due to opportunistic marketing of alternative and quack medicines to gullible and often desperate men. Differentiating fact from fiction and finding reliable, transparent information on the subject remains difficult.

Healthy hair on the scalp has a two-stage life cycle: a growth period of two to six years, during which hair grows about 0.3 mm per day, followed by a dormant period of two to four months. After this the hair falls out, and a new hair emerges from the same hair follicle. (Hair on other parts of the body has a shorter life cycle and therefore does not grow as long.) Different hairs are in different phases in this cycle, so that on any given day only about 50–150 hairs fall out, which is less than 0.1% of the total number of hairs on the scalp.

The dominant form of hair loss in men is called androgenetic alopecia, or male pattern baldness. It generally follows a fixed pattern of progression: the corners of the hairline recede first, giving rise to an 'M'-shaped hairline. This is followed by a thinning of the hairline generally and also the crown (the top of the head). Eventually the exposed areas of the hairline and crown join, leaving hair at the back and sides only, which itself may continue to thin. This is the course to total baldness; in most men hair loss will tail off at some intermediate point.

Hair loss is not caused by the sudden loss of hair but rather increasingly diminished growth of individual hairs over time. In the early stages, the number of hairs remains constant, and what appears as hair loss is in fact a reduction in the thickness and rate of growth of new hairs. Each generation of new hair grows back finer, shorter, often lighter-coloured than before. As the condition progresses, hair appears wispy, then like peach fuzz, and eventually cannot be seen at all.

There are several commonly believed myths about hair loss. One is that the incidence of hair loss in a man is solely determined by the maternal grandfather. Although it is heritable, there is at present no way to accurately predict who will lose his hair or when he will lose it. A recent study has found that men whose fathers exhibit hair loss are 2–2.5 times as likely to suffer from hair loss as those whose fathers have a full head of hair. Another myth is that wearing hats, caps or bandannas promotes hair loss, for which there is no support. It is often claimed that stress or significant mental exercise can initiate or hasten hair loss, but the evidence for this is scant.

TREATMENTS

All hair-loss drugs are more successful at preventing the decay of healthy hair follicles than reviving dormant follicles which produce fine, wispy hair. So the earlier hair loss is treated, the greater is the amount of hair that is likely to be maintained. Right now, baldness is more preventable than reversible.

The primary contributing factor in male pattern baldness is believed to be the androgenic hormone dihydrotestosterone (DHT). Increased levels of DHT are known to inhibit hair growth, although how this occurs remains poorly understood. Higher testosterone levels are not in themselves correlated with increased likelihood of hair loss.

In what might appear to be a stroke of fortune for drug companies, hair-loss treatments do not cure hair loss once and for all; rather the medicine has to be taken indefinitely. If the treatment is terminated, the rate of hair loss will return to its pre-treatment levels. Bear in mind, however, that the state of the art in treating baldness is changing rapidly, and today's maintenance will likely prove to be a stop-gap until the arrival of superior, possibly permanent treatments.

Finasteride, marketed as Propecia, is, along with Minoxidil, the only US Food and Drug Administration-approved hair-loss drug. This does not imply that other treatments are not effective; gaining FDA approval is expensive and requires additionally that a drug's side effects are understood and minimal. Propecia is currently accepted as the most effective treatment for hair loss, with 30–75% of users reporting constant or increased hair levels. It works by inhibiting the production of DHT, and is administered in the form of a pill taken daily.

Minoxidil, marketed as Regaine in the UK and Rogaine in the US, has been shown to slow or stop hair loss in 25–40% of patients. It was originally developed as a high-blood-pressure treatment, with increased hair growth an unintended side effect. Despite its commercial success, how it combats hair loss is not well understood. It is applied as a cream directly to the afflicted area, usually once or twice a day. Despite Homer Simpson's immediate results with Dimoxinil (Simpson and Delilah, episode 7F02), both Propecia and Regaine require three to six months' use before clear results appear.

As with most aspects of men's appearance, an air of indifference is essential to wearing thin hair. At some point, manipulating thinning hair to hide the head must come to an end. Yul Brynner shaved his head completely and made baldness chic. Zinedine Zidane knew when to make the cut, as did Andre Agassi, both of whom keep their hair close-cropped. John Malkovich and Sean Connery kept their hair mid-length but never wore a comb-over.

JOHN THOMAS

Circumcision The ancient Egyptians practised circumcision, and the Book of Jeremiah (9:26) adds the Jews, Edomites, Ammonites and Moabites. The Ancient Greeks thought circumcision unbecoming, and associated it with satyrs, the promiscuous man-goat race that wandered the forest. While the early Christian Church frowned upon the practice, by medieval times it was prohibited: '[The Holy Roman Church] strictly orders all who glory in the name of Christian, not to practise circumcision either before or after baptism, since... it cannot possibly be observed without loss of eternal salvation,' declared Pope Eugenius IV in his 1442 papal bull. The curious popularity of circumcision in the English-speaking world largely originated in the late 19th century in the United States, where by the turn of the century the removal of the foreskin was associated with all sorts of remedial and preventive medicine. Although circumcision is now believed to confer no significant medical benefits, the majority of males are circumcised for non-religious reasons in the United States, the Philippines and South Korea. Circumcision rates amongst newborns are:

Australia 12%	Canada 11%	England 6%	USA 65%

Dressing is the persistent self-positioning of a man's jewels to the same side of his trousers. A man is said to 'dress to the left' or 'dress to the right' if he predominantly falls to the left or right trouser leg. The best time to tell which side you're on is while sitting down. When making a suit (p. 61), some tailors assemble the crotch of the trousers asymmetrically to account for this bias. There are a number of theories to account for dressing, none of which have been substantiated: the direction of dress corresponds with left-/right-handedness; it is the side of the lower testicle (see *High ball*, opposite); it is a by-product of wearing trousers twisted at the waist.

Shoe size A number of features are said to predict the size of a man's privy parts, including: height, length of nose, distance between thumb and finger at 90° and shoe size (p. 55). A recently published study casts doubt on the last and most persistent of these theories, namely, that the size of the foot and penis correlate. (J. Shah & N. Christopher, *British Journal of Urology International*, **90**, 586 (2002).) The two urologists conclude: 'The median stretched penile length for the sampled population was 13 cm and the median UK shoe size was 9 (European 43). There was no statistically significant correlation between shoe size and stretched penile length.'

ON THE BALL

Zoe: How's the nuts?
Bloom: Off side. Curiously they are on the right. Heavier I suppose. One in a million my tailor, Mesias, says.

James Joyce, Ulysses

High ball (For the cylindrical drinking vessel *highball*, see ❦ Glasses, p. 20.) The Ancient Greeks were well aware that a man's testicles were not symmetrical, but that one—usually the left—descended lower than the other. This anatomical subtlety is borne out in their sculpture. Of 187 statues considered by the psychologist I. C. Mc-Manus, 51% show the left testicle to be lower and 22% the right, the remainder being of equal descent ('Right-left and the scrotum in Greek sculpture', *Laterality*, **9**, 189 (2004)). This correlates with modern-day observations. Chang et al. (*Journal of Anatomy*, **94**, 543 (1960)) found the left testicle to be lower in 62% of subjects and the right in 27%, the rest being indistinguishable. The reason for this bias to the left is not known, but Bloom's explanation above can be dismissed. It is widely accepted that, surprisingly, the right testicle tends to be both heavier and larger.

Blue balls Although sometimes dismissed as an old wives'—or rather husbands'—tale, blue balls is well recognized, if not fully under-stood or documented. It is a painful ache in the scrotum, caused by prolonged, significant sexual arousal, and affects many adolescent and mature men, though infrequently. While the pathophysiology is not understood, J. M. Chalett and L. T. Nerenberg conjecture that, in tandem with persistent pelvic venous dilation, 'testicular venous drainage is slowed, pressure builds and causes pain' ('"Blue Balls"', *Pediatrics*, **106**, 843 (2000)). The discomfort ceases on release or sub-sides on its own after one or two hours. Circumstantial evidence suggests that the name may derive from a blue tint in the scrotum caused by reduced circulation, de-oxygenated blood being darker than oxygenated.

Varicocele Generally painless and harmless, a varicocele is the enlarge-ment of the blood vessels that drain blood from one of the testicles. As with varicose veins frequently found in women, a varicocele is caused by the malfunction of the one-way valves in the vessels. When the valves can no longer counteract the force of gravity, blood pools in the lower veins. The condition affects approximately 15% of men, the large majority of cases involving the left testicle, and feels like a soft testicular lump. There are usually no symptoms, although the varicocele may seem to disappear whilst lying down when the blood drains away from it.

There is an unstated code of behaviour in men's public loos which, while more instinctive than prescriptive, is surprisingly universal.

No pairing Unlike women, men visit the lavatory entirely for practical reasons, and it is suspect to immediately follow a friend to the loo.

No talking Terse conversation in the loo can take place before and after, but not during, use of the urinals.

No looking Eyes should be aimed straight ahead or down in concentration; glances towards your neighbour are very suggestive.

No touching Hands should be in front of you. A bump of the elbows can be deflated by a sober apology, but without turning the head.

URINAL OCCUPATION RULES

When faced with an array of urinals to choose from, which one should you take? The basic idea is that the distance between users should be maximized, at the same minimizing a newcomer's chance of getting too close. The latter makes the endmost urinals highly desirable. Never go between two men if it can be avoided. Below are sample situations for seven urinals, where ○ means vacant and ♦ occupied, and the best strategy for each. (In order to write the exact solution below, we assume any man following you chooses a vacant urinal at random.)

1 2 3 4 5 6 7	*Optimal strategy*
○ ○ ○ ○ ○ ○ ○	1 and 7 are correct, and every man knows this.
♦ ○ ○ ○ ○ ○ ○	7 is correct, but 6 is often picked to avoid showing paranoia.
♦ ○ ○ ○ ○ ○ ♦	Urinal 4 maximizes the distance from others.
♦ ○ ○ ♦ ○ ♦ ○	7 promises at most 1 neighbour in the case of a newcomer.
♦ ○ ♦ ♦ ○ ○ ♦	Only 6 is free of second-nearest neighbours.
♦ ○ ♦ ♦ ○ ♦ ♦	An unpleasant scenario, but 2 is the lesser of two evils.
♦ ○ ○ ○ ○ ♦ ○	3 and 4 may seem identical, but 3 will on average be further from a newcomer ($E(3) = 0.650$, $E(4) = 0.656$ below).

❧ *For geeks* Let N be the total number of urinals, labelled from left to right by $k = 1, 2, \ldots, N$, of which $q + 1$ are vacant. Assume on average one new man approaches a random vacant urinal (without applying any strategy) during the typical period of occupation. As he may come in at any point after you, the average intersection of his and your occupation time is $1/2$. Further assume the interaction between men is repulsive with an inverse square law. Then the optimal unoccupied urinal k is the one which minimizes $E(k)$ below, which is composed of a weak repulsive uniform charge (first term) and a stronger repulsive charge at occupied sites (second term):

$$E(k) = \frac{1}{2q} \sum_{i=1, i \neq k}^{N} \frac{1}{(k-i)^2} + \frac{2q-1}{2q} \sum_{i \text{ occupied}} \frac{1}{(k-i)^2}.$$

Sleep is one of the great neutralizers of life's injustices. Not because it provides a respite from life itself, but rather because it acts as a buffer period during which the unfortunate or the ambitious can gain an edge on others by *not* sleeping. There is, of course, a limit to how far sleep can be reduced without negative physiological effects. For most people, this cut-off is around five hours. A study of men who received four hours a night found signs of diminished ability to process carbohydrates after 16 nights. Severe sleep deprivation is likely to cause death. Experiments on rats have shown that total deprivation for several weeks results in an inability to regulate body temperature, even if sleep is reintroduced. Death from septic shock quickly follows.

Staying awake for extended periods of time, usually for prolonged industry, is usually achieved by (i) an increase of motivation or (ii) the use of stimulants. Sleep-deprived individuals asked to perform mental activity showed remarkable improvement if the incentive to perform well was increased sufficiently. The offer of a cash reward in proportion to achievement led subjects to perform as if they had been fully rested. This suggests that lack of sleep does not so much diminish our ability to concentrate, but rather raises our incentive threshold.

By far the most common stimulant is caffeine, found in the seeds and leaves of a number of trees and shrubs. The typical caffeine contents of various substances are shown below. The amount of caffeine in tea and coffee, the most common sources of the drug, depends significantly on leaf and bean variety, production and preparation. Note that the usual serving size varies from the 250 ml or 40 g used below.

Average daily UK intake (mg caff.)	280	*Lethal dose for 50% (mg caff.)*	10,000
Caffeine tablets	*mg caff./pill*	*Coffee & tea*	*mg caff./250 ml*
Vivarin	200	Coffee, brewed (typical)	140
Stay Alert gum	100	Coffee, instant (typical)	100
No Doz	100	Tea, black (typical)	85
Pro Plus	50	Tea, fruit (Pickwick)	80
Soft drinks	*mg caff./250 ml*	Tea, green (typical)	60
Red Bull	82.5	Coffee, decaffeinated (typical)	5
Jolt Cola	50.0	*Chocolate*	*mg caff./40 g*
Mountain Dew	39.1	Unsweetened choc. (typical)	35
Diet Coke	32.8	Hershey's Special Dark	29.2
Dr Pepper	29.6	Semi-sweet chocolate (typical)	25
Pepsi-Cola	26.4	Milk chocolate (typical)	10
Diet Pepsi-Cola	25.4	Hershey's Bar	9.4
Coca-Cola	24.0	Kit Kat	5.7

The most effective method of lifting weights—and by this is meant high-resistance anaerobic exercise for size and strength—is to use free weights instead of machines whenever possible. Of course, some exercises are difficult or impossible to perform without machines—leg curls, for instance. But free weights or the body's own weight should be used for most exercises. Part of the reason is that machines invariably lock the motion into a fixed path, negating the subconscious effort put into symmetry and balance. This means that the auxiliary muscles that keep the motion from wandering off course are neglected. The result is a body without tie-ins between muscle groups and left-right symmetry. As a practical advantage, free weights are universal in the sense that they can be done identically in any gym.

Weight training is usually organized as follows:

Session	Visit to the gym	2–6 times per week
Exercise	Focus on specific muscles, see opposite	6–12 per session
Set	Period of continuous exertion	3–5 per exercise
Rep	Repetition of the same movement	7–12 per set

Sessions may always incorporate the same exercises, or cycle through different major muscle groups: legs and abdominals one session, arms and shoulders the next, for example.

Standard Olympic bars have a solid 1-inch-diameter central segment and 2-inch-diameter ends for loading similarly sized metal plates. The bar itself weighs 20 kg. Plates are available in the various weights below. This binary system has the advantage that all resistance levels, from 20 to 97.5 kg in 2.5 kg intervals, can be symmetrically loaded with only two plates of each size. Despite being 44.1 lb, 20 kg plates are usually taken to be 45 lb for the purposes of reckoning. As a rule of thumb, a fit man should be able to bench-press his own weight.

Plate sizes (kg)	1.25	2.5	5	10	20
(lb)	2.75	5.51	11.0	22.0	44.1

❦ *For geeks* The single-repetition maximum is the highest weight one can push, pull or lift. It can be calculated for any exercise from one's performance at a lower weight as follows. Let r be the maximum number of repetitions that can be done at some weight w and

$$C(r) = -0.00186r^2 + 0.0561r + 0.957.$$

Then $C(r) \times w$ is one's true single-repetition maximum. For example, if one can bench press 135 lb just 8 times, then, from the table below, one's maximum for a single repetition is 1.287×135 lb = 173.7 lb.

Reps r	2	3	4	5	6	7	8	9	10
$C(r)$	1.062	1.109	1.152	1.191	1.227	1.259	1.287	1.311	1.332

EXERCISES BY PRINCIPAL MUSCLE WORKED

Below are the 30 most classic lifting exercises. A moderate routine might be 3–4 sets per exercise, 8 exercises per session and 3 sessions per week; for intensive training, 10 exercises per session and 6 sessions per week. The 10 most essential exercises are marked * .

Biceps
  * Standing barbell curls   A bent barbell works best. Keep the elbows fixed.
    Seated dumbbell curls   Rest elbow in hand, one arm at a time.
    Dumbbell curl on incline bench   Keep upper arms vertical with the floor.
    Chin-ups   With palms facing in and a close grip (see p. 16).
Triceps
  * Tricep extensions   Use bent grip from overhead cable. Keep elbows fixed.
    French press   Lock elbows straight above, lower barbell to neck.
    Parallel bar dips   Isolates the triceps with body's own weight (see p. 16).
Forearms
  * Wrist curls   With forearms flat on bench lift barbell with palms-up grip.
    Reverse wrist curls   Like wrist curls but with palms-down grip.
Chest
  * Bench press   Wider grip for pectorals, closer grip for triceps.
    Incline press   Works upper pecs for armour-plated look.
    Bent-arm flyes   Lying on bench, lift dumbbells from sides to above chest.
    Machine flyes   Start with arms just over 180° apart. Good for definition.
Shoulders
  * Military press   Aka shoulder press. In front of or behind neck.
    Dumbbell lateral raises   While standing, raise dumbbells to horizontal.
    Upright rows   While standing, lift barbell with close grip to chest.
    Bent-over cable laterals   With arms crossed, use two floor-level pulleys.
Calves
    Standing calf raises   Keep knees locked. Beware of back strains.
  * Seated calf raises   Use heavy loads. Do not rock back and forth.
    Calf-extensions on leg press   Put balls of feet on lower edge of foot plate.
Thighs
    Leg press   Contract until legs are 70° or 80° at the knee.
  * Squats   Foundation exercise for working the quadriceps.
  * Leg curls   Isolates the back of the thighs.
    Leg extensions   Focuses on the front of the thigh and above the knee.
Abdominals
  * Sit-ups   Performed on a decline adds considerable resistance.
    Crunches   Either lying on your back or with a vertical bench.
    Bent-knee leg raises   Lying on back, lift and contract legs.
Back (including lats)
  * Wide-grip chins   With palms facing out. Also try behind neck.
    Bent-over rows   With back parallel to floor lift barbell to waist.
    Seated rows   Done with cable and T-bar with close grip.

James Bond (p. 144), often away from home for days at a time, exercised in his room in the mornings to rouse himself from self-pity or (more often) a hangover. A typical routine, described in Ian Fleming's *From Russia with Love*, includes '20 slow press-ups, enough straight-leg lifts to make his stomach muscles scream, 20 toe touches and finally arm and chest exercises combined with deep breathing until he is dizzy'. With a couple of sturdy chairs and a bar or broomstick one can do considerably more.

Press-ups The most versatile weights-free exercise of all. With the hands directly under the shoulders, the triceps are emphasized; a wider placement works the pectoral muscles. The difficulty can be increased by raising the feet off the ground, e.g., on the front of a chair or, higher still, the back of a chair. As the body approaches vertical (a handstand), this exercise approaches a military press with the body's own weight—not easy. Try to reach sets of 50.

Pull-ups One of the most natural and effective of all exercises, and the most difficult of those without weights. There are two kinds: hands facing in (also known as chin-ups), with a closer grip, and hands facing out, with a wider grip. Hands-in mainly works the biceps, then lats, and also expands the chest. Hands-out works the lats, then biceps. If you can do three sets of 12 in five minutes, rejoice.

Chair dips Excellent for isolating the triceps. Put two chairs back-to-back, just further apart than the width of your shoulders. Standing between them, put your hands on the chair backs and, raising your legs, rest your entire weight on the chairs. Lower yourself as much as possible, then extend the arms. This exercise will be difficult at first but should advance quickly. Aim for sets of 20.

Reverse bench (rows) Good for the back, similar in its effect to seated rows. Put two chairs back-to-back, four feet apart, and place a bar or broomstick across the backs of both. Lie on your back with your chest under the bar and grip it overhand, pulling yourself slowly to the top. The resistance can be increased by putting your feet on a chair. The back should not touch the floor between repetitions.

Triceps extensions Another focus on the triceps, but also the back and lats. Put two chairs front-to-front, three or four feet apart. Place your heels on the seat of one and your hands, behind your back, on the corners of the other. Lower yourself as far as you can and then fully extend the arms. Work towards sets of 30; if these become easy, put a couple of heavy books on your lap.

Bent-knee sit-ups Still one of the best exercises for the upper abdominals. Keep knees bent and fix your feet under, say, a sofa. If you can do 50 in one go, hold a couple of books against your chest.

DRINKING & SMOKING

George Best I spent ninety per cent of my money on women, drink and fast cars. The rest I wasted.

Ernest Hemingway An intelligent man is sometimes forced to be drunk to spend time with his friends.

Benjamin Franklin Beer is proof that God loves us and wants us to be happy.

Anonymous Thus dost thou every taste and genius hit, / In smoke thou'rt wisdom; and in snuff thou'rt wit.

Bob Dole We know smoking tobacco is not good for kids, but a lot of other things aren't good. Drinking's not good. Some would say milk's not good.

Homer Simpson I like my beer cold... my TV loud... and my homosexuals flaming.

Winston Churchill My rule of life prescribed as an absolutely sacred rite smoking cigars and also the drinking of alcohol before, after and if need be during all meals and in the intervals between them.

Arnold Schwarzenegger I have inhaled, exhaled everything.

The Massachusetts Spy The cordial drop, the morning dram, I sing, / The mid-day toddy, and the evening sling.

Richard Braunstein The hard part about being a bartender is figuring out who is drunk and who is just stupid.

Anonymous You don't have to be a beer drinker to play darts, but it helps.

George Gissing A pipe for the hour of work; a cigarette for the hour of conception; a cigar for the hour of vacuity.

Christopher Howse Real ale fans are just like train-spotters, only drunk.

Samuel Johnson A man who exposes himself when he is intoxicated, has not the art of getting drunk.

Jack Handy If you ever reach total enlightenment while drinking beer, I bet it makes beer shoot out your nose.

Joseph Cullman [head of Philip Morris] Some women would prefer having smaller babies.

Abraham Lincoln I believe, if we take habitual drunkards as a class, their heads and their hearts will bear an advantageous comparison with those of any other class. There seems ever to have been a proneness in the brilliant and warm-blooded to fall into this vice.

Pablo Picasso Drink to me. [last words]

MEASURING DRINKS

Measures for drinks have a complex history, and even today different conventions exist in different places: English and American definitions are almost all different. The most common measure for mixed drinks is the shot (see ❧ Glasses, p. 20), about which there is much misinformation. Despite the recent preponderance of 40ml, below is the historically more correct (and more generous) definition of 1 1/2 oz, which is 42.6 ml in the UK. This matters little when cocktails recipes are given in relative (so many parts of this and that), rather than absolute, terms, as is the case in this book (see ❧ Cocktails, p. 35).

	UK definition		*US definition*	
	fl. oz (UK)	*ml*	*fl. oz (US)*	*ml*
dash	1/48	0.592	1/48	0.616
teaspoon (tsp)	1/8	3.55	1/6	4.93
tablespoon (tbsp)	1/2	14.2	1/2	14.8
fluid ounce or pony	1	28.413	1	29.574
shot, jigger or bar glass	3/2	42.6	3/2	44.4
gill	5	142	4	118
cup	10	284	8	237
can of Coke	11.6	330	11.2	330
pint	20	568	16	473
bottle of spirits	24.6	700	23.7	700
bottle of wine	26.4	750	25.4	750

Wine is sometimes sold in larger or smaller volumes than the usual 750 ml bottle. Champagne normally undergoes secondary fermentation in standard bottles and magnums, which are decanted into the different bottles below. An exception is Drappier Champagne, where the final bottle is used throughout the process. They are one of the few producers to sell most of the sizes below—all but the Rehoboam.

Bottles	*Litres*	*Champagne*	*Bordeaux*	*Port*
1/4	0.188	Split	–	–
1/2	0.375	Half-bottle	Fillette	–
1	0.75	Bottle	Bottle	Bottle
2	1.5	Magnum	Magnum	Magnum
3	2.25	–	Marie-Jeanne (approx.)	Tappit Hen
4	3	Jeroboam	Double Magnum	Jeroboam
6	4.5	Rehoboam	Jeroboam	–
8	6	Methuselah	Imperial	–
12	9	Salmanazar	–	–
16	12	Balthazar	–	–
20	15	Nebuchadnezzar	–	–
24	18	Solomon (or Melchior)	–	–
36	27	Primat	–	–

PROOF

The association of the word 'proof' with alcoholic strength derives from an ingenious test of whether or not a spirit is stronger than a certain threshold, namely, 57.15% alcohol by volume. This is the concentration of spirit above which a gunpowder paste made with it will still ignite, thus proving its potency. Today three methods are used to quantify the alcoholic strength of a solution. *Alcohol by volume*, or ABV, is the number of millilitres of ethanol per 100 millilitres of solution. *Proof* is twice this number times a hundred, and *British proof* is approximately 7/8 times the proof, though this is rarely used now. Thus a bottle of whisky at 40% ABV is 80 proof or 70 British proof. The strongest spirit which can be produced using conventional distillation is 95%, available in America under the name Everclear.

Typical drinks servings are listed below. Interestingly, a pint of English beer contains only slightly less alcohol than a shot of absinthe (p. 29). A unit of alcohol, intended to allow comparison of ABV between drinks, is defined differently (and somewhat arbitrarily) in different countries. In Britain a unit is 10.0 ml ethanol, and the recommended weekly intake of alcohol for men is 21 units, or 210 ml ethanol, equivalent to 2.3 bottles of wine or 7.4 pints of beer.

Measure	ABV	Proof	Drinks/ bottle	Vol/ drink(ml)	Ethanol/ drink(ml)
pint of US beer	4%	8	—	473	18.9
pint of UK beer	5%	10	—	568	28.4
glass of wine	12%	24	6	125	15.0
glass of port or sherry	20%	40	10	75	15.0
shot of spirits	40%	80	16.4	42.6	17.0
shot of cask whisky	60%	120	16.4	42.6	25.6
shot of absinthe	70%	140	16.4	42.6	29.8
shot of Everclear	95%	190	16.4	42.6	40.5

ALCOHOLIC COMMUTATION RHYMES

Liquor before beer, in the clear;
Beer before liquor, never sicker.

Whisky before beer, never fear;
Beer before whisky, kind of risky.

Beer before wine, you're fine;
Wine before beer, or dear.

Gin while you sin, always win.

Rum before you run, never fun.

While some of these maxims are at odds, it is widely accepted that grain followed by grape is preferable to the alternative, and that champagne should not follow anything. For a clear head the next day, neat grain spirit, such as whisky (p. 30), throughout the evening is ideal.

Different drinks require different glasses, not only by tradition but also because of variations in serving size, serving temperature and volatility. All glasses should be made of clear glass or crystal. Crystal is cut lead glass, that is, glass with 12–30% lead oxide by weight, which gives the glass a higher refractive index and causes it to sparkle. The different kinds of glasses, shown opposite, are not numerous. They can be divided into (i) stemless glasses; (ii) stemmed glasses for wine; and (iii) stemmed glasses for spirits, liqueurs and their derivatives.

Stemless glasses are cylindrical or have a slightly inverted conical shape, with flat bottoms. The largest is the *pint glass*, which is mostly used for serving beer on draught. It is standardized to hold a pint of beer (568 ml), plus room for the head. In the UK underfilling a pint glass is heavily frowned upon—selling pints 10% short can lead to prosecution. The *pilsner* is used to serve many bottled beers, and has a circular foot attached to the base for added stability. The *beer mug* is thick-walled and sturdy and comes in various sizes. The *highball* and *collins* are used for water, juice and long cocktails, the only difference being that a highball has parallel sides and a collins sloping sides. The *old-fashioned* is stockier and sturdier with a heavy glass base; it is used for neat spirits and short cocktails. Smallest of all is the *shot glass*, in which neat spirits and shooters are served without ice.

There are are many varieties of wine glass, but only a few are necessary to drink any given wine at its best. The spherical *red wine glass* in various sizes is the most familiar, and is sometimes used as a general-purpose vessel for other types of wine. The *white wine glass* is cylindrical near the top; because it is intended to keep the wine cold, large examples are rarely seen. The *champagne flute*, designed to stay cold and minimize carbonation loss, has a small circumference at the top, unlike the largely obsolete champagne bowl with its shallow sides. The *sherry glass* is used for the fortified wines sherry and port which, being stronger, require smaller vessels. Finally, the *tasting glass* is medium-sized and has a small opening to concentrate a wine's aromas.

Of the stemmed glasses used for spirits, liqueurs and cocktails, the *brandy snifter* is the largest, though it is never filled anywhere near capacity. Its contents are warmed by the hand on which the bowl rests. The familiar V-shaped glass is known as a *martini* or *cocktail* glass. It is used for short cocktails served without ice (with ice, use an old-fashioned glass). Liqueurs are served in a *cordial*, a small stemmed vessel similar in volume to a shot glass. A *hurricane* is a curvaceous glass used to serve cocktails made with copious crushed ice. Finally, a *toddy* is for hot drinks, such as Irish coffee. It is in the shape of a mug attached to a stem and base, designed to keep the drink warm.

Pint glass   Pilsner   Beer mug   Highball

Collins   Old-fashioned   Shot glass   Red wine glass

White wine glass   Champagne flute   Sherry glass   Tasting glass

Brandy snifter   Martini or cocktail glass   Cordial   Hurricane   Toddy

Beer is the alcoholic beverage made from fermented grain. Drinks fermented from other sources have other names: fermented honey is called mead; apple juice, cider; grape juice, wine; and pear juice, perry. The ingredients of beer are generally limited to water, malted barley, hops and yeast. Barley is a grain, like wheat, and it is malted by allowing it to germinate (sprout). This releases enzymes which convert its starches to sugars. Hops are the seed vessels of a vine-like plant which impart flavour and bitterness. Yeast causes fermentation—the conversion of sugar to alcohol—of which carbonation is a natural by-product.

Beer can be classified by the kind of yeast used in fermentation. Wild, naturally occurring yeast is used to make *lambics*. Much more often the yeast is cultivated, and if it is top-fermenting the beer is called *ale*; if bottom-fermenting, *lager*.

LAMBICS

Lambics are neither top- nor bottom-fermented, but instead rely on wild yeast native to the area they are brewed in, usually around Brussels. This is one of the oldest styles of brewing, and lambics have a complex, yeasty, tart, dry taste. Examples include Lindemans Cuvée René, Cantillon Gueuze-Lambic and Gueuze Girardin. *Fruit beers* are made from lambics by the addition of fruit, the sugars of which lead to a refermentation. *Kriek* (Kriek Girardin, St Louis Kriek) and *Framboise* are made by adding cherries and raspberries, respectively.

LAGERS

Bottom-fermentation is a more recent innovation than top, and consequently the styles of lager are not as broad. Tell-tale signs of lager are a translucent colour and a clean, crisp taste.

Pilsners Often referred to simply as lagers, these have a light-gold colour and pronounced hop flavour. Ideally, Pilsners should be 5% alcohol by volume, or just under. Examples include Bitburger, Budweiser Budvar and Pilsner Urquell.

Pale lagers (Budweiser, Carlsberg, Heineken) have minimal malt or hop character and are light-gold to straw-coloured. Sometimes called session beers, their chief advantage is that they can be drunk in large volumes without significant taste or intoxication.

Bocks These (Amstel Herfstbock, Paulaner Salvator) are a strong, dark variety of lager with minimal hop character which originated in the German town of Einbeck. Their robust character makes them popular from autumn to early spring. Varieties include the more powerful still *Doppelbock* and *Eisbock*, the latter being strengthened by freezing and removing the ice (water freezes before alcohol).

ALES

Ale, which is top-fermented, is a much older style of beer than lager, with complex roasted and fruity flavours. There is an enormous range of varieties, some of which evade easy classification.

Anglo-American ales Bitter (Fuller's London Pride, Brains SA, Young's Bitter) refers to a lightly carbonated, pale-ale-style beer, usually served on draft, and accounts for a large fraction of the ale sold in Britain. *Old Ale* (Theakston Old Peculier, Adnams Broadside) is stronger with a malty taste and is often sweet. *India pale ale* (IPA) was originally made for export to India, with a strong presence of hops as a preservative for the long voyage. Examples include Brains IPA and Burton Bridge Empire Pale Ale. *Barley wine* (Bass No. 1, Young's Old Nick) usually refers to a brewer's most potent ale, typically 8% or higher. Slightly weaker versions often go by the name of *Winter Warmer* (Fuller's 1845, Young's Winter Warmer).

Porter and stout are made from dark-roasted malt or barley and are dark-brown to black. The lighter-bodied of the two is *porter* (Burton Bridge Porter, Whitbread Porter), which has had a revival after a period of decline. *Stout*, which is more complex and filling, can be further divided into *dry stouts* (Guinness, Murphy's, Beamish) and *sweet stouts* (Young's Oatmeal Stout, Farson's Lacto Milk-Stout).

Belgian-style ales Sometimes called Belgian specialty beers, this is a diverse category of top-fermenting beers produced in and around Belgium. They tend to have distinctive flavours and include many of the most highly esteemed beers in the world. Some of the better known breweries are Leffe, Delirium Tremens, Rodenbach and Duvel. *Abbey ales* are made by breweries associated with a monastery or imitative of that style (L'Abbaye des Rocs, Karmeliet). *Trappist ales* are brewed within the walls of a Trappist monastery under the complete control of the resident monks and are internationally renowned. At present seven abbeys are allowed to carry the 'Authentic Trappist Product' logo: Achelse Kluis, Chimay, De Koningshoeven (La Trappe), Orval, Rochefort, Westmalle and Westvleteren. *Dubbels* are double-fermented and are strong (over 6.5%) and dark with a malty, fruity taste. Stronger yet are *Tripels*, which tend to be pale with a substantial hoppy character.

Wheat beers Beer made from wheat in addition to barley is called wheat beer or white beer (Hoegaarden, Celis White). They are fair and opaque and are often flavoured with orange peel or coriander. One of the most refreshing styles of beer, they are popular in warm weather, sometimes with a slice of lemon.

GRAPE VARIETIES

The simplest classification of wines is by the variety of grapes used to produce them. Some are made from a single grape, others are blended from two or more varieties. Traditionally, six dominant grapes, called noble grapes, were used to make the best wines in the world: the white grapes Sauvignon Blanc, Riesling and Chardonnay; and the black Pinot Noir, Cabernet Sauvignon and Merlot. Today the list of top grapes is longer, owing especially to innovative winemaking in the New World.

Cabernet Sauvignon One of the most widely-planted grapes, it is the basis of red bordeaux, where it is blended with Cabernet Franc and Merlot, and much California red.

Cabernet Franc Mostly grown in France, where it is blended to make red bordeaux.

Chardonnay This is the basis of the burgundy white wines Chablis, Côte d'Or and Mâcon. It is blended with Pinot Noir and Pinot Meunier to make champagne. When made from Chardonnay alone, champagne is called *blancs de blancs*.

Gamay Notable only as the grape of the light red wine Beaujolais.

Gewürztraminer Wine made from this grape has a distinct spicy, aromatic taste which makes it suitable for stronger foods. It is largely grown in cooler climates.

Merlot The basis of the red wines Pomerol and St-Emilion.

Muscat Possibly the oldest variety of all, from which all others have descended. The grapes can be black or white, and are used to make a wide array of wines, all of which exhibit a common distinct taste.

Pinot Noir This is the basis of red burgundy and, when blended, champagne. Outside of France the grape is grown extensively but with less consistent results.

Riesling The premier grape of Germany, and the chief grape used for fine wine production in that country.

Sauvignon Blanc With Sémillon, used to make Graves and Sauternes.

Sémillon Rarely used to make wine on its own, it is mostly blended with Sauvignon Blanc to make Sauternes and other dessert wines and dry wines of varying quality.

Syrah Also known as Shiraz in Australia and South Africa. Used to make the Rhône wines Côte Rôtie and Hermitage, and also blended with other grapes because of its strong, smoky taste.

Tempranillo Used to make Rioja and other Spanish reds, it is the premier red grape of Spain but is little grown outside that country.

Zinfandel Largely produced in California, where it is used to make reds and pale rosé.

WINE CUSTOMS

Opening a bottle This is one of the most satisfying of all drinking rituals. The best corkscrew is the simplest: a metal spiral attached to a perpendicular wooden handle. This offers no leverage but depends solely on strength. The usual technique is to place the bottle between the legs, just above the knees, and hold the neck with the one hand while pulling the corkscrew with the other. If your shoulders are not up to strength, a regime of upright rows (p. 15) will help. In the absence of a corkscrew, pushing the cork *in* with a blunt tool works surprisingly well. Depress it slowly to avoid spraying wine when it gives way. Pouring the first glass is awkward because the cork gets in the way, but subsequent glasses are easy.

Opening a champagne bottle The pressure in champagne and sparkling wine bottles increases with temperature and agitation, so very cold bottles handled carefully release their corks with the least force. First, remove the foil to expose the wire cage. While this is untwisted, keep the thumb over the cork to prevent its spontaneous expulsion. The trick to removing the cork quietly is to hold it with the one hand, with the thumb on top of it, while with the other slowly turning the bottle. Alternatively, there are occasions when it is desirable to project the cork as far as possible, across a room or away from a picnic. The method here is to keep the bottle still and gently massage the cork with the thumb and forefinger wrapped around its base. In both cases keep a glass nearby for any overflow.

Pouring wine An ordinary-sized wine glass should be filled to two-thirds full and refilled when below one-third full. When serving sparkling wine, the glass should be tilted (unless it is already on the table) so as to minimize the loss of gas.

Order of wines The *Larousse Encyclopedia of Wine* gives the following conventions: 'white wine before red, young before old, light before heavy, dry before sweet, minor before fine or rare. White wines accompany the first courses in a meal, red ones the main or later courses.' Exceptions are champagne and white dessert wines, which are sometimes served with pudding. Sherry makes a fine pre-prandial drink, enhanced as it is by smoking. If multiple wines are on offer at dessert, they rotate clockwise in the order of their fineness: port first, followed by claret or other red wine, then dessert wine.

Decanters are sometimes used as attractive replacement vessels for bottled wine and are essential for wines that throw a deposit, such as vintage ports and many old reds. Decanters for wine are round and uncut so that the wine can be seen. Port decanters are round and sometimes cut. Decanters for spirits are generally square and cut.

Spirits are the result of the distillation of wine or other fermented (alcohol-containing) liquids. They can be divided into families according to the source of the mash which is fermented: grape, fruit, grain or sugar. Some spirits, such as vodka, are so highly distilled that the choice of mash has little effect on the end product. Most spirits are bottled at 40–50% alcohol by volume (ABV), which is 80–100 proof. It is difficult to give more specific indications of strengths because they vary from producer to producer.

Spirits distilled from fermented grape juice are called brandy. Other fermented fruit juices, once distilled, are called fruit brandies; hence apples yield apple brandy, pears pear brandy, and so on. The more popular brandies have specific appellations: Cognac and Armagnac are the best known. Grappa and marc are distilled from fermented grape pomace, the solid remains of grapes pressed in the wine-making process. Like all high-proof liquors, brandy, once bottled, ceases to develop.

A broad spectrum of spirits are made from fruits and succulent plants, of which apple and agave are the most popular. Applejack is the traditional American name for apple brandy distilled from cider, potent if not always palatable. In England this is called cider brandy. Calvados, a more refined drink, is made directly from fermented apple or apple and pear juice and aged in oak casks before bottling. Tequila and mezcal are both made from the fermented juice of the agave family of succulents, tequila from the blue agave and mezcal from the maguey plant. Despite their similar origin, the two spirits have different methods of production and markedly different tastes. It is mezcal, not tequila, which sometimes comes with a worm in the bottle, the 'worm' in fact being a moth larva.

The most widely drunk spirits are distilled from grains, such as barley, corn and rye. The purest of these is vodka, which can in principle be made from anything containing starch or sugar. In practice grain or potatoes are most often used. Gin, by which is meant London dry gin, is simply neutral grain spirit flavoured chiefly with juniper and redistilled. Sloe gin is not a spirit but a liqueur, made by infusing sloe berries, a small wild plum, in gin and sugar. Aquavit, sometimes called schnapps, is made like gin: neutral grain spirit is infused with caraway seeds and other spices and redistilled. It is traditionally drunk neat and cold. Malt whisky is made exclusively from barley, yeast and water (see p. 30). The mash used in bourbon must include 51% corn; the mash in rye whiskey, 51% rye.

Of the spirits made from sugar, rum is the best known. It is made from sugar cane or, more often, molasses: the dark, viscous fluid that remains after sugar is crystallized out of sugar cane juice. Whether rum is light or dark depends on how long it is aged in the barrel and how much caramel is added. Cachaça is also made from sugar cane but has a flavour distinct from rum. It is the best-selling spirit in Brazil and is the basis of the caipirinha cocktail.

Spirit	Source	Origin
Grape spirits		
Armagnac	white grapes	Gascony, France
Brandy	grapes	France
Cognac	white grapes	south-west France
Grappa	grape pomace	Italy
Marc	grape pomace	France
Metaxa	grapes	Greece
Pisco	Muscat and other grapes	Peru, Chile
Fruit spirits		
Applejack	cider	New England
Arrack	coconut sap	South-East Asia
Calvados	apples (or apples & pears)	Normandy, France
Cider brandy	cider	England
Kirsch	cherries	Alsace, Germany, Switzerland
Kislav	watermelons	Russia
Mezcal	maguey plant	Mexico
Mirabelle	yellow plums	Lorraine, Alsace, France
Palinka	plums, apples, apricots	Austria, Hungary, Romania
Quetsch	purple plums	Central Europe
Raki	grapes, figs, plums	Turkey
Slivovitz	plums	Balkan countries
Tequila	blue agave	Mexico
Grain spirits		
Aquavit	grain, potatoes (with caraway seeds)	Scandinavia
Bourbon	corn	southern United States
Gin	grain (with juniper)	Netherlands
Jenever	rye, wheat, malted barley	Flanders
Malt whisky	barley	Scotland
Poteen	grain or potatoes	Ireland
Rye whiskey	rye	United States
Schnapps	grain, fruit	Austria, Germany
Shochu	rice, grain, potatoes	Japan
Vodka	grain, potatoes	Russia, Poland
Sugar spirits		
Batavia arrack	sugar cane	Indonesia
Cachaça	sugar cane	Brazil
Rum	molasses	Caribbean

A liqueur is a spirit flavoured with fruit, herbs or spices—collectively called botanicals—to which sugar is added. This final distinction is important: modern gin, which is grain spirit flavoured with juniper, is not a liqueur, but 18th-century gin, which was sweet, is. To be called a liqueur the product must, by European law, contain not less than 100 grams of sugar per litre and be at least 15% alcohol by volume. Most liqueurs are 25–40% ABV, but some are considerably stronger: Elixir Végétal de la Grande-Chartreuse is 71%, although in France it is considered a pharmaceutical product.

There are several ways by which flavouring can be added to a base spirit. Maceration is the combination of cold spirits and botanicals left to blend over a period of time. Infusion is the mixture of warm spirits and botanicals; as with tea, the higher temperature accelerates and enhances the process of extraction. Alternatively, the mixture of alcohol and flavourings can itself be distilled, a process simply called distillation. In this case only essential oils and other volatile flavourings from the botanicals remain in the resulting spirit. In all three cases, the liquor is sweetened by adding sugar.

Liqueurs may be divided into those which are flavoured with fruit, including cocoa and coffee beans, and those flavoured with herbs and spices, such as apricot kernels, attar of roses, vanilla and mint. In practice, many liqueurs are a mixture of the two. Because liqueurs are often flavoured with dozens of different botanicals, they can have complex, subtle tastes which are not easily described. The ingredients themselves are usually heavily guarded secrets, in some cases known by only a handful of people at any one time.

The best liqueurs are the longstanding proprietary brands, many of which have remained more or less unchanged for centuries. Benedictine and Chartreuse have been in production since the 16th and 18th centuries, the latter still at the hands of the Carthusian monks at Chartreuse. In Waugh's *Brideshead Revisited*, Anthony Blanche offers the pale green liqueur to Charles Ryder: 'Real G-g-green Chartreuse, made before the expulsion of the monks. There are five distinct tastes as it trickles over the tongue. It is like swallowing a sp-spectrum.' (The monks returned in 1929.)

Apart from being essential to countless cocktails (see p. 33), liqueurs are usually drunk neat, usually from a cordial or shot glass (see p. 20). Like spirits, they are flammable. This property can be put to effect by lighting a glassful (sambuca is a favourite) and extinguishing it right side up against a wet palm. If done quickly the flame will extinguish at once and the cooling gas will create a partial vacuum, affixing the glass to the palm.

HERB LIQUEURS

Name	Tasting notes	ABV
Chartreuse Elixir Végétal	medicinal, aromatic	71
Absinthe (La Fée)	aniseed, mint, lemon	68
Chartreuse Verte	aromatic, herbs, liquorice	55
Pastis (Ricard)	star anise, liquorice, black pepper	45
Benedictine	mixed spices, honey, citrus, cognac-based	40
Chartreuse Jaune	honey, aromatic	40
Danzig Goldwasser	orange peel, anise, caraway seed	40
Drambuie	honey, orange, aromatic, malt whisky-based	40
Sambuca (Molinari)	aniseed, black liquorice	40
Strega	mint, fennel, aniseed	40
Ouzo (12)	anise, cinnamon	38
Irish Mist	Irish whiskey, honey, heather	35
Galliano	spice, aniseed, citrus, vanilla	30
Royal Mint Chocolate	after dinner mints	28.5
Amaretto (Disaronno)	apricot kernels, almonds, baked cake	28
Parfait Amour	rosewater, orange, vanilla	25
Pimm's No. 1 Cup	citrus, spices, gin-based	25
Frangelico	hazelnut, caramel, butter	24
Advocaat (Warninks)	custard, brandy- & egg-yolk-based	17.2

FRUIT LIQUEURS

Name	Tasting notes	ABV
Cointreau	sweet oranges, bitter orange peel	40
Grand Marnier	burnt oranges, orange peel, cognac-based	40
Midori	honeydew melons	40
Southern Comfort	caramel, citrus	40
Triple sec	oranges, orange peel	30–40
Mandarine Napoleon	candied orange peel, bitter marmalade	38
Jägermeister	mixed spices, liquorice, medicinal	35
Limoncello (Villa Massa)	lemon drops, lemon peel	30
Kahlúa	coffee, dark chocolate, vanilla, sharp then sweet	26.5
Tia Maria	Jamaican coffee, milk chocolate	26.5
Sloe gin (Plymouth)	raspberries, forest fruits, gin-based	26
Campari	bitter orange peel, honey	25
Cherry brandy (Heering)	ripe cherries, almonds, brandy-based	24.7
Peach schnapps (Archers)	sweet peach flesh	23
Malibu	sweetened coconut, suntan lotion, rum-based	21
Pisang Ambon	banana split, overripe bananas	21
Passoã	passion fruit, citrus	20
Baileys	Irish whiskey, cream, dark chocolate	17
Tequila Rose	strawberries, tequila-based	17
Chambord	raspberries, honey, jam	16.5

Drinking & Smoking

To be called a single malt Scotch, a whisky (spelt whiskey in America and Ireland) must satisfy three conditions. *Single*: it must be produced at a single distillery, although it may be mixed from separately aged casks. *Malt*: it must be made entirely from malted (sprouted) barley, to which only yeast and water can be added. Other whiskies and bourbons may contain additional grains, such as corn or rye. *Scotch*: it must be distilled and aged in Scotland. There are curiously few single malt distilleries elsewhere in the world; Peter Jackson (see p. 130) names six, located in Australia, Ireland, Japan, New Zealand and Pakistan. Unlike wine or other spirits, the world of single malt Scotch is small and can be approached with a view to comprehensive familiarity.

Distillery	District	Cls	Distillery	District	Cls
Aberfeldy	Midlands	A	Cragganmore	Speyside	G
Aberlour	Speyside	B	Craigellachie	Speyside	K
Allt-á-Bhainne	Speyside	–	Dailuaine	Speyside	K
Ardberg	Islay	I	Dallas Dhu	Speyside	K
Ardmore	Speyside	C	Dalmore	N Highlands	B
Arran	Island	–	Dalwhinnie	Speyside	F
Auchentoshan	Lowlands	D	Deanston	Midlands	H
Aultmore	Speyside	F	Drumguish	Speyside	–
Balblair	N Highlands	E	Dufftown	Speyside	I
Balmenach	Speyside	K	Edradour	Midlands	E
Balvenie	Speyside	B	Fettercairn	E Highlands	H
Banff	Speyside	L	Glen Albyn	Speyside	J
Ben Nevis	W Highlands	D	Glenallachie	Speyside	F
Benriach	Speyside	F	Glenburgie	Speyside	E
Benrinnes	Speyside	B	Glencadam	E Highlands	L
Benromach	Speyside	F	Glen Deveron	Speyside	F
Bladnoch	Lowlands	E	Glendronach	Speyside	K
Blair Athol	Midlands	C	Glendullan	Speyside	B
Bowmore	Islay	I	Glen Elgin	Speyside	L
Brackla	Speyside	K	Glenesk	E Highlands	K
Braeval	Speyside	–	Glenfarclas	Speyside	I
Bruichladdich	Islay	H	Glenfiddich	Speyside	H
Bunnahabhain	Islay	F	Glen Flagler	Lowlands	–
Caol Ila	Islay	E	Glen Garioch	E Highlands	L
Caperdonich	Speyside	L	Glenglassaugh	Speyside	G
Cardhu	Speyside	F	Glengoyne	W Highlands	J
Clynelish	N Highlands	C	Glen Grant	Speyside	J
Cnoc	Speyside	–	Glen Keith	Speyside	K
Coleburn	Speyside	D	Glenkinchie	Lowlands	F
Convalmore	Speyside	K	Glenlivet	Speyside	B

There are 119 distilleries which now produce or have recently produced single malt Scotch whisky. Some of the distilleries, such as Rosebank, are closed but previous production is still being aged and is available on the market. For each distillery the following information is listed:

Name If the distillery has changed name, the most recent name is given.

District One of the nine regions of Scotland in which the distillery is located: Campbeltown, Island, Islay, Midlands, Lowlands, Speyside, East Highlands, North Highlands and West Highlands.

Classification (Cls) A letter indicating one of 12 similarity classes to which each whisky was assigned (overleaf). If omitted (–), the whisky was not studied.

Distillery	District	Cls
Glenlochy	W Highlands	I
Glenlossie	Speyside	J
Glen Mhor	Speyside	H
Glenmorangie	N Highlands	C
Glen Moray	Speyside	G
Glen Ord	N Highlands	K
Glenrothes	Speyside	K
Glen Scotia	Campbeltown	F
Glen Spey	Speyside	H
Glentauchers	Speyside	H
Glenturret	Midlands	B
Glenugie	E Highlands	A
Glenury Royal	E Highlands	I
Highland Park	Island	B
Imperial	Speyside	L
Inchgower	Speyside	F
Inchmurrin	W Highlands	E
Inverleven	Lowlands	E
Jura	Island	I
Kinclaith	Lowlands	E
Knockando	Speyside	F
Knockdhu	Speyside	K
Ladyburn	Lowlands	H
Lagavulin	Islay	I
Laphroaig	Islay	A
Linkwood	Speyside	J
Littlemill	Lowlands	E
Loch Lomond	W Highlands	–
Lochnagar	E Highlands	L

Distillery	District	Cls
Lochside	E Highlands	B
Longmorn	Speyside	G
Longrow	Campbeltown	I
Macallan	Speyside	B
Mannochmore	Speyside	–
Millburn	Speyside	B
Miltonduff	Speyside	F
Mortlach	Speyside	K
North Port	E Highlands	J
Oban	W Highlands	B
Pittyvaich	Speyside	–
Port Ellen	Islay	C
Pulteney	N Highlands	E
Rosebank	Lowlands	G
St Magdalene	Lowlands	J
Scapa	Island	A
Singleton	Speyside	B
Speyburn	Speyside	D
Springbank	Campbeltown	F
Strathisla	Speyside	B
Strathmill	Speyside	–
Talisker	Island	C
Tamdhu	Speyside	J
Tamnavulin	Speyside	G
Teaninich	N Highlands	L
Tobermory	Island	H
Tomatin	Speyside	K
Tomintoul	Speyside	G
Tormore	Speyside	K
Tullibardine	Midlands	F

Below is a classification of 109 distilleries producing single malt Scotch whisky, based on mathematicians Lapointe and Legendre's statistical study of Jackson's 1989 tasting notes. (At the time of their analysis, the authors had information on 109 of the 119 distilleries above.) The dendrogram is best considered as a tree, viewed from the top down. Thus the trunk is the centre point from which the branches emanate. Two whiskies (leaves) which join near the outer edge are similar in taste, e.g., Glenlivet and Glendullan at 4 o'clock. The closer to the centre a path between two whiskies travels, the less similar they are.

The two main branches from the centre divide the spirits into two classes: 69 'full-gold-coloured, dry-bodied and smoky' whiskies (A–H) and 40 'amber, aromatic, light-bodied, smooth palate and fruity finish' whiskies (I–L). Further out, 12 intermediate branches are labelled A–L; these are the 12 similarity classes indicated overleaf. Drawn from data in F.-J. Lapointe and P. Legendre (see p. 130).

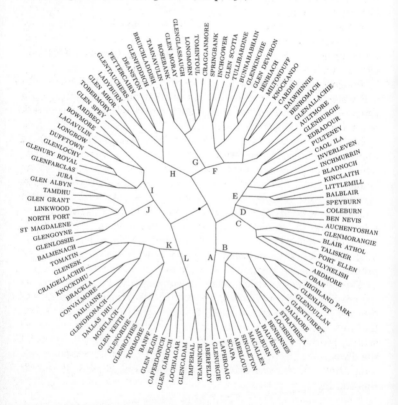

COCKTAIL THEORY

A cocktail is an iced spirit modified by juices, liqueurs, sugar, aromatic wines and bitters, which may or may not be diluted by a sparkling beverage or water. Cocktails fall into three categories: *short drinks*, which are undiluted; *long drinks*, which are diluted with soda water or other carbonated drink; and *punches*, which are diluted with water. Of course, in practice all cocktails are to some extent diluted by adding ice, and are the better for it, but this implicit dilution is not considered in their definition.

Short drinks should be at least 50% spirit by volume. Consequently, they are served in smaller portions, usually in martini or old-fashioned glasses (❦ Glasses, p. 20). They may be further divided into *sours* and *aromatics*. Sours, which do not in general taste sour because sugar is added, have as a modifying agent lemon or lime juice. With aromatics the principal modifying agent is one of the bitters, such as Angostura or Peychaud, or an aromatic wine, such as vermouth.

A long drink differs from a short drink by the addition of a neutral background beverage, generally soda water, but sometimes tonic water, or ginger ale, or Coke. If it is made without citrus juice, it is a *highball*; with lemon juice, a *collins*; and with lime juice, a *rickey*.

Punches, which have the longest lineage, are correctly diluted with still water, although in many recipes this has been replaced by soda water or lemonade. Punches are served from a bowl containing a block of ice; ice is not added to each glass.

Most books on cocktails contain far too many recipes, many of them unpalatable. In fact there are not more than two dozen drinks from which nearly all others can be derived. Start, for example, with the Gimlet: it is made of 4 parts gin, 2 parts lime juice and 1 part sugar syrup. If the gin is replaced with light rum, it is a Daiquiri. Add some crushed mint leaves and soda water and it becomes a Mojito. Substitute bourbon for rum and drop the soda and lime for a Mint Julep. Replace the mint with lemon and it is a Whiskey Sour. Indeed, a thorough understanding of which flavours mix with others, and in what proportions, makes cocktail recipes altogether redundant.

The debate over stirring versus shaking should be laid to rest, as there is little difference between the two: shaking involves slightly less dilution if the ice is much colder than 0 °C. The exception is drinks that froth, such as those made with egg whites, where shaking is essential. More important is whether to strain—keeping the ice out of the drink—or pour—leaving the ice in. Pouring is more common with long drinks. In all cases drinks should be as cold as possible, and to this end they are occasionally served in chilled glasses.

David Embury, the author of the most influential book on cocktails (p. 130), defines a cocktail axiomatically:

1 It must whet the appetite, not dull it;
2 It should stimulate the mind;
3 It must be pleasing to the palate;
4 It must be pleasing to the eye;
5 It must have sufficient alcoholic flavour;
6 Finally it must be well iced.

From these axioms a number of properties of cocktails can be deduced. Axioms 5 and 6 tell us what a cocktail is *not*, namely, anything made without spirits or warm. Thus a kir (white wine and cassis) is not a cocktail, nor is an Irish coffee, which is hot. However desirable a cocktail may be after dinner, it must function as an aperitif before (axiom 1). The variety of cocktail glasses is partly explained by axiom 4, each type of drink being most tempting in its own shape of glass.

The question arises of what should be found in a well-stocked drinks cupboard. From the point of view of mixing drinks, gin and vodka come to mind, both of which mix well with many flavours. But the most useful ingredients must be those that come up most frequently in cocktail recipes. An analysis of the top 100 cocktails in the UK yields a total of 94 different ingredients, distributed as follows (only the top 12 ingredients in each column are listed):

Spirits	%	Other alcohol	%	Non-alcohol	%
vodka	30	Angostura	14	ice	98
gin	18	Cointreau	12	sugar syrup	46
light rum	10	framboise	8	lime juice	28
tequila	8	champagne	6	lemon juice	22
bourbon	7	dry vermouth	5	soda water	12
cognac	7	sweet vermouth	5	orange juice	10
dark rum	6	cassis	4	cranberry juice	8
Scotch whisky	4	Kahlúa	4	apple juice	7
cachaça	3	blackberry liqueur	4	pineapple juice	6
gold rum	2	peach schnapps	4	ginger beer	6
Pisco	2	Baileys Irish Cream	3	egg white	6
Irish whiskey	1	Grand Marnier	3	Rose's lime cordial	5

The distribution of glasses is also of interest. Of the same 100 cocktails, 33% are drunk from a martini glass, 27% a highball, 21% an old-fashioned, 6% a flute, 4% a pilsner, 3% a hurricane and 2% a shot.

All of the drinks listed opposite are given in terms of relative, rather than absolute, measures. This means that a cocktail can be made in as large or small a quantity as desired.

A DOZEN COCKTAILS FOR LIFE

These 12 classic drinks have stood the test of time. Proportions can and should be adjusted to suit individual tastes. The glass and garnish for each are shown to the right.

CAIPIRINHA

8 parts Cachaça	*old-fashioned*
1/2 to 1 lime/drink	*straw*
3 parts sugar syrup	

Muddle cut lime in glass. Add rest and crushed ice and stir.

COSMOPOLITAN

6 parts vodka	*martini*
3 parts Cointreau	*orange peel*
6 parts cranberry juice	
1 part lime juice	

Shake with crushed ice and strain into glasses.

GIMLET

4 parts gin	*martini*
2 parts lime juice	*lime slice*
1 part sugar syrup	

Shake with crushed ice and strain into glasses.

MANHATTAN

5 parts bourbon	*martini*
1 part dry vermouth	*orange peel*
2 dashes Angostura/drink	

Shake with crushed ice and strain into glasses.

MARGARITA

2 parts tequila	*martini*
1 part Cointreau	*lime slice*
1 part lime juice	

First salt glass rims. Shake with crushed ice and strain into glasses.

MARTINI

| 7 parts gin | *martini* |
| 1 part dry vermouth | *lemon peel* |

Shake with crushed ice and strain into glasses.

MINT JULEP

3 parts bourbon	*highball*
1 part sugar syrup	*straw*
10 mint leaves/drink	
1 dash Angostura/drink	

Bruise mint leaves with bourbon. Add rest and crushed ice and stir.

MOJITO

4 parts light rum	*highball*
4 parts soda water	*straw*
1/2 lime/drink	
10 mint leaves	
1 part sugar syrup	

Muddle cut lime and mint in glass. Add rest and crushed ice and stir.

OLD-FASHIONED

5 parts bourbon	*old-fashioned*
1 part sugar syrup	*orange slice*
2 dashes Angostura/drink	

Shake with crushed ice and pour (with ice) into ice-filled glasses.

SIDECAR

2 parts Cognac	*martini*
1 part lemon juice	*lemon peel*
1 part Cointreau	

Shake with crushed ice and strain into glasses.

SINGAPORE SLING

8 parts gin	*highball*
4 parts cherry brandy	*straw*
2 parts lemon juice	*cherry*
1 part sugar syrup	
1 dash Angostura/drink	

Shake with crushed ice, pour (w. ice) into glasses, top w. soda water.

WHISKEY SOUR

2 parts bourbon	*old-fashioned*
1 part lemon juice	*lemon slice*
1 part sugar syrup	
2 dashes Angostura/drink	

Shake with crushed ice and pour (with ice) into glasses.

SMOKING ETIQUETTE

The introduction of the smoking ban in England in the summer of 2007 will of course change the way men smoke. One thing is certain: there will be more smoking in private residences and out of doors. Here is a guide to smokers' rights and wrongs.

Indoor smoking First, is it acceptable to ban guests from smoking in one's house? James Leavey, editor of the *FOREST Guide to Smoking in London* (1996), advises:

> There are those who will not permit any smoking in their home. It is their prerogative but of course their smoking guests may consider this anti-social. It is very unkind to confront a heavy smoker in your home with the fact that he or she will have to suffer a smoke-free evening. Better to warn your guests when you invite them, so they can decide whether or not to turn down your invitation.

John Morgan, author of the latest *Debrett's*, concurs. 'If you as the host hate the habit, you can quite legitimately never invite smokers to your table. However, it is not appropriate to forbid a guest to smoke in your house once he or she is there.' On the other hand, a sensitive smoker will realize when his habit is not welcome and will adjust his behaviour accordingly, standing near an open window or keeping his cigarettes to a minimum. It is not unheard of for one guest to indicate annoyance at another's smoking. As host, the easiest solution is to isolate not the smoker but the complaining guest: 'Let's step outside for a chat on the balcony while John finishes his cigarette.'

Second, when is it acceptable to light up indoors? The presence of ashtrays is a sure sign that smoking is allowed, although their absence does not necessarily imply the opposite. If you cannot see an ashtray, ask the host. Smoking while others at your table are eating is bad manners, though a cigarette between meals is perfectly acceptable. The possession of portable ashtrays, which are available in smart and ingenious designs, does not confer a licence to smoke anywhere. At formal dinners, during which the Loyal Toast is to be given, it is inappropriate to smoke before glasses have been raised.

Ash and butts The question of where one can dispose of ash and butts is a tricky one. Certainly it is acceptable to flick your ash onto the ground or pavement out of doors. Dropping butts is an unattractive habit but there are occasions when this is the only option. If there is no ashtray or bin nearby, it is acceptable in public, though not private, outdoor spaces. Indoors the policy is similar, but more stringent by one degree. When necessary, ash can be dropped on public, though not private, hard floors; butts must be properly disposed of.

Sharing and caring One of the attractions of smoking is the instant camaraderie felt between smokers. Asking an unknown smoker for a light or cigarette is perfectly acceptable and is likely to initiate conversation. When the occasion arises, a man should light a woman's cigarette directly, but offers the lighter to a man for him to light his own. A cigar is always lit by the smoker himself.

The problem of cigarette odour is a long-standing one. *Manners for Men*, first published in 1897, identifies the problem:

> Some men have a knack of ridding their clothes and themselves of the fumes of smoke in a wonderful way. Perhaps one reason of this is that the tobacco they use is of a mild sort. Perhaps the diligent use of the clothes-brush is another. But there are also men round whom cling the odours of stale tobacco with a very disagreeable constancy. Why it should be so I cannot pretend to say.

The same applies to rooms. For smelly spaces, 'neutradol is particularly effective, doesn't smell like a tart's boudoir and one squirt obliterates most known smells', suggests James Leavey. Keep in mind also that it is not so much smoking, but ash and ashtrays, that are the source of unpleasant odours.

THE PROS AND CONS OF SMOKING

By European law, cigarette packets must include conspicuous warnings of the health risks associated with smoking. FakeFags (fakefags.co.uk) offers alternative messages for those who are already familiar with the risks of smoking.

Government warning	*FakeFags sticker*
Smoking kills	You could get hit by a bus tomorrow
Smokers die younger	My gran smokes 40 a day and she's 93
Smoking causes fatal lung cancer	Live fast, die young
Smoking causes ageing of the skin	You will get fat if you stop smoking
Smoking is highly addictive, don't start	At least I don't smoke crack
Smoking when pregnant harms your baby	It's OK, I'm not pregnant
Smoking can cause a slow and painful death	You've got to die of something
Smoking seriously harms you and others around you	Non-smokers may cause irritation
Smoking can damage the sperm and decreases fertility	Smoking makes you look sexy
Smoking clogs the arteries and causes heart attacks and strokes	Smoking supports the NHS
Stopping smoking reduces the risk of fatal heart and lung diseases	Nobody likes a quitter

The first thing to consider when smoking a cigar is not the brand but the size. Size effects the intensity of flavour, prescribes the occasion and determines the duration: a typical cigarillo can be smoked in under 10 minutes, while a giant may last over two hours. The length of a cigar is measured in inches and the diameter, or ring gauge, in 64ths of an inch. Although there is no prescription as to which cigars should be smoked by whom, it is loosely accepted that 'the ring gauge should match your age'. Thus a 24-year-old man might smoke a 3/8 inch cigarillo, a 32-year-old a 1/2 inch panatella and a 48-year-old a 3/4 inch Churchill. The smallest cigarillos tend to have ring gauges in the low 20s, which is probably the earliest age to be seen smoking cigars.

There is a longstanding tradition of associating names with certain cigar sizes and some names have specific meaning in the cigar industry. Nevertheless there is no set convention and some names conflict or are redundant. Below is an attempt to rationally divide the entire size range, taking into account present usage. Measurements between sizes belong to the larger size.

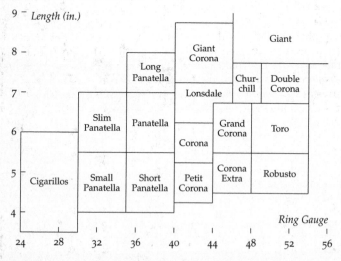

Typical dimensions of each size are as follows:

Cigarillo	4×26	Petit Corona	5×42	Robusto	5×50
Small Panatella	5×32	Corona	5.5×42	Toro	6×50
Slim Panatella	6×34	Lonsdale	6.5×42	Churchill	7×48
Short Panatella	5×38	Giant Corona	7.5×44	Double Corona	7.5×50
Panatella	6×38	Corona Extra	5.5×46	Giant	8.5×52
Long Panatella	7.5×38	Grand Corona	6.5×46		

The introduction of the national indoor smoking ban in the summer of 2007 is of course cause for smokers' sorrow. But even this dark cloud brings with it some cause for hope: snuff. With the exception of fire, the smokeless tobacco offers all of the attractions of smoking: the kick, the kit, the ceremony and the camaraderie. With year-to-year sales in the UK already on the increase, the clampdown on smoking might bring snuff use back to levels not seen since it was taken up by the early 19th-century gentility and early 20th-century coal miners. The motto of Wilson of Sharrow, snuff producers since 1737, is timely: 'Smoke when you can, snuff when you can't.'

Snuff is finely powdered tobacco leaf and stalk which is not ignited but sniffed directly into the nose. It comes in many varieties, falling roughly into three classes: natural, perfumed and medicated. Perfumed snuff is scented with the essential oils of fruits or flowers; medicated, with menthol or eucalyptus or aniseed. First-time users might have a tendency to sneeze, but this dies off with experience. Snuff is stored in a snuffbox, a small lidded container with any one of a number of (preferably airtight) closing mechanisms. While snuffboxes of considerable value are available, an experienced snuff taker uses a sober metal or wooden box which can be lost without regret.

There are two common ways of taking snuff. The first is executed by placing a small amount of snuff, pinched from the source, in the depression on the back of the left hand between the forefinger and outstretched thumb. From here it is sniffed into both nostrils or one nostril at a time. In the case of the latter it is helpful, if inelegant, to close the other nostril with the right hand. Note that to sniff is not to snort: unlike other powdered substances, snuff is not meant to reach the sinuses or beyond. The second method is described in a mid-20th-century snuff pamphlet:

> Take the snuff box in the right hand.
> Pass it to the left hand.
> Rap the snuff box.
> Open the box and inspect the contents.
> Present box to surrounding company with a courteous bow.
> Receive it back with the left hand.
> Gather up the snuff in the box by striking the side with middle and forefinger.
> Take a pinch with the right hand.
> Hold the snuff for a second or two between fingers before taking.
> Carry the pinch to the nose.
> Snuff with precision by both nostrils and without grimaces or distortion of the features.
> Close snuff box with a flourish.

The attraction to pipe smoking is not based on nicotine—like cigars, pipes are not inhaled—but association and ritual: the routine filling of the bowl; the warmth of the briar; the subconscious fascination with fire. Pipe smoke itself is more instinctly pleasant than the smoke from rolled tobacco. Cigars are typically smoked in company, pipes in solitude.

Pipes can be made from briar, meerschaum, clay, corncob or calabash (gourd). Of these, briar is by far the most popular. It is the hardened root burl of the Mediterranean heath tree. The most distinctive feature of a pipe is whether the stem is bent or straight. Bent stems are easier to hold in the mouth (they exert less torque on the teeth) while straight are presently smarter. The style of stem does not determine the shape of the bowl, which comes in many varieties. Pipe authority Richard Carleton Hacker classifies bowls into eight types:

Apple: an elegant, spherical, comparatively squat bowl.

Billiard: classic shape; height of bowl equals length of shank.

Bulldog: a bevelled top with carved ridge and diamond-shaped stem.

Canadian: a long shank and short bit, thus more difficult to make.

Dublin: wider at the top than base, with a flat or concave rear.

Freehand: a freeform style inspired by the individual briar stock.

Pot: the shortest and broadest of the bowls, with a rounded bottom.

Poker: a flat-bottomed, clean-cut, cylindrical bowl.

The main skill in smoking a pipe is knowing how to fill and light it. This determines how easily the pipe draws, how long the tobacco lasts, and how much dottle (ash and partially burnt tobacco) remains at the end. Keep in mind that pipes, like cigars, go out from time to time and must be relit. Here are instructions for filling and lighting:

First fill the bowl of the pipe until it slightly overflows by dropping in loose strands of tobacco, taking care to disentangle clumps.

Using a pipe tool or the head of a nail, tamp down the tobacco with light force until it has been reduced to about half its volume.

Again, drop loose tobacco into the bowl until it overflows.

Tamp the tobacco until it is just below the surface of the bowl.

Light the pipe, ideally with a horizontal match, and take in several short puffs of smoke. Stop and wait for the coals to die out. This is known as the charring light.

Tamp down once more, creating a layer of charred tobacco. This essential step ensures that the bowl of tobacco lights evenly.

Light the pipe a second time, as before, and continue to draw.

WOMEN

PRECEDENCE

All else being equal, women take precedence over men, and this is the basis of a number of customs. Men are introduced to women, as in 'Daisy Buchanan, may I introduce Jay Gatsby,' or, more simply, 'Marge, this is Homer.' It is the woman rather than the man who initiates, and thereby determines, the form of recognition—a kiss, a handshake or nothing—on greeting and departing. Women are in general served food before men, and their glasses are filled first (unless the table is large, in which case wine is served around the table clockwise). It is correct for men to rise when a woman arrives or departs, although the coming and going of a man does not justify this. A man lights a woman's cigarette (see p. 37), carries her heavy bags and offers his seat if she is forced to stand, though the last can be dispensed with in busy settings, such as the Underground.

Walking with a woman can be easily formulated. In general, a man walks to the right of a woman, unless the couple is walking beside a road, in which case the man puts himself between the woman and the road. If the couple passes another man, the man keeps to the side of the woman, and allows the man to walk into the street, but if they pass a woman, the man walks into the street himself.

The etiquette of opening doors is motivated first by considerations of labour, then of precedent. Thus if the door opens in, the man opens it and allows the woman to walk through first. But if the door opens out, the man walks through and the women follows. If others are coming from the opposite side, in the first case the man holds the door open and the others take precedence, but in the second the woman then the man precede. In the case of revolving doors, both on account of labour and of them opening out, the man is the first to enter.

PROVISION

One of the most innate chivalric tendencies is the provision—though not necessarily the preparation—of food. This can be seen in the actual procurement of fish and fowl, of course, but is also symbolized by the carving of meat at the dinner table.

Today provision often takes the form of paying for dinner and drinks. Whatever the arguments might be for going Dutch, a woman who insists on splitting the bill is either romantically uninterested or tedious. In early courtship it is correct to pay even when a woman offers once or twice, though if three times a man must concede. The foxiest females seem most willing to let men cover the costs. French women never offer to pay for dinner—nor lunch, for that matter—and are certainly no less desirable than *les Anglaises*. Having said that, a constant outlay on women can cause near-bankruptcy, and for men who find themselves pinching pennies, it is advisable to *only pay for women you fancy*. A thoughtful woman will recognize any financial disparity and contribute accordingly after the first few outings.

Wine remains a male preserve, despite the increasing number of female oenologists. At a restaurant the man chooses the wine; though he may ask the woman for input, he is under no obligation to do so. He fills the woman's glass when low and each time he fills his own, even if only symbolically. A sensitive woman will nurse a half-full glass rather than refuse when she has had her fill.

PROTECTION

The custom of returning a woman home after an evening out remains correct in principle, but varies in practice according to the circumstances. It is correct to walk or drive a woman to her door if she does not live far away, but if she does it is impractical to make a significant detour, as well as alarming from the woman's point of view. Better to send her home in a taxi. The man is not required to pay, unless he insists on her taking a taxi as opposed to, say, a bus. When entertaining a group, a man's first priority is to his guests, and it is his guests who should look after the safe return of any women.

When is a man welcome inside a woman's house after returning her? 'If a woman does not want a man to come in, then gentle but clear suggestions. . . should be put into the conversation,' explains John Morgan in the latest *Debrett's* (1996). 'If a man is asked in, he must not assume that he has the green light for sex, although a woman who does this shouldn't be surprised if he does.'

An insult to a man's girlfriend or wife in his presence is always a gross offence. The Code Duello, the most widely accepted set of prescriptions on duelling and honour, states: 'Any insult to a lady under a gentleman's care or protection [is] to be considered as, by one degree, a greater offence than if given to the gentleman personally, and to be regulated accordingly.' Offences are, in increasing order of severity, an insult, a lie and a blow.

WWII POSTAL ACRONYMS

Although the recent surge of interest in abbreviations and acronyms was motivated by texting (see p. 142), it is not unprecedented. During the Second World War, servicemen adopted a number of sentimental acronyms in their censored letters home. Unlike FUBAR and SNAFU, these were usually in the form of place names.

BOLTOP	Better on lips than on paper
BURMA	Be undressed ready my angel
CHINA	Come home I need affection
HOLLAND	Hope our love lasts and never dies
ITALY	I trust and love you
MALAYA	My ardent lips await your arrival
MEXICO CITY	May every x I can offer carry itself to you
NORWICH	[K]nickers off ready when I come home
SIAM	Sexual intercourse at midnight
SWALK	Sealed with a loving kiss
WALES	With a love eternal sweetheart

CONVERSATION HEARTS

The famous pastel-coloured, heart-shaped sweets with words printed on them have been produced by NECCO (New England Confectionery Company) since 1902. Each year 8 billion hearts are made, which is 25 hearts for every English-speaking woman in the world. On each heart is a one- to three-word phrase, printed in red in all capitals. The total number of phrases is not known, but every year a few new ones are added and a few are decommissioned. There is a curious abundance of imperatives: MARRY ME, LOVE HER. Other phrases are not obviously connected with the holiday they commemorate: BOOK CLUB, WHIZ KID. While some of the original expressions are still found (BE TRUE, SWEET TALK), a number of more sober ones have been included (GET REAL, WISE UP). Recent phrases include:

:-)	DEAR ONE	I DO	LOVE ME	PEN PAL	U R A 10
#1 FAN	DIVA	I HOPE	LOVE YOU	REAL LOVE	U R A QT
ALL MINE	DREAM GIRL	I WILL	LOVER BOY	ROMEO	U R A STAR
AMORE	EMAIL	I'M SURE	MARRY ME	SMILE	UR KIND
ANGEL	FAX ME	IN STYLE	MISS YOU	SO FINE	VENUS
ASK ME	FIRST KISS	IT'S LOVE	MY BABY	STAR DUST	VOGUE
BE GOOD	FOR YOU	KISS ME	MY GIRL	SURE LOVE	WAY
BE MINE	GET REAL	LET IT BE	MY LOVE	SWEET TALK	WHIZ KID
BE TRUE	GO GIRL	LET'S KISS	MY MAN	THANK YOU	WISE UP
BOOK CLUB	GOT LOVE	LET'S READ	MY WAY	TIME OUT	WRITE ME
CALL ME	HI LOVE	LOVE	NICE GIRL	TLC	YES DEAR
COOL	HOW NICE	LOVE HER	ONE I LOVE	TRES CHIC	YOU & ME
CUTIE PIE	HUG ME	LOVE HIM	ONLY YOU	TRUE LOVE	YOU RULE

A woman's beauty is notoriously difficult to define, dependent as it is on non-physical attributes such as style and demeanour. Jacqueline Kennedy and Princess Diana, not technically classically beautiful, were two of the most photographed women of the last century. Even a strict physical interpretation of the term must concede that beauty waxes and wanes with a woman's effort.

Without attempting to define beauty, we can nevertheless quantify it. Our starting point is Helen of Troy, the offspring of the Greek god Zeus and Leda, wife of the king of Sparta. Helen, whose abduction sparked the Trojan War, was the most beautiful woman in the world in around the 12th century BC. In Christopher Marlowe's *The Tragical History of Doctor Faustus*, Mephistopheles calls up a vision of Helen, and Faustus reponds:

> Was this the face that launched a thousand ships
> And burned the topless towers of Ilium?

From this we can deduce two things: the extent of Helen's beauty, and its effect. The population of the earth in the 12th century BC is estimated to be at most 100 million, making her the most beautiful of 50 million women. If Helen's beauty launched a thousand ships, we may infer that the most beautiful of 50 thousand women would launch a single ship. The military vessels of the time were simple galleys powered by 25 oars on each side, 50 oarsmen in all. Accordingly, the pick of a thousand women would bring a single oarsman to risk his life in war. Let such a beauty be the colloquial 'perfect 10' on a scale of 0 to 10. We call a single point on this scale a *Helena* (Ha).

The beauty of a thousand women is not, of course, uniformly distributed; there are invariably more 8s than 9s, more 7s than 8s, and so on. Like the Richter scale for measuring earthquakes, beauty is logarithmic, but with a base of 2 rather than 32. This means that, for beauty to increase by one Helena, the woman must be the most beautiful of twice as many women. Thus if a woman is the most striking of 2 women, her beauty is 1 Helena; of 4 women, 2 Helenas; of 8 women, 3 Helenas; and, in general, of 2^N women, N Helenas. Equally, a woman's beauty in Helenas is the number of rounds she is likely to win in the classic locker-room game, *Who would you rather sleep with?*, played as a knockout tournament. Whilst 10 Helenas would cause a man to risk his life, a woman's beauty does occasionally exceed 10, there being no set limit to this attribute. The beauty of Helen herself is $\log_2(50,000,000) = 25.6$ (50 million is $2 \times 2 \times 2 \ldots \times 2$, between 25 and 26 times). Thus we define one Helen (H) to be 25.6 Helenas (Ha).

Some examples of women's beauty are as follows:

Woman	Number	Ha	H
Best of a dozen	12	3.6	0.14
Most beautiful of a martyr's 72 virgins	72	6.2	0.24
Would cause a man to risk his life	1,000	10.0	0.39
Best beauty seen in a lifetime	10^5	16.6	0.65
Helen of Troy	5×10^7	25.6	1.00
Miss World	3.2×10^9	31.6	1.23
Most beautiful woman who ever lived	2×10^{10}	34.2	1.34

It frequently happens that a man prefers women close in age to himself (or $1/2$ his age + 7, see p. 50). In assessing a woman's beauty, he should compare her with women whose difference in age will not bias him one way or the other. Of any large population of women, $1/2$ of women have beauty 0 Ha, $1/4$ have 1 Ha, $1/8$ have 2 Ha, and so on. This contrasts with the more common but less systematic beauty scale in which 0 is plain, 5 average and 10 stunning. Alas, Helenas can only measure beauty, not homeliness.

It is one thing to believe a woman to be beautiful, another to proclaim it. Flattery is best offered to the intermediate, not the extreme.

> Women who are either indisputably beautiful, or indisputably ugly, are best flattered, upon the score of their understandings; but those who are in a state of mediocrity, are best flattered upon their beauty, or at least their graces; for every woman who is not absolutely ugly thinks herself handsome; but not hearing often that she is so, is the more grateful and the more obliged to the few who tell her so; whereas a decided and conscious beauty looks upon every tribute paid to her beauty only as her due; but wants to shine, and to be considered on the side of her understanding; and a woman who is ugly enough to know that she is so, knows that she has nothing left for it but her understanding, which is consequently and probably (in more senses than one) her weak side.
>
> *Letters to His Son*, Philip Stanhope, 4th Earl of Chesterfield

Paradoxically, beauty seems to safeguard modesty. The more that a woman is admired and surrounded by men, the less likely she is to indulge in casual passion; whereas a woman whose beauty is contested, finding herself unable to compete with the beautiful head-on, will compensate by offering easy access. Beauty has its price, of course. As a kept animal, used to daily provision without toil, loses its instinct to find food in the wild, a beautiful woman, accustomed to men's attention, can forget how to earn it through kindness. Perhaps this explains Shakespeare's inversion of Marlowe:

> Is she worth keeping? Why, she is a pearl
> Whose price hath launch'd above a thousand ships.
>
> *History of Troilus and Cressida*

The first thing to keep in mind during early courtship is that men chase and women are chased. A man finds this both pleasurable and instinctive; he is

Like the hunter who chases the hare
Through heat and cold, o'er hill and dale,
Yet, once he has bagged it, he thinks nothing of it;
Only while it flees away does he pound after it.

Ariosto, *Orlando Furioso*, X, vii, translated by M. A. Screech

Men chase what they desire. Intelligent women recognize this, and invert it: a man who does not chase does not desire. The best-selling book *The Rules* by Ellen Fein and Sherrie Schneider lists 'time-tested secrets for capturing the heart of Mr. Right', shown below. The central message is that playing hard to get provides a litmus test for a man's interest. The chase-chased courtship asymmetry is not male chauvinism—it is an essential ritual in forming stable matches.

The second thing is that men fall in love more quickly than women. Where a woman takes her time and considers what is real, a man runs with first impressions and invents the rest according to his fantasy. This invention is both intoxicating and intimidating; ultimately it makes men fear women. In Lermontov's *A Hero of Our Time*, the practised seducer Pechorin tells us: 'Women ought to wish that all men knew them as well as I because I have loved them a hundred times better since I have ceased to be afraid of them and have comprehended their little weaknesses.' Hence the importance in early conquest of approaching women with insouciance, as one might a potential male friend. This requires acting, but the game is short-lived—it need only last until love (or its absence) has replaced infatuation.

The Rules for Women

Don't talk to a man first (and don't ask him to dance).

Don't stare at men or talk too much.

Don't meet him halfway or go Dutch on a date.

Don't call him and rarely return his phone calls.

Always end phone calls first.

Don't accept a Saturday night date after Wednesday.

Always end the date first.

Stop dating him if he doesn't buy you a romantic gift for your birthday or Valentine's Day.

Don't see him more than once or twice a week.

No more than casual kissing on the first date.

Don't tell him what to do.

Let him take the lead.

Don't expect a man to change or try to change him.

Don't open up too fast.

Don't live with a man (or leave your things in his apartment).

Don't date a married man.

Be easy to live with.

Except perhaps on Sadie Hawkins Day (p. 159), on a first date a man invites a woman by suggesting a fixed plan, without negotiation as to where to meet or what to do. It is not a time to be original in your choice of venue. A first date should merely be a setting for easy and unimpeded conversation, hence the custom of having it in a public place. Dinner is ideal: it is conducive to talking; it affords the chance to drink alcohol; there is no set time to finish by. If you do not have plans for afterwards, such as music or the theatre or the cinema, it is wise to begin with separate drinks beforehand, which brings a sense of motion to the evening.

While it remains correct to collect a girl by car, it is more common—and often more practical in a big city—to meet her at a pre-arranged location. In this case it is essential to arrive ten minutes early. By the time the girl arrives, you should be seated and have in hand a drink and a slim novel (Pushkin or Turgenev are ideal). In any event do not talk to others or use your mobile phone; you may appear interested in things, not other people.

You should have a reservation at a restaurant and know how to get there, which may require reconnaissance beforehand. (If you find yourself stuck with nowhere in mind, choose one on the spot using the algorithm below.) A schoolboy error is the over-ambitious choice of restaurant. Apart from being expensive, it is intimidating for the woman, who tends to think that allowing you to pay a large bill obligates her affection, and usually has the reverse effect. You pay the bill, of course (see p. 42), even if she offers; to split is to accept defeat.

The end is as important as the beginning. The essential thing—and remember we are talking about the *first* date—is to show no interest in her physically. Your restraint should grow in proportion to her beauty. A pretty girl considers a man's affection her due (see p. 45). Her desirableness rebuffed, a man becomes more, not less, fascinating to her. Which makes a second date straightforward by comparison.

CHOOSING THE BEST RESTAURANT

♣ *For geeks* Consider the familiar experience of walking down a street looking to dine. One would like, on the one hand, to sample many restaurants before making a choice, and on the other, to avoid passing a good candidate in the hope of something better. What strategy maximizes the probability of choosing the best restaurant? If there are N restaurants on the street, the optimal policy is to walk past the first $1/e \simeq 37\%$, then pick the next one better than all of those. (Here e is the base of the natural logarithm, 2.718.) This is a universal strategy, and can be equally applied to accepting an offer or buying a house or, in the case of women, accepting a marriage proposal.

Benjamin Franklin's *Poor Richard's Almanack* was one of the best-selling books in New England before the War of Independence. As well as astronomical data, a calendar of the year, prognostications and verse, *Poor Richard* offered many maxims on moderation in vice (see the Almanack, pp. 73–100). Many concerned the restraint of sensuality. Privately, however, he held more pragmatic views. In a letter to 'My dear Friend', thought by some to be his son, Franklin contrasts relations with an older woman and a younger.

REASONS TO PREFER OLD MISTRESSES TO YOUNG

1. Because as they have more knowledge of the world and their minds are better stored with observations, their conversation is more improving and more lastingly agreeable.

2. Because when women cease to be handsome, they study to be good. To maintain their influence over men, they supply the diminution of beauty by an augmentation of utility... And hence there is hardly such a thing to be found as an old woman who is not a good woman.

3. Because there is no hazard of children, which irregularly produced may be attended with much inconvenience.

4. Because through more experience, they are more prudent and discreet in conducting an intrigue to prevent suspicion. The commerce with them is therefore safer with regard to your reputation. And with regard to theirs, if the affair should happen to be known, considerate people might be rather inclined to excuse an old woman who would kindly take care of a young man, form his manners by her good counsels, and prevent his ruining his health and fortune among mercenary prostitutes.

5. Because in every animal that walks upright, the deficiency of the fluids that fill the muscles appears first in the highest part. The face grows lank and wrinkled, then the neck, then the breast and arms, the lower parts continuing to the last as plump as ever. So that covering all above with a basket, and regarding only what is below the girdle, it is impossible of two women to know an old from a young one. And as in the dark all cats are grey, the pleasure of corporal enjoyment with an old woman is at least equal, and frequently superior, every knack being by practice capable of improvement.

6. Because the sin is less. The debauching a virgin may be her ruin, and make her for life unhappy.

7. Because the compunction is less. The having made a young girl *miserable* may give you frequent bitter reflections, none of which can attend making an old woman *happy*.

8thly and lastly. They are *so grateful!!*

Although the association of rings and marriage is ancient, before WWII women wore wedding rings and men did not. Married soldiers away from home took to the idea of wearing a band as a reminder of their fidelity, and today over half of newlywed men wear a wedding ring. The ring itself, which is invariably a plain gold band, is worn on the same finger as the women's, that is, the third finger of the left hand. An engagement ring is normally given to a woman on or soon after proposing. While there is much talk today about letting the woman choose the design, more admirable is the man who without warning proposes with ring in hand. There are various rules of thumb as to how much an engagement ring should cost, ranging from two weeks' to two months' salary. In the UK, two-thirds of a month is more typical.

Often an engagement ring is flanked by one of the five cardinal gemstones: amethyst, diamond, emerald, ruby and sapphire (amethyst is no longer considered valuable following the discovery of large deposits in Brazil and elsewhere). During the 19th century a popular form of engagement ring made use of different gemstones to form an *acrostic*, a sequence of words whose initial letters form a message. The most popular spelled REGARDS, making use of the five cardinal stones and garnet: ruby, emerald, garnet, amethyst, ruby, diamond, sapphire. Another spells LOVE: lapis lazuli, opal, vermarine, emerald, though the colour coordination and inclusion of vermarine makes such a combination suspect. Much better is EROS: emerald, ruby, opal, sapphire.

This method of encoding a message can be generalized. The most desirable gemstones, including the five cardinal stones, are listed below. Their initials comprise half the letters of the alphabet: A B C D E G L M O P R S T. Any word composed from these letters, such as ADORE, corresponds to a series of gemstones, although less than 1% of all seven-letter words, for example, can be so constructed. By associating with each birthstone the number of its month, we also have a way of moving from numbers to stones to letters (cf. text message input, p. 141). Thus, 4527 → diamond, emerald, amethyst, ruby → DEAR.

a	alexandrite	green-red			m	moonstone	white		
a	amethyst	purple	Feb	2	o	opal	variegated	Oct	10
a	aquamarine	pale blue	Mar	3	p	pearl	white	Jun	6
b	bloodstone	pale blue			p	peridot	pale green	Aug	8
c	cat's eye	brown			r	ruby	red	Jul	7
c	citrine	yellow			s	sapphire	blue	Sep	9
d	diamond	clear	Apr	4	s	sardonyx	pale green		
e	emerald	green	May	5	t	topaz	yellow	Nov	11
g	garnet	dark red	Jan	1	t	tourmaline	variegated		
l	lapis lazuli	dark blue			t	turquoise	sky blue	Dec	12

WHOM TO MARRY

Consanguinity has always constrained who can marry whom. According to *The Book of Common Prayer*, a man may not marry his

mother	wife's mother	mother's father's wife
daughter	wife's daughter	wife's father's mother
sister	father's wife	wife's mother's mother
father's mother	son's wife	wife's son's daughter
mother's mother	father's sister	wife's daughter's
son's daughter	mother's sister	daughter
daughter's daughter	brother's daughter	son's son's wife or
father's daughter	sister's daughter	daughter's son's wife
mother's daughter	father's father's wife	

In the UK laws prohibiting some of the more arcane combinations above have been relaxed. Despite popular belief, a man may marry his cousin, and first-cousin marriage is legal is most countries. Laws prohibiting first-cousin marriage usually predate modern genetic theory, although one-half of American states have yet to repeal them. Scientists seem particularly disposed to first-cousin love, with Albert Einstein marrying Elsa Einstein and Charles Darwin marrying Emma Wedgwood.

WHEN TO MARRY

The most common rule of thumb for the ideal age of your bride at marriage is $1/2$ your age + 7. (For women readers, it's (your age - 7) × 2.) Thus for a man of 30, a bride of 22 is most suitable; for a man of 40, a bride of 27. The formula adjusts for women's comparatively advanced emotional strength and matches the fertile period of a woman (14–47) to that of a man (14–80). Proponents suggest it also reduces the risk of later infidelity on the side of men: 'I like my whiskey old and my women young,' in the words of Errol Flynn. (For a list of single malts, see p. 30.)

Man's age at marriage (a)	16	24	32	40	48	56	64	72
Woman's age at marriage ($1/2\,a + 7$)	15	19	23	27	31	35	39	43

An alternative guide to marriage ages, and one which gives less disparate numbers, matches the Fibonacci and Lucas numbers. These sequences dictate the notable stages of a man's and woman's life, respectively (see p. 5).

Man's age at marriage	F_n	21	34	55	89
Woman's age at marriage	L_{n-1}	18	29	47	76

WEDDING ANNIVERSARIES

The first widely accepted list of wedding anniversary gifts was published by Emily Post in her best-selling book *Etiquette* in 1922. It listed eight anniversaries: 1, 5, 10, 15, 20, 25, 50 and 75. '[The gifts] need not, however, be of value; in fact the paper, wooden and tin wedding presents are seldom anything but jokes. Crystal is the earliest that is likely to be taken seriously by the gift-bearers. Silver is always serious, and the golden wedding a quite sacred event.' In later editions Post increased the list to the years 1–15, and multiples of 5 up to 60. Today these are the only years for which broad conventions exist. Some freedom in choosing what to give can be had by giving two or three alternative objects whose sum is the requisite anniversary. Thus cotton and bronze might be given for a 10th anniversary instead of tin.

1	paper	9	pottery	25	silver
2	cotton	10	tin	30	pearl
3	leather	11	steel	35	coral
4	linen	12	silk	40	ruby
5	wood	13	lace	45	sapphire
6	iron	14	ivory	50	gold
7	wool	15	crystal	55	emerald
8	bronze	20	china	60	diamond

STABLE MARRIAGE PROBLEM

♣ *For geeks* Imagine that you have to pair off some number N of men and the same number of women into N happy marriages. The only information you have access to is each individual's ranking of the N members of the opposite sex: a person's first choice is ranked 1, second choice 2, and so on. The problem is to pair off the men and women into N couples such that there is no man and woman who would rather have each other than their present partners; such a matching is called stable. At the same time, you would like to minimize the average rank of an individual's spouse.

In the optimal stable matching, the average rank of one's spouse is small compared to N for large N—most people are stably *and* happily married. However, this assumes that two persons' rankings of the opposite sex are uncorrelated. When a common notion of attractiveness is introduced, the rankings become similar, and the competition more severe. The overall effect is to make people *less* happy: In the limit that the rankings of the opposite sex are identical—a universal sense of beauty—the average rank of one's spouse grows to at least $1/2\ N$. For details, see G. Caldarelli and A. Capocci, *Physica A*, **300**, 325 (2001).

James Bond's (p. 144) romantic ideology is one of the defining characteristics of the British icon, about which we are only given a superficial picture. But Bond's relationship with women closely mirrors that of his creator, Ian Fleming, whose birthday centenary occurs in 2008, and Fleming's understanding of women *is* well documented.

Early on Fleming began his lifelong habit of approaching women 'like a glass of champagne', there to be drunk. During a year in Switzerland after leaving Sandhurst, Fleming became engaged to Monique Panchaud de Bottomes, the first and last time he fell in love (she would later become Bond's Swiss mother Monique Delacroix). But his mother did not approve and, when she threatened to disinherit him, Fleming was forced to break the engagement. 'I'm going to be quite bloody-minded about women from now on,' he wrote. 'I'm just going to take what I want without any scruples at all.'

Fleming became notorious for his reckless approach to love and passed without scruple from one affair to the next. Anyone looking for commitment was quickly rebuffed, and there is no evidence that women shaped him in any profound way. Like Bond in *On Her Majesty's Secret Service*, Fleming eventually married, if reluctantly. The woman was Lady Ann O'Neill, who was pregnant with his child. The marriage was plagued with mutual infidelity from beginning to end. It also included, if not bondage, sadomasochism: 'I loved cooking for you and sleeping beside you and being whipped by you... I long for you even if you whip me because I love being hurt by you and kissed afterwards,' wrote Ann in an early letter to Fleming. Vivienne Michel, the heroine and narrator of *The Spy Who Loved Me*, reflects Fleming's sentiments when she says: 'All women love semi-rape. They love to be taken. It was [Bond's] sweet brutality against my bruised body that made his act of love so piercingly wonderful.'

Looking for 'something to take my mind off the shock of getting married for the first time at the ridiculous age of 43', Fleming began his first Bond novel, *Casino Royale*. In it we see Fleming's approach to women, borne out in Bond's 'conventional parabola' of seduction: the 'sentiment, the touch of the hand, the kiss, the passionate kiss, the feel of the body, the climax in the bed, then more bed, then less bed, then the boredom, the tears and the final bitterness...' For Bond as for Fleming, the thrill of women was in the chase and in carnal satisfaction, although, in the case of Bond, the latter usually marked the end of the relationship. 'Women have their uses for the release of tension. And for giving a momentary release from loneliness. The only time people are not alone is just after making love,' Fleming wrote in a letter, capturing Bond's hollow outlook on romance precisely.

DRESS

❦ ON DRESS

Franz Kafka I merely try casually in a hit-or-miss way to dress well.

Hardy Amies Great style is insouciance—it is very vulgar to be impressed by your own clothes.

E. M. Forster All men are equal. All men, that is, who possess umbrellas.

August Luchet Last briefly and change often, appear rather than be—that is what suffices.

Lord Chesterfield Take great care always to be dressed like the reasonable people of your own age, in the place where you are; whose dress is never spoken of one way or another, as either too negligent or too much studied.

Paris Hilton The only rule is don't be boring and dress cute wherever you go.

Gore Vidal Style is knowing who you are, what you want to say, and not giving a damn.

Anne Hollander I have come to believe that male dress was always essentially more advanced than female throughout fashion history, and tended to lead the way, to set the standard.

Kotzebue Everything a man of fashion puts on his body must be broken in, nothing should appear new.

Honoré de Balzac In order to be fashionable, one must enjoy rest without having experienced work...Like steam engines, men regimented by work all look alike...The man instrument is a social zero.

Beau Brummell If John Bull turns round to look after you, you are not well dressed; but either too stiff, too tight, or too fashionable.

Jules Barbey d'Aurevilly Eccentricity is the rebellion of the individual against the established order, sometimes against nature itself, and that way madness lies. Dandyism, on the other hand, plays games with the rules while continuing to respect them.

George Meredith Cynicism is intellectual dandyism.

Lord Tennyson What profits now to understand / The merits of a spotless shirt / A dapper boot / A little hand / If half the little soul is dirt?

Jan Tschichold Today, good taste is often erroneously rejected as old-fashioned because the ordinary man, seeking approval of his so-called personality, prefers to follow the dictates of his own peculiar style rather than submit to any objective criterion of taste.

SHOE SHINE

Polishing shoes requires perseverance. It is not a single shine that determines a shoe's appearance but rather frequent polishing over a long period. The trick is to polish lightly but often, which eventually levels the pores and irregular surface of the leather. Black shoes, having no colour of their own, should reflect light and therefore should be highly polished. Black toecap shoes are sometimes polished to a moderate shine, with the toecaps themselves polished excessively (spit shine, see below). With brown shoes it is not gloss but patina that should be emphasized, and this can only be achieved with time and regular polish in a colour just lighter than the shoe itself. The combination of polish and wear produces a complex patchwork of colours and tones.

There are two main methods of polishing. The first is described on the back of the Kiwi tin: 'Apply polish with a cloth or brush. Let dry for one to two minutes, then brush to a bright shine. For heightened gloss, apply another light coat, sprinkle with water and buff with a soft cloth.' A cloth applies polish more evenly than a brush and is disposable, whereas a brush is quicker and reaches into crevices but must be cleaned with soap and water. The brush used to give lustre to the dried polish should be a separate, larger brush made of horse hair. The gloss can be enhanced by a final buff with a nylon stocking.

A more laborious method, known as a spit shine or sweating, is used to obtain the mirror-like finish particularly prized on black shoes. The finish is much more handsome than patent leather, whose gloss comes from a plastic coating. The technique involves no brushes, but is entirely done with a cloth wrapped around the fingers and kept moist (not wet) by dipping it into water. Using the cloth, rub a small amount of polish vigorously but lightly into a small area of the shoe until it is no longer cloudy. Repeat this process many dozens of times until the leather begins to resemble a black mirror.

KIWI COLOURS

In 1906 Australians William Ramsay and Hamilton McKellan introduced their black boot polish, called Kiwi. The first successful polish for brown shoes—dark tan—followed in 1908 and during the First World War Kiwi was adopted by the British army. Kiwi polish is now commonly available in 12 varieties.

1 Black	5 Dark Tan[1]	9 Tan
2 Blue	6 Mahogany	10 White
3 Brown	7 Mid Tan	11 Parade Gloss Black
4 Cordovan	8 Neutral	12 Parade Gloss Brown

[1]Closer in colour to brick red.

SHOE SIZE

Shoe size is one of the least standardized of all measurements, largely because, for a given size, the length of the foot and the length of the last are not the same. (The last is the shape that a shoe is made around.) The most common units of shoe size are the barleycorn (1/3 inch) and the Paris point (2/3 cm). In the UK, shoe size is equal to the length of the last in barleycorns minus the constant 25.25. The same applies to the US, except that the constant is 24.75. In Europe, shoe size is the length of the last in Paris points. Thus the equivalence between UK and US sizes and EU sizes is only approximate.

last (in)	UK size	US size	EU size	last (cm)	last (in)	UK size	US size	EU size	last (cm)
10.25	5 1/2	6	39	26.0	11.58	9 1/2	10	44	29.3
10.42	6	6 1/2	40	26.7	11.75	10	10 1/2	45	30.0
10.58	6 1/2	7	40	26.7	11.92	10 1/2	11	45	30.0
10.75	7	7 1/2	41	27.3	12.08	11	11 1/2	46	30.7
10.92	7 1/2	8	42	28.0	12.25	11 1/2	12	47	31.3
11.08	8	8 1/2	42	28.0	12.42	12	12 1/2	47	31.3
11.25	8 1/2	9	43	28.7	12.58	12 1/2	13	48	32.0
11.42	9	9 1/2	44	29.3	12.75	13	13 1/2	49	32.7

SHOELACES

There are many different ways of lacing a shoe, and the number of ways grows quickly with the number of eyelets. Of course, some lacings are better than others. The shortest and the strongest are:

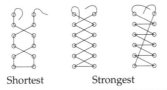

Shortest   Strongest

✤ *For geeks* A lacing of n pairs of eyelets is a closed path of $2n$ line segments through the $2n$ eyelets. To count as a genuine lacing, at least one of the two lace segments connecting to each eyelet must also connect to the opposite column of eyelets. Then the number of different ways to lace a shoe is

$$L(n) = \frac{(n!)^2}{2} \sum_{k=0}^{m} \frac{1}{n-k} \binom{n-k}{k}^2,$$

where $m = n/2$ if n is even and $m = (n-1)/2$ if n is odd. For example, for $n = 2$, 3 and 4 pairs of eyelets, the number of lacings is $L(2) = 3$, $L(3) = 42$ and $L(4) = 1080$. In all cases the shortest and strongest lacings are of the same form as above. For details, see Burkard Polster on p. 131.

The original function of the shirt was to protect the expensive and difficult-to-clean suit from the body. Hence the popularity of cotton—easily laundered and pleasant against the skin. Silk remains an indulgence, wool a mortification. Today a shirt (and here we limit ourselves to shirts with buttons) serves two purposes: as an undergarment with a suit, and as an outer garment without one.

Worn with a suit, a shirt should contrast with its dark cloth and therefore be light-coloured—white and light blue and pink, for example. Checks on a light background are popular, as are stripes, especially in England. There should be no breast pocket, and embroidered initials, if present, should never be seen. Of particular importance are the collar and cuffs which, under the jacket, are the shirt's only visible parts. Cutaway collars look handsome with knots of all sizes; less widely spread collars require smaller knots. Double cuffs (also known as French cuffs, though the French infrequently wear them) are more formal than button cuffs but are sometimes worn casually in London. Short-sleeved shirts are worn at barbecues and the beach; with a suit it is an act of sartorial terrorism, even if Ian Fleming always wore them thus. Rolling up one's sleeves, on the other hand, is to be encouraged, with both button and double cuffed shirts alike. Chaps roll to below the elbow, blokes to above.

Without a jacket, the shirt becomes the outer garment, and for this reason undershirts are sometimes seen, especially amongst Americans and Italians. A breast pocket is handy—it takes the place of the pockets on the jacket. The tie is usually discarded and the collar, no longer framing a knot, may be buttoned down. The top placket buttons are invariably undone, two buttons now being more common than one. Stronger colours, and the bold checks favoured by Americans, are all on display alongside the more civilized colours of 'dress' shirts.

NUMBER OF SHIRTS

❧ *For geeks* The minimum number of shirts and trousers to pack (in addition to clothes worn) on a trip lasting *Days* days is

$$Shirts = \sqrt{Days} \quad \text{and} \quad Trousers = \sqrt[3]{Days}.$$

Thus, for $1, 2, 3, 4, \ldots, 365$ days, one should pack $1, 1, 2, 2, \ldots, 19$ shirts and $1, 1, 1, 2, \ldots, 7$ pairs of trousers. Combining these, the relation between the number of shirts and trousers in one's possession is

$$Shirts^2 = Trousers^3.$$

Thus a man with 5 pairs of trousers should have 11 shirts; with 10 pairs of trousers, 32 shirts.

IRONING A SHIRT

Along with polishing shoes (p. 54), ironing a shirt is one of the two domestic arts a man should know. Ironing well is less about doing it correctly (many variations give the same result) than doing it quickly and sufficiently. The first thing to consider is that different fibres burn at different temperatures. Most irons have a temperature setting which lists the materials directly. The standard recommended values are:

⌁	110 °C	230 °F	acetate, acrylic, modacrylic, nylon, spandex
⌁	150 °C	302 °F	polyester, rayon, silk, triacetate, wool
⌁	200 °C	360 °F	cotton, linen

Steam speeds up ironing; with it, and some practice, a shirt can be ironed in five minutes. Alternatively, a spray bottle can be used to keep the shirt damp as you go, although this is less effective than steam. Some particular considerations: Dark fabrics should be ironed on the wrong side to avoid shine. Ties are steamed, never ironed.

Collar (25 s.) Keep the collar flat (there is no need to iron in a crease where it turns down). Iron the underside first, then the outside. Move from the tips of the collar towards the centre to prevent creasing at the edges.

Cuffs (45 s.) Iron the non-showing side first, then the showing side, being sure to iron from the edges inwards. Double cuffs should be ironed flat—again there is no need to iron in a crease.

Yoke (25 s.) This part of the shirt covers the shoulders, and is the trickiest part to get to. Use the narrow end of the ironing board.

Sleeves (90 s.) Start from the shoulder and finish near the cuff, ironing in the gauntlet pleats leading into it. Most sleeves are creased, but there is no consensus as to whether they should be. (Creases are avoided with the aid of a narrow board inserted into the sleeve.)

Back (45 s.) Despite its size, this uninterrupted piece of cloth is one of the fastest to iron. Remember that the bottom half will be tucked in and need not be ironed.

Front (70 s.) The bottom half can be neglected. Ironing around the buttons need not be perfect since the inside placket will not show.

If time is short and a jumper or jacket is worn, the time can be reduced to 2 min 20 s by ironing the collar, cuffs and front only.

A stiff shirt is worn with evening dress (p. 63) and, by some, a dinner jacket (p. 62). The stiffness comes from starch, which is usually applied by a dry-cleaner. At a pinch it can be done at home by repeated applications of spray starch, after each of which the shirt is ironed on the wrong side (to avoid yellowing). Only the front, collar and cuffs are starched. DIY starching of detachable collars is hopeless and they should be done professionally.

JEANS THEORY

Although the origin of denim work clothes is disputed, it was during the second half of the 19th century that they became widespread. The invention of jeans arguably came with the introduction of copper re-inforcing rivets by Jacob Davis and Levi Strauss in 1873. It was not until the 1950s, however, that jeans were in any sense fashionable and worn outside their manual-labour context. Wearing jeans was a minor act of rebellion, a supposed association with the proletariat.

Jeans today are so ingrained in popular culture that it is difficult to view their symbolism objectively. The old motivation—association with Everyman—remains partially true. Today part of the attraction is that jeans attenuate the formality of the overall costume, thereby allowing one to dress smartly with impunity. Andy Warhol was not the first person to combine jeans with a suit jacket and tie, but he made the juxtaposition popular. Today a blazer or pinstripe jacket with a worn pair of jeans does not draw attention. It suggests spontaneity—not for the first time we see the desire for studied indifference.

Along with the other quintessentially male garment, the suit, jeans are the most common element of Western men's dress. Everyone knows about jeans, but few understand them. A fair definition is *close-fitting blue denim trousers*, which we consider in detail.

Close-fitting Despite the short-lived popularity of bagginess in the 1990s, jeans are fundamentally close-fitting. A slim fit is inherent in their design: jeans do not have pleats; they grip the hips rather than suspend from the natural waist; the generous vertical pockets found on suit trousers are replaced with horizontal ones; jeans conform rather than drape, and for this reason need not be ironed. The narrow cut emphasizes a man's breadth of chest and muscularity. 'The tightness of fit, the showing of a good leg, fitted in with the Edwardian look of the modern dandy and the humbler Teddy Boy. The shape of course affected that of all trousers, which were belted low over the hips,' writes Hardy Amies.

Blue The overwhelming majority of jeans are blue jeans. Black and white jeans resurface once a decade or so, but in such small quantities as to be negligible. It is perhaps not coincidental that blue is the dominant colour of the suit. In jeans the blue is made from indigo, a natural dye derived from plants in the genus *Indigofera*, or a synthetic equivalent. The exposed thread (weft) is dyed blue and the perpendic-ular, covered thread (warp) is left white, a tell-tale sign of which is the diagonal stripe pattern on the reverse. It is a common misconception that the fading of jeans results from the dark weft being worn through, exposing the white warp, which only happens with extreme wear. Fading is in fact the result of the poor adhesive properties of indigo dye. Tiny fragments of indigo are embedded in, rather than bonded to, the cotton fibres. Friction results in the loss of dye fragments, hence the particular fading properties of denim with washing and wearing.

Denim The cloth itself is a kind of heavy cotton twill with a pronounced diagonal rib. Denim is a contraction of *serge de Nîmes*: Nîmes is a southern French city; serge is a kind of weave with diagonal ribs, now used more to describe wool cloths (James Bond liked his suits made from blue serge, p. 145). The cloth is known to shrink, usually about 3% over the first couple of years, which is about an inch for a 34-inch inseam. Denim shrinks further when dried at high temperature (although this is largely reversible through ordinary wear). For this reason jeans should be hung up to dry.

JEANS PRACTICE

Unlike with most clothes, with jeans the appearance of age through fading and wear is not only accepted but encouraged. This is not new: Jules Barbey d'Aurevilly, writing in 1844, describes Georgian swells who distressed the surface of their newly made clothes with glass-paper: 'They were at the end of their impertinence, they just couldn't go any further... They had their clothes distressed before they put them on, all over the cloth...' Today this worn look is more often ready-made, with jeans sold in various states of decline. Just how much wear is acceptable varies from year to year. The recent look of extreme distress, faded legs and frayed edges has been replaced by more moderately worn cloth in uniform shades. The most flattering cut of jeans is straight-leg, with boot cut (though not flairs) an acceptable and sometimes practical alternative. In either case, it is essential that jeans are worn slightly longer than one's usual trousers.

The oldest jeans companies, Levi's, Lee and Wrangler, continue to be the most successful, though only Levi's are much seen in urban settings. Their straight-leg, undecorated jeans are perhaps the only branded article of clothing that is truly egalitarian. The most dramatic shift in how denim is worn has, of course, been the meteoric rise in popularity of high-end jeans like Diesel and True Religion. Designers are giving unprecedented attention to fit and details, whilst firmly maintaining the proletarian, utilitarian look. Importantly, the brand itself takes second place to cut and cloth, which discourages analogies with the designer-jeans fad twenty years earlier. The situation is more reminiscent of traditional men's tailoring, which relies on sober detailing and above all else fit; it too puts limited stock in labels. Will bespoke jeans be widely available soon?

The Western civilized world—and much of the Eastern—has adopted English national dress. In 1649 King Charles I was executed and with him went doublet and hose. The history of the suit—in its earliest form a knee-length coat, waistcoat and breeches—begins with the Restoration. Unlike in France, where the aristocracy was concentrated at court, the English nobility was scattered about the countryside. Sport played a decisive role in shaping fashion, and by the late 18th century the frock coat was cut away for riding. A hundred years later the tails were removed altogether and the suit in its modern form appeared.

The suit is foremost a masculine garment, both in its simplicity of decoration and emphasis of the male form. Its matching fabric in muted colours forms the backdrop against which the colour and finery of women's clothes are displayed. The V shape rising from the tapered trousers to the jacket's padded shoulders sets man distinctly apart from woman.

The suit jacket comes in two varieties: single- and double-breasted. Single-breasted jackets have notched lapels and usually two or three or four buttons, two being dated and four showbiz. Only the top, middle and middle two buttons are done up, respectively, these being level with the natural waist and the jacket's narrowest point. Double-breasted jackets have peaked lapels and the jacket fronts overlap, with only the top working buttons done up. The number of vents is largely a matter of taste, although single-breasted jackets tend to have none or one; double, none or two.

There is less scope for variation in trousers. Turn-ups (called cuffs in America), while perfectly acceptable, are presently not *la mode*. If present, they are 1¹/₂ inches deep. Belts, appropriate with separate jacket and trousers, interrupt the matching fabric of the suit; in their place side fasteners or braces are preferable. Vertical front pockets, and one back pocket, are correct. Waistcoats are made of the same fabric as the suit, apart from with morning coats (p. 64). Like the jacket it should have (notched) lapels. By tradition the lowest waistcoat button is not fastened.

The single most important aspect of a good suit is fit. Always begin with the shoulders. Here the suit should be close-fitting, with little space for the cloth to indent against the arms. The collar must not gape at the back. The arm holes should be high and the sleeves narrow. The jacket should be just long enough to cover the seat entirely. A close-fitting garment around the legs has always been important in defining the masculine figure, first in the form of hose, then breeches, then trousers. Accordingly, trousers should be cut narrow through the seat and thigh and have one or no front pleats—not two.

BUYING A SUIT

Like architecture and typography, a suit is built up out of minor variations on inherited wisdom. Small deviations speak loudly. 'Never in your dress altogether desert that taste which is general,' advises Bulwer-Lytton. 'The world considers eccentricity in great things genius, in small things folly.' Your first couple of suits should be dark blue or dark grey. Black suits, apart from evening clothes and at funerals (and even here navy is perfectly correct), look cheap. First learn to wear with ease a plain navy suit, white shirt and solid navy tie, which is not as easy as it sounds. Once you have developed an eye for the basics, you can turn to other cloths—chalk stripes, checks, Prince of Wales, tweeds, corduroy, even velvet.

Price does not guarantee that a suit will look good, and indeed the most expensive suits, selected without a practised eye, are often unattractive and ill-fitting. There are a number of details that signify a well-made suit: pocket flaps; sewn rather than fused canvas lining; a button as opposed to zip fly; side adjusters instead of belt loops; working cuff buttons; matching lining inside the pocket flaps and jacket; a thread behind the buttonhole on the left lapel to hold stems.

Whilst most men's suits are ready-made, having a suit tailored brings with it the possibility of improved fit and the choice of cloth, lining, vents, pockets and button placement. There are two kinds of tailoring: made-to-measure and bespoke. A made-to-measure suit costs half again the price of a suit off-the-peg. The suit is made to a fixed pattern, but adapted to one's basic measurements: chest, waist, arms, legs and back. These details are sent away and made into a suit. When the finished product is returned, only small further changes can be made, like waist size or trouser length. A bespoke suit, on the other hand, is stagewise assembled on site over the course of a number of fittings (and costs twice as much as made-to-measure). Attention to detail is paramount, and much effort will be made to ensure a perfect fit. But beware of the tailor's eye for human defects: few men are constructed in the image of Ideal Man (p. 4), and the tailor will spot and adjust for any peculiarities ruthlessly.

Keep in mind that a tailor is only as demanding as his client, so it is important to be a stickler for details. When having clothes made one learns by mistakes, and your first suit will not be your favourite, so it is wise to begin with an inexpensive tailor. The principal signs that a suit has been tailored is the absence of a label and the choice of lining, which is customarily bolder than ready-made linings. Burgundy is traditional, with crimson, salmon pink and bottle green also smart. Light and royal blue tend to conflict with blue shirts.

BLACK TIE

Men's formal clothes invariably have their roots in sporting and military costume, first being accepted as day wear and eventually as clothes for the evening. The dinner jacket does not, as is often thought, derive from the evening tailcoat but from a Victorian lounge jacket popular in the late 1800s. The short jacket was later worn as informal evening wear and in the 1920s made a fashionable alternative to the tailcoat by the Prince of Wales. A dinner jacket is also known as *black tie*, a *tuxedo* in America, and *dress for dinner*, the last only found on invitations.

Dinner jackets come in three varieties: single-breasted, with peaked lapels; single-breasted, with a shawl collar; and double-breasted, which is always peaked. Unlike a black suit, a dinner jacket never has notched lapels. A closer inspection reveals that the silk facings of the lapels and collar are one of two types: *satin*, a smooth, glossy weave; or *grosgrain*, a matte silk weave with pronounced ribs. Both are permissible on all three jacket styles, with the exception of double-breasted, which today tends to show grosgrain. A white dinner jacket should not be worn, not in the summer, not by the sea.

Trousers are cut in the same material as the jacket with a silk braid running down the outside leg. Formal clothes require that the place where the trousers and the shirt meet be covered. This is the job of the waistcoat, also in black. Alternatively, a black cummerbund—originally an Indian sash worn around the waist (kamar-band)—is worn, with the folded pleats facing up. A double-breasted jacket looks after itself.

Dinner jackets are worn with a white marcella (piqué) shirt or, at a pinch, plain white broadcloth. Pleated shirts, while sometimes worn, have an aged look; 'You can revive a passing fashion of 100 years ago,' writes Hardy Amies, 'not one of ten.' The unstarched shirt collar should turn down, although there has been a revival of stiff wing collars. The bow tie is undecorated and black, never coloured, and comes today in three shapes (p. 68). Its weave should reflect the silk facings of the jacket: satin if the lapels are satin and barathea (a textured, basket weave) if the lapels are grosgrain. The bow should be tied by hand; for the clumsy there are ties with detachable bands which can be first tied around the leg in full view. Shirt studs and cufflinks are worn.

Shoes are of course black, with patent black lace-ups or black toe-caps correct; black brogues, less so. Slip-ons (whether they bear a penny or a tassel or a snaffle) are naff. Socks should be long enough to cover the calf. Pocket handkerchiefs are essential and should be silk and coloured; off-white is acceptable, just.

WHITE TIE

Despite appearances, the evening tailcoat is double-breasted. It evolved from the riding coat such that the two halves could never be fastened. Hence the two rows of buttons still seen today. Tailcoats are black, of course, but also sometimes midnight blue, which under artificial light appears blacker than black; true black by comparison can have a greenish tinge. The coat fronts should just cover the waistband of the trousers and the tails should reach the back of the knee.

White tie trousers differ from black tie trousers in two respects. Foremost, they are cut to be worn at the natural waist. This is because the white waistcoat must cover the trousers' waistband without extending below the coat fronts worn over it. Second, by tradition, the trousers have two silk braid stripes running down the outside seam of each leg—dinner jacket trousers have one.

The shirt is made of marcella or, less commonly, plain broadcloth and is starched stiff at the front and cuffs. The best shirts have a loop which attaches to the fly of the trousers to keep it from billowing out. A stiff wing collar is essential, and this means it must be detachable—it is very difficult to make an attached collar stiff. Although the collar should be at least 13/4 inches high, most shops' collars are too short, New & Lingwood being an exception. Like the shirt, the waistcoat is cut from white marcella and is worn stiff. It has a deep opening and only closes at the base, with studs. The waistcoat may have a back, usually in satin, or be backless and attach behind with an adjustable band. The marcella bow is tied like any other bow tie, a task which is near impossible if the thing is over-starched.

Shoes are patent leather, either lace-ups or (less commonly) court pumps with a ribbed satin bow, though well-polished toecaps would pass muster. Socks are now black and handkerchiefs off-white, although some colour can be displayed by a man who knows the rules. It is not ostentatious to wear a pocket watch, the fob (chain) being attached to a purpose-made hole in the waistcoat; if worn, the wristwatch is removed. Cufflinks and studs for the shirt and waistcoat are traditionally gold (not silver) or mother of pearl, with semi-precious and precious stones also seen. Decorations are worn in the presence of a member of the royal family or if they are indicated on the invitation, as in 'Evening dress—decorations'.

Few things are more ruined by poor fit than evening clothes. Second-hand (which is to say, old; see p. 72) dinner jackets and tailcoats seem to fit best, probably because they were made by hand. But beware of the matching trousers which, if made before 1950, are likely to have a hint of Oxford bags—a sartorial crime.

The morning coat has tails, of course, but it is not shaped like a tail-coat. It is closer to a frock coat with the corners cut away, with continuous curves from lapels to tail; hence a morning coat is sometimes called a cutaway. Morning coats come in two colours: grey, worn with matching grey trousers; or black, usually in a herringbone weave, worn with grey and black striped or black and white houndstooth trousers. Black is the smarter of the two, reminding us of the Regency coat and breeches from which it descends. These did not match either, the coat being dark and the trousers light.

A white shirt, dove-grey waistcoat and black-and-white tie are correct, if uninspired. Much more handsome is the incorporation of colour, which also helps dispel the hired look. Solid, checked and striped shirts are suitable in any light colour, although blue is a wise starting point. The collar, however, should be white, preferably stiff. A stiff turn-down collar is attached by studs, and weaving a necktie through it is not easy. A coloured shirt calls for a coloured waistcoat, in buff (a light brownish yellow) or cream or pale blue or pink even, preferably made of linen. The waistcoat should have lapels, but whether it is single- or double-breasted is purely a matter of taste; since the wedding of Charles, Prince of Wales and Camilla Parker Bowles, double has been somewhat more fashionable. The use of colour means one can choose one's tie more liberally, in navy or burgundy, for example. It should be in heavy silk and, if not plain, woven rather than printed, fixed to the shirt with a tie tack (p. 71).

It is acceptable to wear a cravat instead of a necktie, tied in an overhand knot and pinned in place with a stick pin. Nevertheless a tie is the less studied and smarter of the two. It forms a link between the morning coat and the modern suit, without which a morning suit risks looking like fancy dress. A man should feel as much at ease in formal clothes as in any others, but he needs reference points. A grey or preferably black top hat can be worn or carried. Shoes are black toecaps. If ever there was a time to wear a buttonhole, this is it.

Don't want to compete with the groom? George Brummell's rejection of fine feathers brought an end to male peacocks. Unless otherwise instructed, it is not out of place to wear a morning suit at any traditional English wedding. But disregard the dictum that the principal male members of the wedding party should dress alike, probably inspired by the for-hire companies which rent to them. Indeed the opposite is true: exercising the limited freedoms in morning dress is one of the principal pleasures in wearing it. If buying a new morning suit is prohibitively expensive, fine old ones can be bought second-hand for little more than the cost of hiring (p. 72).

Like most elements of Western men's dress, the tie has its origins in England. 'If we, the Brits, cannot claim to have invented the modern tie,' argues Hardy Amies, 'no other nation can either.' The earliest record of the tie in its modern form is in 1850s England, where it was worn by young men as sporting attire. The style became fashionable at once, eclipsing the cravats and stocks popular at the time. Much has been said about the demise of the tie, and throughout the last hundred years its death has been repeatedly prophesied. It should be kept in mind, however, that knotted neckcloths have been standard attire for men for 350 years, and if the tie does vanish, something knotted around the neck will almost certainly replace it.

We will not talk about the colour or pattern of ties here, apart from saying that a solid navy tie in woven or knitted silk never goes amiss. As for the shape of a tie, a width of 3–3 1/2 inches is in natural proportion with the typical man's suit. While most ties available today are wider than this, the best tie makers, such as Hermès and many of the shops along Jermyn Street (p. 109), have consistently produced ties of the ideal width. The length of the tie should not, of course, descend below the waistband. More contentious is whether or not the thin blade should be tucked into the label behind the wide blade.

It is often said that ties should never be dry-cleaned, but this is not quite true. It is not the cleaning but the inevitable pressing afterwards which most harms a tie, and the latter can be avoided if a cleaner is warned beforehand. Nonetheless there is no need to have a tie cleaned apart from visible marks or stains.

The death of a much-loved tie invariably results from the fraying of the wide blade's edges, which usually happens long before any other part of the tie wears out. The solution is to have the tie shortened by half an inch, which many alterations tailors will do if asked. It is a somewhat delicate operation but, if done with care, it can double a tie's life. A truly worn-out or unwanted tie can be turned into a belt. It is simple to make. You cut off the wide blade such that the tie is a few inches longer than the circumference of your waist, and sew the cut end around two identical metal rings, about 1 1/2 inches in diameter and 1/6 inch thick. The belt is 'buckled' by weaving the opposite end through the rings as shown. Pulling on this end tightens the belt.

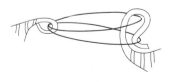

TIE KNOTS

A tie of conventional length can be tied into 85 different knots, excluding knots which are mirror images of others. These correspond to all the ways of arranging the six symbols $L_\otimes, L_\odot, R_\otimes, R_\odot, C_\otimes, C_\odot$, where L, R and C stand for left, right and centre and $\odot$ and $\otimes$ indicate out of, and into, the page (an arrow tip and an arrow tail). The only rules are that the $\otimes$s and $\odot$s must alternate and the same letter cannot appear twice in a row ($L_\odot L_\otimes$, for example, is illegal). Moreover, a knot must begin with $L_\otimes$ or $L_\odot$ and end with $R_\odot L_\otimes C_\odot T$ or $L_\odot R_\otimes C_\odot T$.

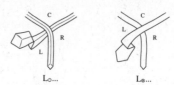

$L_\odot...$ $L_\otimes...$

Two ways to start a tie knot.

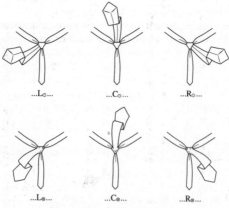

$...L_\odot...$ $...C_\odot...$ $...R_\odot...$

$...L_\otimes...$ $...C_\otimes...$ $...R_\otimes...$

Six possible tie knot moves.

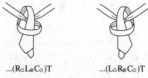

$...(R_\odot L_\otimes C_\odot)T$ $...(L_\odot R_\otimes C_\odot)T$

Two ways to end a tie knot.

Of the 85 possible knots, 15 stand out:

Oriental	Nicky	Half-Windsor	Cavendish	Grantchester
Four-in-hand	Pratt	St Andrew	Christensen	Hanover
Kelvin	Victoria	Plattsburgh	Windsor	Balthus

The three traditional knots (numbers 2, 7, 31) and a couple of others are listed below. For the comprehensive treatise on necktie knots, see *The 85 Ways to Tie a Tie* (❦ Books, p. 131).

No.	Size	Centres	Sequence	Knotted	Name
2	4	1	$L_\otimes R_\odot L_\otimes C_\odot T$	n	four-in-hand
4	5	2	$L_\odot C_\otimes R_\odot L_\otimes C_\odot T$	n	Nicky
7	6	2	$L_\otimes R_\odot C_\otimes L_\odot R_\otimes C_\odot T$	y	half-Windsor
31	8	3	$L_\otimes C_\odot R_\otimes L_\odot C_\otimes R_\odot L_\otimes C_\odot T$	n	Windsor
54	9	3	$L_\odot R_\otimes C_\odot L_\otimes R_\odot C_\otimes L_\odot R_\otimes C_\odot T$	y	Hanover

No.   Number of the knot.

Size   Number of moves (not including T) or half-turns, which corresponds to the size of the knot.

Centres   Number of centre moves C. The number of centres divided by the size corresponds to the width of the knot.

Knotted   Knotted status. If the knotted tie is removed and both ends are pulled, it will form a trefoil knot (y) or unknot itself (n).

Example: Nicky

♣ *For geeks*   The number of different tie knots K that can be tied with h moves or half-turns is

$$K(h) = \tfrac{1}{3}(2^{h-2} - (-1)^{h-2}).$$

For example, only 1 knot can be tied with 3 half-turns: the Oriental; 1 knot can be tied with 4 half-turns: the four-in-hand; and 3 can be tied with 5 half-turns: the Kelvin, Nicky and Pratt. Assuming the standard tie is long enough to allow at most 9 moves, the total number of knots is

$$\sum_{h=1}^{9} K(h) = 85.$$

From Thomas Fink and Yong Mao,
'Designing tie knots by random walks', *Nature*, **398**, 31 (1999);
'Tie knots, random walks and topology', *Physica A*, **276**, 109 (2000).

BOW TIE

Despite its longer lineage than the necktie, today the bow tie is worn almost exclusively with formal clothes. Some men persist in wearing a bow tie with a jacket or suit, but at a cost: against the backdrop of modern men's dress, bow ties appear studied or eccentric. They confer a diminished impression of authority. A man's dress is made remarkable only by its absence of defect. Conspicuous inconspicuousness is the rule, and the bow tie does nothing if not draw attention. 'If you insist on wearing a bow tie to business—and bow tie wearers are a stubborn lot—I suggest you wear it with the proper accessories,' writes John Molloy in *Dress for Success*. 'A red nose and a beanie cap with a propeller.'

Bow ties worn with a dinner jacket or tailcoat are black silk or white cotton, and can be found in three shapes: the butterfly, the batswing and the one-hander (left to right). All are tied the same way.

Unlike a necktie, both ends of a bow tie can be manipulated to form a knot, making bow tie knots potentially much more complicated than tie knots. The only known knot which can be tied with conventional bow ties is the usual reef bow (p. 118) below. The granny bow causes the tied bow to sit vertically rather than horizontally. Alternative knots may exist, but have yet to be discovered. The author welcomes candidates for new knots—or a proof of their impossibility. Of course, bow ties should be self-tied rather than ready-tied. '[The bow tie] and the stiff wing collar are the direct descendants of Beau Brummell's starched cravats. He had trouble tying these. How could the rising

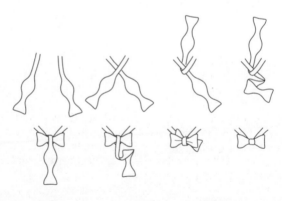

middle classes cope? ...I cannot blame men for buying "made-up" ties, sin though it is to wear one,' writes Hardy Amies.

The tied bow has four layers of cloth emanating from each side of the knot, three of which form the bow (shown top-down below) and one of which goes around the neck. Pulling on the three bow layers produces different effects, essential to optimizing all but the most expertly tied knots.

A Pulling here increases one side of the bow whilst decreasing the other side half as much.

B Pulling here increases one side of the bow whilst tightening the knot.

C Pulling here increases one side of the bow whilst decreasing the other side twice as much.

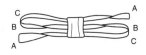

CRAVAT AND ASCOT

The modern cravat is a long, rectangular neckcloth, pleated in the centre to form a neckband. It is made of silk, usually in a print of polka dot, paisley or foulard. Despite being a direct descendant of the plain white linen neckcloths of Brummell and the Regency, it is rarely found in plain colours. Continentals often wear it casually around the neck and tucked under an open-collared shirt, a practice which has not caught on in Britain, where cravats are limited to weddings with a morning suit (p. 64). Cravats are tied as follows:

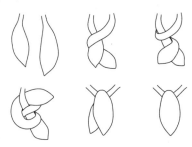

Apart from its narrower blades, the Ascot differs from the cravat most noticeably in the knot used to tie it. It is tied in a reef knot (p. 118) with the descending blades of equal length, one carefully folded over the other and fixed with a pin. It is mostly worn with morning dress at weddings and the eponymous horse race.

HANDKERCHIEFS

Contrary to popular belief, the purpose of the handkerchief is not aesthetics but utility. It has for centuries been a practical accessory: to catch a sneeze, open a bottle or dry up tears. During the First World War, the handkerchief was kept tucked into the jacket sleeve because the uniform pockets buttoned down. It has since returned to the breast pocket, and whether it is on display or not, that is where it belongs. 'The most important [rule] is that it must look as though you use it; and you must. To have a handkerchief showing in the breast pocket and another one for use is to provide the most "naff" gesture a man can make,' writes Hardy Amies in *The Englishman's Suit*. The second is that it must not look like a piece of origami; tricorns, shells and bird bases should be avoided. If it is to be arranged it must be done with studied indifference.

Apart from being square and having rolled edges, a handkerchief can be made from just about anything: silk, linen, even cotton, the backs of old shirts proving a thrifty source. It should of course not match the tie but rather in its lustre oppose it: linen or cotton for satin ties, silk for matt or wool ties. 'Of course it's extravagant to blow one's nose in a silk handkerchief, but we are talking about style and not economics,' writes Amies. 'There are now quite beautiful coloured cotton handkerchiefs... of the bandanna type... Very good to add a touch of the country squire.'

BANDANNAS

The word 'bandanna' is derived from the Hindi word *bādhnū*, an Indian method of selectively dyeing cloth by tying it in knots. It now refers to the cotton and sometimes silk squares printed with simple patterns of paisley or polka dots. Bandannas are bigger than handkerchiefs, typically 22 inches square as opposed to 16. They are worn in the breast or front trouser pockets; beware of using the back pocket unless you are familiar with the gay semiotics of the 'hanky code'.

Bandanna uses: babushka · bandage · bandanna doll · Barbie parachute · belt (two tied together) · bib · blindfold · bottle apron · cat cape · cheesecloth · coffee filter · cold compress · cravat · dish cloth · dog kerchief · dust mask · gag · gang allegiance · garotte · gift wrap · glasses cleaner · handcuffs · headband · hobo pack · lunch box · muffler · napkin · nappy · neckerchief · origami · pillow cover · pirate costume · placemat · polish rag · pot holder · poultice · scarf · shoe shine cloth · shoo away bugs · sit upon · sling · smokescreen mask · splint · strainer · sweat band · tie a ponytail · towel · touch football (American) · tourniquet · washcloth · whip · Wild West costume · wrap breakables

BUTTONHOLES

Like most details of the men's suit, the buttonhole on the left lapel is not fanciful. It descends from a true button hole, an artefact of the high-fastening lapels of the 18th century—buttoning descended but the button holes did not. Putting the buttonhole to unintended use is not new: in the early 18th century the ends of the lace cravats popular at the time were pulled through it, a style known as the Steinkerk. Today the buttonhole is used to hold a flower, though a sprig of ivy will not be out of place. Well-tailored suits have a loop inside the lapel to hold the stem. It is incorrect to pin a flower to a lapel without a buttonhole. A hole can easily be added by a tailor, the only exception being the shawl-collared dinner jacket, whose lapel never fastened. The buttonhole flower itself should look as though it came from the neighbour's garden, not arranged by a florist. Carnations and thistles are smart, as are paper poppies in November (but flags in America only). Orchids are camp. A rose is worn on St George's Day.

HARDWARE

Cufflinks One of the simplest types of cufflinks, and also the smartest, is two metal ovals joined by a chain. There are countless other varieties, some of which have ingenious designs. But there is a fine line between the smart and the naff, and the inexperienced are best advised to stick to the plainest designs. It is completely acceptable to detach the link from one side of the cuff and roll up the sleeves. But beware of single-faced cufflinks, which are on such occasions even more likely than usual to fall out.

A *tie bar* is used to restrain the necktie, usually for the sake of formality or safety. It is a hairpin-shaped piece of metal or other material which slides over the shirt and tie, keeping the latter immobilized. *Tie clips* are similar but spring-loaded. Both are hopelessly dated.

Tie tacks, on the other hand, are seeing a revival. They are made of a circular metal disk which attaches to a base under the shirt by way of a pin. They are often worn with a morning coat (p. 64). Budd (p. 108) and Benson & Clegg offer affordable specimens in plain metal.

A *collar bar* is a piece of metal which clasps both sides of the collar and forces the tie knot forward, causing the tie to billow.

Collar bones, or collar stiffeners, are inserted into the collars of many shirts to keep the points of the collar from curling. These are typically plastic, sometimes metal, best of all bone.

Studs close the front of formal shirts in place of buttons, resembling small dumbbell-shaped cufflinks.

Collar studs, not visible, attach detachable collars to the shirt.

As fashion goes, men's dress is not complicated. Like architecture or typography, it is a mixture of a lot of system and a little trend. It is built up of a hierarchy of formality, each level evolving at a pace in inverse proportion to its sobriety. Casual clothes—those seen on the streets of London, New York, Berlin and Tokyo—evolve most quickly, with currents visibly shifting from year to year. The turnover for jackets is longer—velvet jackets have now become mainstream, and more two-button jackets are being made. Suits change more slowly yet, and on the time scale of a decade only motion in the details is detectable: shoulders, vents, buttoning. Least volatile of all are formal clothes, like the dinner jacket and morning suit. They *do* evolve, but very slowly.

The good news for men is that hand-me-down and second-hand jackets, suits and evening clothes are as desirable now as when they were made. They are frequently finer and smarter than clothes bought off the peg today, partly because many of the garments were bespoke and hand-stitched, partly because in previous years more attention was given to fit. There are a handful of shops which specialize in good second-hand clothes for men, none of which is well known (although Hackett began as just such a shop in the early 1980s). Frequently stocked are retro items such as 1950s print ties and high-fastening pin-stripe jackets.

The key to finding what fits is to try on everything in your size and just above and below it. Many bespoke items will be label-less, so the clothes are usually sifted into sizes by appearance. A simple alteration can solve many problems, but it is wise to have it altered by a specialist alterations tailor rather than on the premises.

Old Hat, 66 Fulham High St, London SW6   *0207 610 6558*

Old Hat is owned by David Saxby, described by *The Chap* magazine as Britain's sartorial agony uncle. It's full of second-hand jackets, suits, dinner and smoking jackets, tailcoats, morning coats and old hats, all at extremely good prices. Second-hand suits are £50–100. Old Hat also make their own traditional tweed jackets, waistcoats and accessories, mostly sold from their Fulham Road shop. Foreign labels are frowned upon.

Old Hat (previously Bertie Wooster), 284 Fulham Rd, London SW10   0207 352 5662

In April 2006 Old Hat took over the Bertie Wooster shop on Fulham Road. Bertie Wooster was founded by George Cazenove and named after the narrator of P. G. Wodehouse's Jeeves stories. Not much has changed: Bertie Wooster specialized in top-tailored second-hand and own-label clothes at modest prices, and Old Hat continues the tradition. A recent customer looking to drop off some clothes was told, 'No Ralph Lauren or Armani, please. We prefer tailors off the Row.'

An

ALMANACK

for the year

2 0 0 7

being a guide to

THE HEAVENS

including

MOTIONS OF THE SUN AND MOON,
ASPECTS OF THE PLANETS, ASTRONOMICAL PHENOMENA,
NAMES OF MONTHS AND MEAN WEEKLY WEATHER

&

THE WORLD

including

HOLIDAYS AND INAUSPICIOUS DAYS, CIVIL DAYS,
FEASTS, FASTS AND HOLY DAYS, PROPERTIES OF MONTHS,
AGES OF MAN AND ADVICE FROM POOR RICHARD

The calendar is based on the time it takes for the Earth to rotate around its axis (the day), the moon to revolve around the Earth (the synodic month) and the Earth to revolve around the sun (the tropical year); to this should be added the pre-Mosaic seven-day cycle of the week. Apart from the day and week, none of these is commensurate, but instead have the relations:

$$1 \text{ tropical year} = 12.368 \text{ synodic months};$$
$$1 \text{ synodic month} = 29.531 \text{ days; and}$$
$$1 \text{ tropical year} = 365.242 \text{ days.}$$

The excess of the tropical year over 365 days, namely, 5h 48m 45s, has been the cause of some inconvenience, and the history of the Western calendar is largely the struggle to resolve it. Combining with this the week and month, which dictate most of the year's religious and cultural events, was sufficiently complicated to motivate an annual guide to the year, known since medieval times as an almanack.

Early almanacks, usually 12 or 24 pages long, provided astronomical and meteorological data alongside the dates of holidays, holy days and festivals. In addition, within their densely set lines could be found law and university terms, advice on personal improvement, prognostications and verse. This almanack is set out as follows:

LEFT-HAND PAGE: THE HEAVENS

Time	All times are given in Greenwich Mean Time (GMT), also known by astronomers as Universal Time (UT). For British Summer Time (BST), add 1 hour.
Month names	In various languages and Roman numerals (RN).
Moon	The moon phase dates and times are accurate worldwide, although the hour must be adjusted outside GMT. If there are two full moons in a single month, the second is called a blue moon; on average this occurs once every 2.5 years.
Weekly weather	Values are derived from the 30-year daily averages measured at Royston Iceni Weather Station (N 52°03′, W 0°0′).
Day of year	Of which there are 365 in 2007, it being a common year.
Day of month	Of which there are 31, 28, 31, 30, 31, 30, 31, 31, 30, 31, 30, 31.
Day of week	The first day of the week, Sunday, is denoted ☉.
Sun rise & set	As observed at London Bridge (N 51° 30′, W 0° 05′). This and the moon data are from the Astronomical Applications Department, US Naval Observatory.
Length of day	The amount of time that the sun is above the horizon.
Moon rise & set	As observed at London Bridge.
Moon phase	The illuminated fraction of the moon's disc, measured per cent. Quarter moons correspond to 50% illumination.
Planetary ephemerae	Conjunctions, oppositions, eclipses, solstices, equinoxes and meteor showers. See p. 150 for definitions.

SYMBOLS AND ABBREVIATIONS

b.	begins	☉	Sun	☻	Bank holiday
e.	ends	☽	Moon	☺	Inauspicious day
E	England	♂	Conjunction	℞	Red-Letter day
w	Wales	☍	Opposition	℗	Flag day
s	Scotland	●	New moon	†	Holy day
I	Ireland	☽	First quarter	✠	Saint's day
US	United States	○	Full moon	🜊	Ages of man
BD	Birthday	☾	Last quarter	⚇	For geeks
ᛋ	Sunday	☺	Holiday	✐	Poor Richard

RIGHT-HAND PAGE: THE WORLD

Month attributes	The man of signs is an association of man's body with the signs of the Zodiac, from the head (Aries) to the feet (Pisces), popular in medieval medicine. ☙ For age, see *Ages of man* below. ☙ A seasonal drink is given for each month with the intent of broadening tastes.
Labours cycle	Early almanacks printed verses that linked each month with its practical concerns. (In R. H. Robbins, ed., *Secular Lyrics of the XIVth and XVth Centuries*, 1955.)
🜊 *Ages of man*	The 16th-century *Kalendar of Sheepehards* partitions man's life into 12 stages of six years, each associated with a month. (In B. Blackburn & L. Holford-Strevens, listed on p. 131.)
☺ *Holiday*	Traditional and popular UK holidays. American holidays are marked US.
☻ *Bank holiday*	Applies to the entire UK unless otherwise indicated.
☺ *Inauspicious day*	Unlucky or unpleasant days.
℞ *Red-Letter day*	Important civil days and holy days on which senior judges wear scarlet.
℗ *Flag day*	The Union flag is flown.
† *Holy day*	Christian holy days and fasts.
✠ *Saint's day*	Church of England and Roman Catholic solemnities and feast days.
ᛋ *Sunday*	Sundays are counted as follows: after Epiphany, in Lent, after Easter, after Trinity, in Advent and after Christmas.
🜊 *Ages of man*	Ages and events in the typical man's life mapped onto the year (1 month = 6 years).
⚇ *For geeks*	Curious properties of times, days and dates.
✐ *Poor Richard*	Advice from the most famous of all almanacks, Benjamin Franklin's *Poor Richard's* (see p. 48).

Latin	French	Spanish	German	Italian	Welsh	Irish	RN
Ianuarius	janvier	enero	Januar	gennaio	Ionawr	Eanáir	i

Phase		Day	Hour	Week	Av. max.	Av. min.	Av. precip.
Full moon	○	3	13:57	31 Dec–6	6.9 °C	2.4 °C	0.59 in
Last quarter	☾	11	12:45	7–13	6.5 °C	2.0 °C	0.43 in
New moon	●	19	4:01	14–20	6.2 °C	2.0 °C	0.30 in
First quarter	☽	25	23:01	21–27	6.7 °C	2.3 °C	0.57 in
				28–3 Feb	6.6 °C	2.1 °C	0.47 in

Day of yr	mo	wk	☀ rise	☀ set	Length of day	☽ rise	☽ set	☽ phase	Planetary ephemerae
1	1	M	8:06	16:02	7:56	13:27	6:32	92	
2	2	Tu	8:06	16:03	7:57	14:21	7:44	97	
3	3	W	8:06	16:04	7:58	15:30	8:39	99	Quadrantids peak
4	4	Th	8:06	16:05	7:59	16:48	9:16	100	(3 Jan) Perihelion 20:00
5	5	F	8:05	16:06	8:01	18:08	9:42	98	
6	6	Sa	8:05	16:07	8:02	19:26	10:00	94	Saturn 0.9°S of ☽ 18:00
7	7	☉	8:05	16:09	8:04	20:41	10:14	88	Mercury at sup. ☌ 6:00
8	8	M	8:04	16:10	8:06	21:52	10:25	81	
9	9	Tu	8:04	16:11	8:07	23:02	10:34	73	
10	10	W	8:03	16:13	8:10		10:44	64	
11	11	Th	8:02	16:14	8:12	0:11	10:54	55	
12	12	F	8:02	16:16	8:14	1:22	11:06	46	
13	13	Sa	8:01	16:17	8:16	2:36	11:21	36	
14	14	☉	8:00	16:19	8:19	3:52	11:41	27	
15	15	M	8:00	16:20	8:20	5:09	12:11	19	
16	16	Tu	7:59	16:22	8:23	6:20	12:54	12	
17	17	W	7:58	16:23	8:25	7:21	13:55	6	Mars 4.5°N of ☽ 2:00
18	18	Th	7:57	16:25	8:28	8:06	15:12	2	
19	19	F	7:56	16:26	8:30	8:38	16:40	0	
20	20	Sa	7:55	16:28	8:33	9:01	18:10	1	Venus 0.8°N of ☽ 17:00
21	21	☉	7:54	16:30	8:36	9:18	19:39	4	(20 Jan) Aquarius ♒
22	22	M	7:53	16:32	8:39	9:31	21:07	10	
23	23	Tu	7:52	16:33	8:41	9:44	22:33	19	
24	24	W	7:50	16:35	8:45	9:56	23:59	28	
25	25	Th	7:49	16:37	8:48	10:10		39	
26	26	F	7:48	16:38	8:50	10:28	1:27	51	
27	27	Sa	7:46	16:40	8:54	10:51	2:55	62	
28	28	☉	7:45	16:42	8:57	11:24	4:19	72	
29	29	M	7:44	16:44	9:00	12:11	5:34	81	
30	30	Tu	7:42	16:46	9:04	13:14	6:34	89	
31	31	W	7:41	16:47	9:06	14:28	7:16	95	

All times shown in Greenwich Mean Time.

Birthstone	Zodiac (b.)	Man of Signs	Age	Drink
Garnet	Aquarius ♒	Legs, ankles	0–6	Whisky

By thys fyre I warme my handys;

🜂 The fyrste moneth is Januarye, the childe is without might tyll hee bee 6 yeere olde, he can not helpe him selfe.

Day of mo	wk	Holidays, civil days, days of note	Holy days, Poor Richard, ages of man [yrs]
1	M	● ☺ *New Year's Day*	✠ Circumcision of Our Lord
		☺ *Handsel Monday*	🜂 Is born [0]
2	Tu	● (s)	
3	W		✍ *Creditors have better memories than Debtors.*
4	Th		
5	F		
6	Sa	☺ *Twelfth Day* · The Ashes Cricket ends	† Epiphany
7	⑤	World Darts Championship begins	
		1st ⑤ after Epiphany · ✠ Baptism of the Lord	
8	M	☺ *Plough Monday*	
9	Tu		✍ *Keep your mouth wet, feet dry.*
10	W		
11	Th	Hilary law term begins	
12	F		
13	Sa	✍ *No man e'er was glorious, who was not laborious.*	
14	⑤		2nd ⑤ after Epiphany
15	M		
16	Tu		🜂 Is 10^8 seconds [3.2]
17	W		
18	Th		
19	F		
20	Sa	⚲ BD of Countess of Wessex	
21	⑤	🜂 First memories [4] · 3rd ⑤ after Epiphany	
22	M	✍ *Hear no ill of a Friend, nor speak any of an Enemy.*	
23	Tu		
24	W		
25	Th	☺ *Burns Night*	℞ ✠ Conversion of St Paul
26	F		
27	Sa	♣ Berry Day (see p. 165)	
28	⑤		4th ⑤ after Epiphany
29	M		
30	Tu	✍ *Never spare the Parson's Wine, nor Baker's Pudding.*	
31	W		🜂 Is 6 years

Latin	*French*	*Spanish*	*German*	*Italian*	*Welsh*	*Irish*	RN
Februarius	février	febrero	Februar	febbraio	Chwefror	Feabhra	ii

Phase		*Day*	*Hour*	*Week*	*Av. max.*	*Av. min.*	*Av. precip.*
Full moon	○	2	5:45	4–10	7.6 °C	2.7 °C	0.45 in
Last quarter	☾	10	9:51	11–17	6.5 °C	1.1 °C	0.31 in
New moon	●	17	16:14	18–24	7.1 °C	1.3 °C	0.28 in
First quarter	☽	24	7:56	25–3 Mar	8.3 °C	2.3 °C	0.41 in

Day of yr	*mo*	*wk*	✷ *rise*	✷ *set*	*Length of day*	☽ *rise*	☽ *set*	☽ *phase*	*Planetary ephemerae*
32	1	Th	7:39	16:49	9:10	15:48	7:45	98	
33	2	F	7:38	16:51	9:13	17:07	8:05	100	Saturn 0.9° S of ☽ 23:00
34	3	Sa	7:36	16:53	9:17	18:23	8:20	99	
35	4	𝔖	7:35	16:55	9:20	19:35	8:32	97	
36	5	M	7:33	16:56	9:23	20:46	8:42	93	
37	6	Tu	7:31	16:58	9:27	21:56	8:51	87	
38	7	W	7:30	17:00	9:30	23:06	9:01	80	
39	8	Th	7:28	17:02	9:34		9:12	72	Neptune ✷ ☌ 10:00
40	9	F	7:26	17:04	9:38	0:18	9:25	63	
41	10	Sa	7:24	17:06	9:42	1:33	9:42	54	Saturn at ☍ 18:00
42	11	𝔖	7:22	17:07	9:45	2:48	10:07	44	
43	12	M	7:21	17:09	9:48	4:01	10:42	35	
44	13	Tu	7:19	17:11	9:52	5:06	11:34	25	
45	14	W	7:17	17:13	9:56	5:58	12:43	17	
46	15	Th	7:15	17:15	10:00	6:36	14:06	9	Mars 3.6° N of ☽ 1:00
47	16	F	7:13	17:16	10:03	7:02	15:37	4	
48	17	Sa	7:11	17:18	10:07	7:22	17:09	1	
49	18	𝔖	7:09	17:20	10:11	7:37	18:40	0	
50	19	M	7:07	17:22	10:15	7:50	20:09	3	Venus 2.5° S of ☽ 18:00
51	20	Tu	7:05	17:24	10:19	8:03	21:39	8	Pisces ♓
52	21	W	7:03	17:26	10:23	8:17	23:09	15	
53	22	Th	7:01	17:27	10:26	8:33		25	
54	23	F	6:59	17:29	10:30	8:54	0:40	35	Mercury at inf. ☌ 5:00
55	24	Sa	6:57	17:31	10:34	9:24	2:08	46	
56	25	𝔖	6:55	17:33	10:38	10:07	3:27	57	
57	26	M	6:53	17:35	10:42	11:05	4:31	68	
58	27	Tu	6:51	17:36	10:45	12:15	5:17	77	
59	28	W	6:49	17:38	10:49	13:33	5:49	85	

All times shown in Greenwich Mean Time.

Birthstone	Zodiac (b.)	Man of Signs	Age	Drink
Amethyst	Pisces ♓	Feet	6–12	Martini

And with my spade I delfe my landys.

♊ The 6 yeere that is the first time of the springinge of all flowres, and so the childe till 12 yeere groweth in knowledge and learning, and to doo as he is taught.

Day of mo	wk	Holidays, civil days, days of note	Holy days, Poor Richard, ages of man [yrs]
1	Th		✠ St Brigid
2	F	☺ *Candlemas Day*	♈ ✠ Purification of the Blessed Virgin
		☺ *Groundhog Day* (US)	
3	Sa	Six Nations Rugby begins	
4	☉	Super Bowl XLI	5th ☉ after Epiphany
5	M		♊ Reaches age of reason [7]
6	Tu	♇ ♈ Accession of HM the Queen	
7	W		
8	Th		✍ *Those who are fear'd, are hated.*
9	F		
10	Sa		
11	☉		6th ☉ after Epiphany
12	M		✍ *Be slow in chusing a Friend, slower in changing.*
13	Tu		
14	W	☺ *St Valentine's Day*	
15	Th		✍ *None are deceived, but they that confide.*
16	F		
17	Sa		
18	☉		7th ☉ after Epiphany
19	M	♇ BD of Duke of York	
20	Tu	☺ *Shrove Tuesday*	
21	W		Lent begins · ♈ † Ash Wednesday
22	Th		✠ Chair of St Peter
23	F		✍ *Love, Cough, & a Smoke, can't be well hid.*
24	Sa		✠ St Matthias
25	☉		1st ☉ in Lent
26	M		
27	Tu		✍ *Fish & Visitors stink after three days.*
28	W	Scottish term day	♊ Is 12 years · † Ember Day

Latin	French	Spanish	German	Italian	Welsh	Irish	RN
Martius	mars	marzo	März	marzo	Mawrth	Márta	iii

Phase		Day	Hour	Week	Av. max.	Av. min.	Av. precip.
Full moon	○	3	23:17	4–10	9.8 °C	3.3 °C	0.27 in
Last quarter	☾	12	3:54	11–17	10.3 °C	3.7 °C	0.43 in
New moon	●	19	2:43	18–24	10.7 °C	3.6 °C	0.41 in
First quarter	☽	25	18:16	25–31	11.4 °C	3.7 °C	0.34 in

yr	Day of mo	wk	✳ rise	✳ set	Length of day	☽ rise	☽ set	☽ phase	Planetary ephemerae
60	1	Th	6:47	17:40	10:53	14:51	6:12	92	
61	2	F	6:44	17:42	10:58	16:08	6:28	96	Saturn 1.1°S of ☽ 2:00
62	3	Sa	6:42	17:43	11:01	17:21	6:40	99	Tot. lunar eclipse 23:24
63	4	⑤	6:40	17:45	11:05	18:32	6:50	100	
64	5	M	6:38	17:47	11:09	19:42	7:00	99	
65	6	Tu	6:36	17:49	11:13	20:53	7:09	96	Uranus ✳ ♂ 0:00
66	7	W	6:33	17:50	11:17	22:04	7:20	92	
67	8	Th	6:31	17:52	11:21	23:17	7:32	86	
68	9	F	6:29	17:54	11:25		7:47	79	
69	10	Sa	6:27	17:56	11:29	0:32	8:08	71	
70	11	⑤	6:24	17:57	11:33	1:45	8:38	62	
71	12	M	6:22	17:59	11:37	2:53	9:21	52	
72	13	Tu	6:20	18:01	11:41	3:49	10:21	42	
73	14	W	6:18	18:02	11:44	4:32	11:36	32	
74	15	Th	6:15	18:04	11:49	5:02	13:02	22	
75	16	F	6:13	18:06	11:53	5:24	14:32	13	Mars 1.9°N of ☽ 2:00
76	17	Sa	6:11	18:08	11:57	5:41	16:03	6	Merc. 1.4°N of ☽ 3:00
77	18	⑤	6:09	18:09	12:00	5:55	17:34	2	
78	19	M	6:06	18:11	12:05	6:08	19:06	0	Part. solar eclipse 2:31
79	20	Tu	6:04	18:13	12:09	6:22	20:39	1	(21 Mar) Aries ♈
80	21	W	6:02	18:14	12:12	6:37	22:13	5	Vernal equinox 0:09
81	22	Th	6:00	18:16	12:16	6:57	23:46	12	(21 Mar) Venus 4.0°S
82	23	F	5:57	18:18	12:21	7:24		21	of ☽ 15:00
83	24	Sa	5:55	18:19	12:24	8:03	1:12	31	
84	25	⑤	5:53	18:21	12:28	8:57	2:24	42	Summer Time b. 1:00
85	26	M	5:50	18:23	12:33	10:05	3:17	53	
86	27	Tu	5:48	18:24	12:36	11:22	3:53	63	
87	28	W	5:46	18:26	12:40	12:40	4:18	73	
88	29	Th	5:44	18:28	12:44	13:57	4:36	81	Saturn 1.2°S of ☽ 4:00
89	30	F	5:41	18:30	12:49	15:10	4:49	88	
90	31	Sa	5:39	18:31	12:52	16:21	5:00	94	

All times shown in Greenwich Mean Time. For Summer Time, add 1 hour.

Birthstone	Zodiac (b.)	Man of Signs	Age	Drink
Aquamarine	Aries ♈	Head	12–18	Trappist ale

Here I sette my thynge to sprynge;

♈ Marche is the buddinge time, and in that 6 yeere of Marche the Childe waxeth bygge and apte to doo seruice, and learne scyence from 12 to 18, such as is shewed hym.

Day of mo	wk	Holidays, civil days, days of note	Holy days, Poor Richard, ages of man [yrs]
1	Th	☺ *National day of Wales*	♇ ℞ ✠ St David
2	F		† Ember day
3	Sa		† Ember day
4	⑤		2nd ⑤ in Lent
5	M		
6	Tu		✑ *Three good meals a day is bad living.*
7	W		
8	Th		✑ *Do me the favour to deny me at once.*
9	F		
10	Sa	♇ BD of Earl of Wessex	✠ St John Ogilvie
11	⑤	Cricket World Cup begins	3rd ⑤ in Lent
12	M	♇ ☺ *Commonwealth Day*	
13	Tu		
14	W		
15	Th	✑ *He is not well bred, that cannot bear Ill-Breeding in others.*	
16	F		
17	Sa	☺ *National day of Ireland*	✠ St Patrick
18	⑤	☺ *Mothering Sunday*	4th ⑤ in Lent
19	M	● (1)	✠ St Joseph
20	Tu		
21	W	Spring begins · Length of day = night	♈ Can marry & smoke [16]
22	Th		✑ *Hope of gain Lessens pain.*
23	F		
24	Sa		
25	⑤	English quarter day Summer Time begins 1:00	℞ † Annunciation · 5th ⑤ in Lent
26	M		♈ Can drive [17]
27	Tu		
28	W		
29	Th		
30	F		✑ *He that would travel much, should eat little.*
31	Sa		♈ Is 18 years; can drink

Latin	French	Spanish	German	Italian	Welsh	Irish	RN
Aprilis	avril	abril	April	aprile	Ebrill	Aibreán	iv

Phase		Day	Hour	Week	Av. max.	Av. min.	Av. precip.
Full moon	○	2	17:15	1–7	11.8 °C	3.9 °C	0.46 in
Last quarter	☽	10	18:04	8–14	12.4 °C	3.7 °C	0.46 in
New moon	●	17	11:36	15–21	13.4 °C	4.4 °C	0.30 in
First quarter	☽	24	6:36	22–28	14.4 °C	5.5 °C	0.46 in

yr	Day of mo	wk	☀ rise	☀ set	Length of day	☽ rise	☽ set	☽ phase	Planetary ephemerae
91	1	♋	5:37	18:33	12:56	17:31	5:09	97	
92	2	M	5:35	18:35	13:00	18:41	5:19	100	
93	3	Tu	5:32	18:36	13:04	19:52	5:29	100	
94	4	W	5:30	18:38	13:08	21:04	5:40	98	
95	5	Th	5:28	18:40	13:12	22:19	5:54	95	
96	6	F	5:26	18:41	13:15	23:32	6:13	91	
97	7	Sa	5:23	18:43	13:20		6:40	84	
98	8	♋	5:21	18:45	13:24	0:42	7:17	77	
99	9	M	5:19	18:46	13:27	1:41	8:10	68	
100	10	Tu	5:17	18:48	13:31	2:28	9:18	58	
101	11	W	5:14	18:50	13:36	3:02	10:37	48	
102	12	Th	5:12	18:51	13:39	3:26	12:02	37	
103	13	F	5:10	18:53	13:43	3:45	13:30	27	
104	14	Sa	5:08	18:55	13:47	4:00	14:59	17	Mars 0.5°S of ☽ 2:00
105	15	♋	5:06	18:56	13:50	4:13	16:28	9	
106	16	M	5:04	18:58	13:54	4:26	18:00	3	
107	17	Tu	5:01	19:00	13:59	4:40	19:34	0	
108	18	W	4:59	19:01	14:02	4:58	21:11	1	
109	19	Th	4:57	19:03	14:06	5:22	22:44	4	
110	20	F	4:55	19:05	14:10	5:57		9	Venus 3.3°S of ☽ 8:00
111	21	Sa	4:53	19:06	14:13	6:46	0:06	17	Taurus ♉
112	22	♋	4:51	19:08	14:17	7:51	1:09	27	(21 Apr) Lyrids peak
113	23	M	4:49	19:10	14:21	9:07	1:53	37	
114	24	Tu	4:47	19:11	14:24	10:27	2:22	47	
115	25	W	4:45	19:13	14:28	11:45	2:42	57	Saturn 1.1°S of ☽ 10:00
116	26	Th	4:43	19:15	14:32	13:00	2:57	67	
117	27	F	4:41	19:16	14:35	14:11	3:08	76	
118	28	Sa	4:39	19:18	14:39	15:21	3:18	83	
119	29	♋	4:37	19:20	14:43	16:31	3:28	90	
120	30	M	4:35	19:21	14:46	17:41	3:38	95	

All times shown in Greenwich Mean Time. For Summer Time, add 1 hour.

Birthstone	*Zodiac (b.)*	*Man of Signs*	*Age*	*Drink*
Diamond	Taurus ♉	Neck, throat	18–24	Gimlet

And here I here the fowlis synge.

🦢 Aprill is the springing tyme of flowres, and in that 6 yeere he groweth to mans state in heyght and bredthe, and waxeth wise and bolde, but then beware of sensualitie, for he is 24.

Day of		*Holidays,*	*Holy days,*
mo	*wk*	*civil days, days of note*	*Poor Richard, ages of man [yrs]*
1	⑤	☺ *All Fools' Day*	† Palm Sunday · 6th ⑤ in Lent
2	M		
3	Tu		✍ *Beware of the young Doctor and the old Barber.*
4	W	Hilary law term ends	
5	Th		† Maundy Thursday
6	F	●	† Good Friday
7	Sa	The Boat Race	† Lent ends
8	⑤	☺ *Easter*	† Easter Sunday
9	M	● (E, W, I)	Easter Monday
10	Tu		
11	W		✍ *Read much, but not too many Books.*
12	Th		
13	F	☺ *Friday the 13th*	
14	Sa		
15	⑤		🦢 Can drink in US · 1st ⑤ after Easter
16	M	✍ *Keep your eyes open wide before marriage, half shut afterwards.*	
17	Tu	Easter law term begins	
18	W		
19	Th		✍ *Love well, whip well.*
20	F		
21	Sa	♇ ♏ BD of HM the Queen	
22	⑤	London Marathon	2nd ⑤ after Easter
23	M	☺ *National day of England*	♇ ✠ St George
24	Tu		
25	W		♏ ✠ St Mark
26	Th		
27	F		✍ *Happy's the Wooing that's not long a doing.*
28	Sa		
29	⑤		3rd ⑤ after Easter
30	M		🦢 Is 24 years; Youngest Prime Minister (Pitt)

Latin	French	Spanish	German	Italian	Welsh	Irish	RN
Maius	mai	mayo	Mai	maggio	Mai	Bealtaine	V

Phase		Day	Hour	Week	Av. max.	Av. min.	Av. precip.
Full moon	○	2	10:09	29 Apr–5	15.1 °C	6.0 °C	0.41 in
Last quarter	☾	10	4:27	6–12	16.1 °C	6.6 °C	0.30 in
New moon	●	16	19:27	13–19	17.4 °C	7.4 °C	0.39 in
First quarter	☽	23	21:03	20–26	17.7 °C	8.3 °C	0.56 in
				27–2 Jun	18.7 °C	9.0 °C	0.46 in

	Day of		☀	☀	Length	☽	☽	☽	
yr	mo	wk	rise	set	of day	rise	set	phase	Planetary ephemerae
121	1	Tu	4:33	19:23	14:50	18:53	3:49	98	
122	2	W	4:31	19:24	14:53	20:07	4:02	100	
123	3	Th	4:29	19:26	14:57	21:21	4:20	100	Mercury at sup. ☌ 4:00
124	4	F	4:28	19:28	15:00	22:32	4:44	98	Eta Aquarids peak
125	5	Sa	4:26	19:29	15:03	23:35	5:18	94	
126	6	☉	4:24	19:31	15:07		6:06	88	
127	7	M	4:22	19:33	15:11	0:25	7:09	81	
128	8	Tu	4:20	19:34	15:14	1:03	8:24	72	
129	9	W	4:19	19:36	15:17	1:29	9:45	63	
130	10	Th	4:17	19:37	15:20	1:49	11:09	52	
131	11	F	4:15	19:39	15:24	2:05	12:34	41	
132	12	Sa	4:14	19:40	15:26	2:18	14:00	30	
133	13	☉	4:12	19:42	15:30	2:31	15:27	20	Mars 3.1°S of ☽ 1:00
134	14	M	4:11	19:44	15:33	2:44	16:58	12	
135	15	Tu	4:09	19:45	15:36	3:00	18:32	5	
136	16	W	4:08	19:47	15:39	3:21	20:07	1	
137	17	Th	4:06	19:48	15:42	3:50	21:37	0	
138	18	F	4:05	19:50	15:45	4:32	22:51	2	
139	19	Sa	4:04	19:51	15:47	5:31	23:45	7	
140	20	☉	4:02	19:52	15:50	6:46		14	Venus 1.7°S of ☽ 1:00
141	21	M	4:01	19:54	15:53	8:07	0:21	22	Gemini II
142	22	Tu	4:00	19:55	15:55	9:28	0:45	32	Saturn 0.8°S of ☽ 19:00
143	23	W	3:58	19:57	15:59	10:46	1:02	41	
144	24	Th	3:57	19:58	16:01	11:59	1:15	51	
145	25	F	3:56	19:59	16:03	13:10	1:26	61	
146	26	Sa	3:55	20:00	16:05	14:20	1:36	70	
147	27	☉	3:54	20:02	16:08	15:30	1:46	78	
148	28	M	3:53	20:03	16:10	16:41	1:56	85	
149	29	Tu	3:52	20:04	16:12	17:54	2:09	91	
150	30	W	3:51	20:05	16:14	19:08	2:25	96	
151	31	Th	3:50	20:06	16:16	20:21	2:47	99	

All times shown in Greenwich Mean Time. For Summer Time, add 1 hour.

Birthstone	*Zodiac (b.)*	*Man of Signs*	*Age*	*Drink*
Emerald	Gemini ♊	Arms, shoulders	24–30	Wheat beer

I am as lyght as byrde in bowe;

Maye is the season that flowers byn spreade, and bee then in theyr vertue with sweet odours. In these 6 yeeres he is in his most strength, but then let him geather good maners betyme, for if his tary past that age it is an hap if euer he take them, for then he is 30 yeare.

Day of mo	*wk*	*Holidays, civil days, days of note*	*Holy days, Poor Richard, ages of man [yrs]*
1	Tu	☺ *May Day*	ℜ ✠ SS Philip & James
2	W		
3	Th		✍ *He's a Fool that makes his Doctor his Heir.*
4	F		✠ Beatified Martyrs of England & Wales
5	Sa		
6	𝔖		4th 𝔖 after Easter
7	M	☻	✍ *Love your Enemies, for they tell you your Faults.*
8	Tu		
9	W	⚐ Europe Day	
10	Th	Eurovision Song Contest, Helsinki	
11	F		✍ *Would you persuade, speak of Interest, not of Reason.*
12	Sa	Eurovision Song Contest, Helsinki	
13	𝔖	☺ *Mother's Day* (US)	† Rogation Sunday · 5th 𝔖 after Easter
14	M		† Rogation Day · ℜ ✠ St Matthias
15	Tu		† Rogation Day
16	W		† Rogation Day
17	Th		ℜ † Ascension Day
18	F		
19	Sa	FA Cup Final	
20	𝔖		6th 𝔖 after Easter
21	M		
22	Tu		✍ *In success be moderate.*
23	W		
24	Th		✍ *An undutiful Daughter, will prove an unmanageable Wife.*
25	F	Easter law term ends	
26	Sa		
27	𝔖		† Whit Sunday (Pentecost) · 7th 𝔖 after Easter ✠ St Augustine of Canterbury
28	M	☻ · Scottish term day	
29	Tu	☺ *Oak Apple Day*	
30	W		† Ember Day
31	Th		Is 30 years · ✠ Visitation of the BVM

Latin	French	Spanish	German	Italian	Welsh	Irish	RN
Iunius	juin	junio	Juni	giugno	Mehefin	Meitheamh	vi

Phase		Day	Hour	Week	Av. max.	Av. min.	Av. precip.
Full moon	○	1	1:04	3–9	19.2 °C	10.1 °C	0.49 in
Last quarter	☾	8	11:43	10–16	19.3 °C	10.2 °C	0.40 in
New moon	●	15	3:13	17–23	20.3 °C	10.9 °C	0.33 in
First quarter	☽	22	13:15	24–30	20.8 °C	11.4 °C	0.50 in
Full moon	○	30	13:49				

	Day of		☀	☀	Length	☽	☽	☽	
yr	mo	wk	rise	set	of day	rise	set	phase	Planetary ephemerae
152	1	F	3:49	20:08	16:19	21:28	3:18	100	
153	2	Sa	3:48	20:09	16:21	22:22	4:03	99	
154	3	☉	3:48	20:10	16:22	23:03	5:02	96	
155	4	M	3:47	20:11	16:24	23:33	6:14	91	
156	5	Tu	3:46	20:12	16:26	23:54	7:34	84	
157	6	W	3:46	20:13	16:27		8:57	76	Jupiter at ☍ 0:00
158	7	Th	3:45	20:13	16:28	0:11	10:20	66	
159	8	F	3:45	20:14	16:29	0:25	11:43	56	
160	9	Sa	3:44	20:15	16:31	0:37	13:07	44	
161	10	☉	3:44	20:16	16:32	0:50	14:33	33	
162	11	M	3:44	20:17	16:33	1:04	16:03	23	
163	12	Tu	3:43	20:17	16:34	1:22	17:35	14	
164	13	W	3:43	20:18	16:35	1:46	19:07	7	
165	14	Th	3:43	20:18	16:35	2:21	20:28	2	
166	15	F	3:43	20:19	16:36	3:12	21:32	0	
167	16	Sa	3:43	20:19	16:36	4:20	22:16	1	
168	17	☉	3:43	20:20	16:37	5:41	22:45	5	
169	18	M	3:43	20:20	16:37	7:05	23:06	10	Venus 0.6°S of ☽ 15:00
170	19	Tu	3:43	20:21	16:38	8:26	23:20	18	Saturn 0.4°S of ☽ 8:00
171	20	W	3:43	20:21	16:38	9:42	23:32	26	
172	21	Th	3:43	20:21	16:38	10:56	23:43	35	Summer solstice 18:07
173	22	F	3:43	20:21	16:38	12:06	23:53	45	(21 Jun) Cancer ♋
174	23	Sa	3:43	20:22	16:39	13:16		54	
175	24	☉	3:44	20:22	16:38	14:27	0:03	64	
176	25	M	3:44	20:22	16:38	15:39	0:15	73	
177	26	Tu	3:44	20:22	16:38	16:53	0:30	81	
178	27	W	3:45	20:22	16:37	18:07	0:50	87	
179	28	Th	3:45	20:21	16:36	19:17	1:17	93	Mercury at inf. ☌ 18:00
180	29	F	3:46	20:21	16:35	20:16	1:57	97	
181	30	Sa	3:47	20:21	16:34	21:02	2:51	99	Blue moon

All times shown in Greenwich Mean Time. For Summer Time, add 1 hour.

Birthstone	Zodiac (b.)	Man of Signs	Age	Drink
Pearl	Cancer ♋	Chest	30–36	Pimm's No. 1 Cup

And I wede my corne well inow.

☝ In June he beginneth to close his mynde, and then hee waxeth rype, for then he is 36 yeere.

Day of mo	wk	Holidays, civil days, days of note	Holy days, Poor Richard, ages of man [yrs]
1	F		† Ember Day
2	Sa	ℙℜ Coronation Day	† Ember Day
3	⚈		† Trinity Sunday
4	M		✍ *He that speaks much, is much mistaken.*
5	Tu	Trinity law term begins	☝ First marriage [31]
		♟ Time, date is 12:34 5-6-7	
6	W		
7	Th		† Corpus Christi
8	F		☝ Is 10^9 = 1 billion seconds [31.7]
9	Sa		✠ St Columba
10	⚈	ℙℜ BD of HM the Duke of Edinburgh	1st ⚈ after Trinity
11	M		ℜ ✠ St Barnabas
12	Tu		
13	W		✍ *Force shites upon Reason's Back.*
14	Th		
15	F		✍ *If Jack's in love, he's no Judge of Jill's Beauty.*
16	Sa		✠ Sacred Heart
17	⚈	☺ Father's Day	2nd ⚈ after Trinity
18	M		
19	Tu		
20	W		
21	Th	Summer begins · Longest day	
22	F		✠ SS John Fisher & Thomas More
23	Sa		✍ *Men take more pains to mask than mend.*
24	⚈	English quarter day	3rd ⚈ after Trinity
			ℜ ✠ St John the Baptist
25	M	Wimbledon Tennis begins	☝ Minimum age of US president [35]
26	Tu		
27	W		✍ *A good Lawyer is a bad Neighbour.*
28	Th		
29	F		ℜ ✠ St Peter
30	Sa		☝ Is 36 years

Latin	French	Spanish	German	Italian	Welsh	Irish	RN
Iulius	juillet	julio	Juli	luglio	Gorffennaf	Iúil	vii

Phase		Day	Hour	Week	Av. max.	Av. min.	Av. precip.
Last quarter	☾	7	16:54	1–7	21.6 °C	11.9 °C	0.55 in
New moon	●	14	12:04	8–14	22.2 °C	12.6 °C	0.36 in
First quarter	☽	22	6:29	15–21	22.2 °C	12.7 °C	0.41 in
Full moon	○	30	0:48	22–28	22.7 °C	12.9 °C	0.29 in

	Day of		☀	☀	Length	☽	☽	☽	
yr	mo	wk	rise	set	of day	rise	set	phase	Planetary ephemerae
182	1	☉	3:47	20:21	16:34	21:36	4:01	100	
183	2	M	3:48	20:20	16:32	22:00	5:20	98	
184	3	Tu	3:49	20:20	16:31	22:18	6:44	93	
185	4	W	3:49	20:20	16:31	22:32	8:09	87	
186	5	Th	3:50	20:19	16:29	22:45	9:32	79	
187	6	F	3:51	20:19	16:28	22:57	10:55	69	Aphelion 18:00
188	7	Sa	3:52	20:18	16:26	23:10	12:19	58	
189	8	☉	3:53	20:17	16:24	23:26	13:46	47	
190	9	M	3:54	20:17	16:23	23:47	15:15	35	
191	10	Tu	3:55	20:16	16:21		16:44	25	
192	11	W	3:56	20:15	16:19	0:16	18:09	16	
193	12	Th	3:57	20:14	16:17	0:59	19:19	8	
194	13	F	3:58	20:13	16:15	2:00	20:10	3	
195	14	Sa	3:59	20:13	16:14	3:15	20:45	0	
196	15	☉	4:00	20:12	16:12	4:38	21:08	0	
197	16	M	4:01	20:11	16:10	6:02	21:25	3	Saturn 0.0° N of ☽ 23:00
198	17	Tu	4:03	20:09	16:06	7:21	21:38	7	Venus 2.7°S of ☽ 10:00
199	18	W	4:04	20:08	16:04	8:37	21:49	13	
200	19	Th	4:05	20:07	16:02	9:50	21:59	21	
201	20	F	4:06	20:06	16:00	11:00	22:10	29	
202	21	Sa	4:08	20:05	15:57	12:11	22:21	38	
203	22	☉	4:09	20:04	15:55	13:23	22:34	48	
204	23	M	4:10	20:02	15:52	14:36	22:52	57	Leo ♌
205	24	Tu	4:12	20:01	15:49	15:50	23:15	66	
206	25	W	4:13	20:00	15:47	17:02	23:50	75	
207	26	Th	4:15	19:58	15:43	18:06		83	
208	27	F	4:16	19:57	15:41	18:58	0:38	90	
209	28	Sa	4:17	19:55	15:38	19:36	1:42	95	Delta Aquarids peak
210	29	☉	4:19	19:54	15:35	20:03	2:59	99	Alpha Capricornids
211	30	M	4:20	19:52	15:32	20:23	4:24	100	peak
212	31	Tu	4:22	19:51	15:29	20:39	5:50	99	

All times shown in Greenwich Mean Time. For Summer Time, add 1 hour.

Birthstone	*Zodiac (b.)*	*Man of Signs*	*Age*	*Drink*
Ruby	Leo ♌	Heart, upper back	36–42	Mint Julep

With my sythe my mede I mowe;

In July he is 42, and he begynneth a lyttle to declyne, and feeleth hym not so prosperous as he was.

Day of mo	*wk*	*Holidays, civil days, days of note*	*Holy days, Poor Richard, ages of man [yrs]*
1	𝔖		✠ St Oliver Plunkett · 4th 𝔖 after Trinity
2	M		✍ *No Wood without Bark.*
3	Tu	☹ *Dog Days begin*	𝔑 ✠ St Thomas
4	W	☺ *Independence Day* (US)	
5	Th		
6	F		✍ *Let thy maid-servant be faithful, strong, and homely.*
7	Sa	☢ Date is 7-7-7 · Tour de France begins	
8	𝔖		5th 𝔖 after Trinity
9	M		
10	Tu		✍ *Necessity never made a good bargain.*
11	W		
12	Th	☻ (I) ☺ *Orangemen's Day*	
13	F	☹ *Friday the 13th*	Mid-life [38.5]
14	Sa		
15	𝔖		6th 𝔖 after Trinity
16	M		
17	Tu	ᑭ BD of Duchess of Cornwall	
18	W		
19	Th		✍ *Nothing but Money is sweeter than Honey.*
20	F	☢ Date numbers repeat: 20-07-2007	
21	Sa		Oldest age for Fields medal (Nobel prize of maths) [40]
22	𝔖		7th 𝔖 after Trinity
23	M		
24	Tu		
25	W		𝔑 ✠ St James
26	Th		
27	F	21st World Scout Jamboree begins	
28	Sa		✍ *A light Purse is a heavy Curse.*
29	𝔖		8th 𝔖 after Trinity
30	M		
31	Tu	Trinity law term ends	Is 42 years

Latin	French	Spanish	German	Italian	Welsh	Irish	RN
Augustus	août	agosto	August	agosto	Awst	Lughnasadh	viii

Phase		Day	Hour	Week	Av. max.	Av. min.	Av. precip.
Last quarter	☾	5	21:20	29 Jul–4	23.3 °C	13.4 °C	0.61 in
New moon	●	12	23:03	5–11	22.8 °C	13.1 °C	0.46 in
First quarter	☽	20	23:54	12–18	23.0 °C	13.1 °C	0.35 in
Full moon	○	28	10:35	19–25	22.1 °C	12.6 °C	0.50 in
				26–1 Sep	20.9 °C	11.5 °C	0.34 in

yr	Day of mo	wk	☀ rise	☀ set	Length of day	☽ rise	☽ set	☽ phase	Planetary ephemerae
213	1	W	4:23	19:49	15:26	20:52	7:16	95	
214	2	Th	4:25	19:47	15:22	21:05	8:41	89	
215	3	F	4:26	19:46	15:20	21:18	10:06	81	
216	4	Sa	4:28	19:44	15:16	21:32	11:33	71	
217	5	☾	4:29	19:42	15:13	21:51	13:01	60	
218	6	M	4:31	19:41	15:10	22:17	14:30	49	
219	7	Tu	4:33	19:39	15:06	22:54	15:56	38	
220	8	W	4:34	19:37	15:03	23:47	17:09	27	
221	9	Th	4:36	19:35	14:59		18:06	18	
222	10	F	4:37	19:33	14:56	0:57	18:45	10	
223	11	Sa	4:39	19:31	14:52	2:17	19:12	4	
224	12	☾	4:40	19:29	14:49	3:40	19:31	1	Perseids peak
225	13	M	4:42	19:27	14:45	5:00	19:45	0	Neptune at ☍ 11:00
226	14	Tu	4:44	19:26	14:42	6:18	19:57	1	
227	15	W	4:45	19:24	14:39	7:32	20:07	4	Mercury at sup. ☌
228	16	Th	4:47	19:22	14:35	8:44	20:17	9	20:00
229	17	F	4:48	19:20	14:32	9:55	20:28	16	
230	18	Sa	4:50	19:18	14:28	11:06	20:40	23	Venus at inf. ☌ 4:00
231	19	☾	4:51	19:16	14:25	12:19	20:55	32	
232	20	M	4:53	19:13	14:20	13:33	21:16	41	
233	21	Tu	4:55	19:11	14:16	14:45	21:45	50	Saturn ☀ ☌ 23:00
234	22	W	4:56	19:09	14:13	15:52	22:26	60	
235	23	Th	4:58	19:07	14:09	16:49	23:23	69	Virgo ♍
236	24	F	4:59	19:05	14:06	17:32		78	
237	25	Sa	5:01	19:03	14:02	18:04	0:34	86	
238	26	☾	5:03	19:01	13:58	18:27	1:56	93	
239	27	M	5:04	18:59	13:55	18:44	3:23	97	
240	28	Tu	5:06	18:56	13:50	18:59	4:50	100	Tot. lunar eclipse 10:37
241	29	W	5:07	18:54	13:47	19:12	6:18	100	
242	30	Th	5:09	18:52	13:43	19:25	7:45	97	
243	31	F	5:11	18:50	13:39	19:39	9:14	91	

All times shown in Greenwich Mean Time. For Summer Time, add 1 hour.

Birthstone	Zodiac (b.)	Man of Signs	Age	Drink
Peridot	Virgo ♍	Belly	42–48	Sauternes

And here I shere my corne full lowe;

🜼 In August he is by that 6 yeere 48 yeere and then he goeth not so lustely as he dyd, but studieth howe to geather to fynde him in his olde age to liue more easely.

Day of mo	wk	Holidays, civil days, days of note	Holy days, Poor Richard, ages of man [yrs]
1	W		🖎 Mine is better than Ours.
2	Th		
3	F		
4	Sa		
5	⑤		9th ⑤ after Trinity
6	M	● (s)	✠ Transfiguration of the Lord
7	Tu		🖎 Men and melons are hard to know.
8	W	World Scout Jamboree ends	
9	Th		
10	F		✠ St Lawrence
11	Sa	Dog Days end	
12	⑤		10th ⑤ after Trinity
13	M		
14	Tu		
15	W	ℙ BD of the Princess Royal	✠ Assumption
16	Th		
17	F		🖎 Love your Neighbour; yet don't pull down your Hedge.
18	Sa		
19	⑤		11th ⑤ after Trinity
20	M		
21	Tu		
22	W		🖎 Gifts much expected, are paid, not given.
23	Th		
24	F		✠ St Bartholomew
25	Sa		
26	⑤		12th ⑤ after Trinity
27	M	● (E, W, I)	
28	Tu	Scottish term day	🜼 Middle of adult life [47.5]
29	W		
30	Th		🖎 If your head is Wax, don't walk in the Sun.
31	F		🜼 Is 48 years

Latin	French	Spanish	German	Italian	Welsh	Irish	RN
September	septembre	septiembre	September	settembre	Medi	Meán Fómhair	ix

Phase		Day	Hour	Week	Av. max.	Av. min.	Av. precip.
Last quarter	☾	4	2:32	2–8	20.7 °C	11.4 °C	0.29 in
New moon	●	11	12:44	9–15	19.2 °C	10.9 °C	0.53 in
First quarter	☽	19	16:48	16–22	18.3 °C	10.7 °C	0.64 in
Full moon	○	26	19:45	23–29	17.8 °C	10.1 °C	0.54 in

yr	Day of mo	wk	✻ rise	✻ set	Length of day	☽ rise	☽ set	☽ phase	Planetary ephemerae
244	1	Sa	5:12	18:48	13:36	19:57	10:44	83	
245	2	☉	5:14	18:45	13:31	20:20	12:15	73	
246	3	M	5:15	18:43	13:28	20:54	13:44	63	
247	4	Tu	5:17	18:41	13:24	21:42	15:02	51	
248	5	W	5:18	18:39	13:21	22:46	16:03	40	
249	6	Th	5:20	18:36	13:16		16:47	30	
250	7	F	5:22	18:34	13:12	0:02	17:17	20	
251	8	Sa	5:23	18:32	13:09	1:24	17:37	12	
252	9	☉	5:25	18:30	13:05	2:44	17:53	6	
253	10	M	5:26	18:27	13:01	4:02	18:05	2	Uranus at ☍ 3:00
254	11	Tu	5:28	18:25	12:57	5:16	18:15	0	Part. solar eclipse 12:34
255	12	W	5:30	18:23	12:53	6:28	18:25	0	
256	13	Th	5:31	18:20	12:49	7:40	18:36	2	Mercury 2.5°N
257	14	F	5:33	18:18	12:45	8:51	18:47	6	of ☽ 14:00
258	15	Sa	5:34	18:16	12:42	10:03	19:01	11	
259	16	☉	5:36	18:14	12:38	11:16	19:20	18	
260	17	M	5:38	18:11	12:33	12:29	19:45	25	
261	18	Tu	5:39	18:09	12:30	13:38	20:20	34	
262	19	W	5:41	18:07	12:26	14:38	21:09	43	
263	20	Th	5:42	18:04	12:22	15:26	22:13	53	
264	21	F	5:44	18:02	12:18	16:02	23:29	63	
265	22	Sa	5:46	18:00	12:14	16:28		73	
266	23	☉	5:47	17:57	12:10	16:48	0:52	82	Autumn. equinox 9:52
267	24	M	5:49	17:55	12:06	17:04	2:18	89	(23 Sep) Libra ♎
268	25	Tu	5:50	17:53	12:03	17:17	3:45	95	
269	26	W	5:52	17:51	11:59	17:30	5:13	99	
270	27	Th	5:54	17:48	11:54	17:44	6:43	100	
271	28	F	5:55	17:46	11:51	18:01	8:16	98	
272	29	Sa	5:57	17:44	11:47	18:23	9:50	93	
273	30	☉	5:59	17:41	11:42	18:53	11:23	86	

All times shown in Greenwich Mean Time. For Summer Time, add 1 hour.

Birthstone	Zodiac (b.)	Man of Signs	Age	Drink
Sapphire	Libra ♎	Lumbar region	48–54	Stout

With my flayll I erne my brede;

🍂 In September he is 54 yeere he then purueyethe against the winter to cherish himselfe withall and keepe neere together the goods yᵗ he gat in his youth.

Day of mo	wk	Holidays, civil days, days of note	Holy days, Poor Richard, ages of man [yrs]
1	Sa		✒ *Many Dishes, many Diseases.*
2	☉		13th ☉ after Trinity
3	M		✠ St Gregory the Great
4	Tu		
5	W		
6	Th		✒ *There's more old Drunkards, than old Doctors.*
7	F	Rugby World Cup begins	
8	Sa		✠ Birthday of the BVM
9	☉		14th ☉ after Trinity
10	M		
11	Tu		
12	W		✒ *Eat to please thyself, but dress to please others.*
13	Th		
14	F		✠ Triumph of the Cross
15	Sa		
16	☉		15th ☉ after Trinity
17	M		
18	Tu		✒ *An old young man, will be a young old man.*
19	W		† Ember Day
20	Th		
21	F		† Ember Day · ✠ St Matthew
22	Sa		† Ember Day
23	☉	☺ *Harvest Festival*	16th ☉ after Trinity
		Autumn begins · Length of day = night	
24	M		
25	Tu		
26	W		
27	Th		✒ *Ill Customs & bad Advice are seldom forgotten.*
28	F		
29	Sa	English quarter day	✠ St Michael & All Angels
30	☉		🍂 Is 54 years · 17th ☉ after Trinity

Latin	French	Spanish	German	Italian	Welsh	Irish	RN
October	octobre	octubre	Oktober	ottobre	Hydref	Deireadh Fómhair	x

Phase		Day	Hour	Week	Av. max.	Av. min.	Av. precip.
Last quarter	☽	3	10:06	30 Sep–6	16.5 °C	9.3 °C	0.51 in
New moon	●	11	5:01	7–13	15.8 °C	8.9 °C	0.52 in
First quarter	☽	19	8:33	14–20	14.2 °C	7.6 °C	0.69 in
Full moon	○	26	4:52	21–27	13.6 °C	7.3 °C	0.57 in
				28–3 Nov	12.4 °C	6.8 °C	0.50 in

yr	Day of mo	wk	☀ rise	☀ set	Length of day	☽ rise	☽ set	☽ phase	Planetary ephemerae
274	1	M	6:00	17:39	11:39	19:37	12:49	76	
275	2	Tu	6:02	17:37	11:35	20:38	13:58	66	Mars 4.7°S of ☽ 20:00
276	3	W	6:03	17:35	11:32	21:52	14:47	55	
277	4	Th	6:05	17:32	11:27	23:12	15:21	44	
278	5	F	6:07	17:30	11:23		15:44	33	
279	6	Sa	6:08	17:28	11:20	0:33	16:00	24	
280	7	☉	6:10	17:26	11:16	1:50	16:13	16	Venus 3.5°S of ☽ 3:00
281	8	M	6:12	17:23	11:11	3:05	16:24	9	(7 Oct) Saturn 1.3°N
282	9	Tu	6:13	17:21	11:08	4:17	16:35	4	of ☽ 16:00
283	10	W	6:15	17:19	11:04	5:28	16:45	1	(8 Oct) Draconids peak
284	11	Th	6:17	17:17	11:00	6:38	16:56	0	
285	12	F	6:18	17:14	10:56	7:50	17:09	1	
286	13	Sa	6:20	17:12	10:52	9:03	17:26	3	
287	14	☉	6:22	17:10	10:48	10:16	17:49	7	
288	15	M	6:23	17:08	10:45	11:26	18:20	13	
289	16	Tu	6:25	17:06	10:41	12:29	19:03	20	
290	17	W	6:27	17:04	10:37	13:20	20:00	28	
291	18	Th	6:29	17:02	10:33	14:00	21:10	37	
292	19	F	6:30	17:00	10:30	14:29	22:28	47	
293	20	Sa	6:32	16:57	10:25	14:50	23:50	57	
294	21	☉	6:34	16:55	10:21	15:07		67	Orionids peak
295	22	M	6:36	16:53	10:17	15:21	1:14	77	
296	23	Tu	6:37	16:51	10:14	15:35	2:39	86	Scorpio ♏
297	24	W	6:39	16:49	10:10	15:48	4:07	93	Mercury at inf. ☌ 0:00
298	25	Th	6:41	16:47	10:06	16:04	5:37	98	
299	26	F	6:43	16:45	10:02	16:23	7:12	100	
300	27	Sa	6:44	16:43	9:59	16:50	8:49	99	
301	28	☉	6:46	16:42	9:56	17:29	10:22	95	Summer Time e. 1:00
302	29	M	6:48	16:40	9:52	18:25	11:41	88	
303	30	Tu	6:50	16:38	9:48	19:37	12:41	80	Mars 3.2°S of ☽ 19:00
304	31	W	6:51	16:36	9:45	20:58	13:21	70	

All times shown in Greenwich Mean Time. For Summer Time, add 1 hour.

Birthstone	Zodiac (b.)	Man of Signs	Age	Drink
Opal	Scorpio ♏	Genitals	54–60	Fish house punch

And here I sawe my whete so rede.

♉ Then is a man in October 60 yeere full, if he haue ought he gladdeth, and if haue nought he weepeth.

Day of mo	wk	Holidays, civil days, days of note	Holy days, Poor Richard, ages of man [yrs]
1	M	Michaelmas law term begins	
2	Tu		
3	W		✍ *Two dry Sticks will burn a green One.*
4	Th		
5	F		
6	Sa		
7	☉		18th ☉ after Trinity
8	M		
9	Tu		✍ *He that speaks ill of the Mare, will buy her.*
10	W		
11	Th		
12	F		
13	Sa		
14	☉	World Conker Championships	19th ☉ after Trinity
15	M		
16	Tu		✍ *Let thy Discontents be Secrets.*
17	W		
18	Th		℞ ✠ St Luke
19	F		
20	Sa		
21	☉	☺ *Trafalgar Day*	20th ☉ after Trinity
22	M		
23	Tu		✍ *Little Strokes, Fell great Oaks.*
24	W		
25	Th		✠ 40 Martyrs of England & Wales
			✠ 6 Welsh Martyrs & Companions
26	F		
27	Sa		
28	☉	Summer Time ends 1:00	21st ☉ after Trinity
			℞ ✠ SS Simon & Jude
29	M		✍ *Man, dally not with other Folks' Women or Money.*
30	Tu		
31	W	☺ *Halloween* (US)	♉ Is 60 years

Latin	French	Spanish	German	Italian	Welsh	Irish	RN
November	novembre	noviembre	November	novembre	Tachwedd	Samhain	xi

Phase		Day	Hour	Week	Av. max.	Av. min.	Av. precip.
Last quarter	☾	1	21:18	4–10	11.1 °C	5.9 °C	0.48 in
New moon	●	9	23:03	11–17	9.7 °C	4.8 °C	0.49 in
First quarter	☽	17	22:33	18–24	8.6 °C	4.2 °C	0.54 in
Full moon	○	24	14:30	25–1 Dec	8.2 °C	3.7 °C	0.44 in

yr	Day of mo	wk	☀ rise	☀ set	Length of day	☽ rise	☽ set	☽ phase	Planetary ephemerae
305	1	Th	6:53	16:34	9:41	22:20	13:48	60	Taurids peak
306	2	F	6:55	16:32	9:37	23:40	14:07	49	
307	3	Sa	6:57	16:31	9:34		14:21	39	
308	4	☉	6:58	16:29	9:31	0:55	14:33	29	Saturn 1.8° N of ☽ 3:00
309	5	M	7:00	16:27	9:27	2:07	14:43	21	Venus 3.1° N of ☽ 20:00
310	6	Tu	7:02	16:25	9:23	3:18	14:53	14	
311	7	W	7:04	16:24	9:20	4:28	15:04	8	
312	8	Th	7:05	16:22	9:17	5:39	15:17	4	
313	9	F	7:07	16:20	9:13	6:51	15:33	1	
314	10	Sa	7:09	16:19	9:10	8:04	15:54	0	
315	11	☉	7:11	16:17	9:06	9:15	16:22	1	
316	12	M	7:12	16:16	9:04	10:21	17:02	4	
317	13	Tu	7:14	16:14	9:00	11:16	17:55	8	
318	14	W	7:16	16:13	8:57	11:59	19:00	14	
319	15	Th	7:18	16:12	8:54	12:30	20:14	22	
320	16	F	7:19	16:10	8:51	12:54	21:33	31	
321	17	Sa	7:21	16:09	8:48	13:12	22:53	40	Leonids peak
322	18	☉	7:23	16:08	8:45	13:26		51	
323	19	M	7:24	16:06	8:42	13:39	0:14	61	
324	20	Tu	7:26	16:05	8:39	13:52	1:37	72	
325	21	W	7:28	16:04	8:36	14:06	3:03	82	
326	22	Th	7:29	16:03	8:34	14:23	4:33	90	
327	23	F	7:31	16:02	8:31	14:46	6:07	96	Sagittarius ♐
328	24	Sa	7:33	16:01	8:28	15:18	7:43	99	
329	25	☉	7:34	16:00	8:26	16:06	9:12	100	
330	26	M	7:36	15:59	8:23	17:13	10:24	97	
331	27	Tu	7:37	15:58	8:21	18:34	11:14	92	Mars 1.7° S of ☽ 6:00
332	28	W	7:39	15:57	8:18	19:59	11:48	84	
333	29	Th	7:40	15:57	8:17	21:23	12:10	75	
334	30	F	7:42	15:56	8:14	22:42	12:27	66	

All times shown in Greenwich Mean Time.

Birthstone	Zodiac (b.)	Man of Signs	Age	Drink
Topaz	Sagittarius ✗	Thighs	60–66	Beaujolais nouveau

At Martynesmasse I kylle my swyne;

🦡 Then is man 66 in Nouember, he stoupeth and goeth softly, and leeseth all his beauty and fayrnesse.

Day of mo	wk	Holidays, civil days, days of note	Holy days, Poor Richard, ages of man [yrs]
1	Th		☺ ℜ † All Saints' Day
2	F		☺ † All Souls' Day
3	Sa		🖎 *He that takes a wife, takes care.*
4	⑥		22nd ⑥ after Trinity
5	M	☺ *Guy Fawkes Day*	
6	Tu		✠ All Saints of Ireland
7	W		
8	Th		✠ All Saints of Wales
9	F		✠ Dedication of Lateran Basilica
10	Sa	ℜ Lord Mayor's Day · ☺ *Sadie Hawkins Day* (US)	
11	⑥	Ᵽ *Remembrance Sunday · Armistice Day*	23rd ⑥ after Trinity
12	M		
13	Tu		🖎 *Pretty & Witty will wound if they hit ye.*
14	W	Ᵽ ℜ BD of HRH Prince of Wales · Bond film *Casino Royale* opens	
15	Th		
16	F		✠ St Margaret of Scotland
17	Sa		
18	⑥		24th ⑥ after Trinity
19	M		🖎 *Good wives and good plantations are made by good husbands.*
20	Tu	Ᵽ Wedding Day of HM Queen	
21	W		🖎 *There are no ugly Loves, nor handsome Prisons.*
22	Th	☺ *Thanksgiving* (US)	
23	F		✠ St Columban
24	Sa		
25	⑥	☺ *Stir-Up Sunday*	✠ Christ the King · 25th ⑥ after Trinity
26	M		
27	Tu		🖎 *The Golden Age never was the present Age.*
28	W	Scottish term day	
29	Th		
30	F	☺ *National day of Scotland*	🦡 Is 66 years · Ᵽ ℜ ✠ St Andrew

Latin	French	Spanish	German	Italian	Welsh	Irish	RN
December	décembre	diciembre	Dezember	dicembre	Rhagfyr	Mí na Nollag	xii

Phase		Day	Hour	Week	Av. max.	Av. min.	Av. precip.
Last quarter	☾	1	12:44	2–8	7.7 °C	3.6 °C	0.39 in
New moon	●	9	17:40	9–15	7.1 °C	3.1 °C	0.58 in
First quarter	☽	17	10:18	16–22	6.9 °C	2.7 °C	0.52 in
Full moon	○	24	1:16	23–29	6.8 °C	2.8 °C	0.48 in
Last quarter	☾	31	7:51				

yr	Day of mo	wk	☀ rise	☀ set	Length of day	☽ rise	☽ set	☽ phase	Planetary ephemerae
335	1	Sa	7:43	15:55	8:12	23:56	12:40	55	Saturn 2.4° N
336	2	☉	7:44	15:54	8:10		12:51	45	of ☽ 13:00
337	3	M	7:46	15:54	8:08	1:08	13:01	36	
338	4	Tu	7:47	15:53	8:06	2:18	13:12	27	
339	5	W	7:48	15:53	8:05	3:29	13:24	19	
340	6	Th	7:50	15:53	8:03	4:40	13:39	12	
341	7	F	7:51	15:52	8:01	5:53	13:58	7	
342	8	Sa	7:52	15:52	8:00	7:05	14:24	3	
343	9	☉	7:53	15:52	7:59	8:12	15:01	1	
344	10	M	7:54	15:51	7:57	9:11	15:50	0	
345	11	Tu	7:55	15:51	7:56	9:58	16:52	2	
346	12	W	7:56	15:51	7:55	10:33	18:05	5	
347	13	Th	7:57	15:51	7:54	10:58	19:22	10	Geminids peak
348	14	F	7:58	15:51	7:53	11:17	20:42	17	
349	15	Sa	7:59	15:51	7:52	11:32	22:01	25	
350	16	☉	8:00	15:52	7:52	11:46	23:21	35	
351	17	M	8:01	15:52	7:51	11:58		45	Mercury at sup. ☌
352	18	Tu	8:01	15:52	7:51	12:11	0:42	56	15:00
353	19	W	8:02	15:52	7:50	12:26	2:06	67	Ursids peak
354	20	Th	8:03	15:53	7:50	12:45	3:35	78	
355	21	F	8:03	15:53	7:50	13:11	5:08	87	(22 Dec) Capricorn ♑
356	22	Sa	8:04	15:54	7:50	13:50	6:39	94	Winter solstice 6:09
357	23	☉	8:04	15:54	7:50	14:47	7:59	98	Jupiter ☀ ☌ 7:00
358	24	M	8:05	15:55	7:50	16:02	9:00	100	Mars 0.9°S of ☽ 3:00
359	25	Tu	8:05	15:55	7:50	17:28	9:42	99	(24 Dec) Mars at ☍ 20:00
360	26	W	8:05	15:56	7:51	18:55	10:10	95	
361	27	Th	8:06	15:57	7:51	20:19	10:30	89	
362	28	F	8:06	15:58	7:52	21:38	10:45	81	Saturn 2.8° N
363	29	Sa	8:06	15:59	7:53	22:52	10:57	72	of ☽ 22:00
364	30	☉	8:06	15:59	7:53		11:08	63	
365	31	M	8:06	16:00	7:54	0:04	11:18	53	

All times shown in Greenwich Mean Time.

Birthstone	Zodiac (b.)	Man of Signs	Age	Drink
Turquoise	Capricorn ♑	Knees	66–72	Wassail bowl

And at Cristesmasse I drynke redde wyne.

🜚 In December he is 72 yeeres, then had he leuer haue a warme fire then a fayre lady, and after this age he goeth into decrepitie to waxe a childe again, and can not welde him selfe, and then young folkes be wery of his company but if they haue much good they beene full lytell taken heede of.

Day of mo	wk	Holidays, civil days, days of note	Holy days, Poor Richard, ages of man [yrs]
1	Sa		♑ He that drinks fast, pays slow.
2	⑤		† Advent begins · 1st ⑤ in Advent
3	M		
4	Tu		
5	W		🜚 Health begins to fail [67]
6	Th		♑ The hasty Bitch brings forth blind Puppies.
7	F		
8	Sa		✠ Immaculate Conception
9	⑤		2nd ⑤ in Advent
10	M		
11	Tu		
12	W		
13	Th		♑ Never praise your cyder or your horse.
14	F		
15	Sa		
16	⑤		3rd ⑤ in Advent
17	M		♑ Beware of meat twice boil'd, and an old foe reconcil'd.
18	Tu		
19	W		† Ember Day
20	Th		♑ After Fish, Milk do not wish.
21	F	Michaelmas law term ends	† Ember Day · ✠ St Thomas
22	Sa	Winter begins · Shortest day	† Ember Day
23	⑤		4th ⑤ in Advent
24	M		† Advent ends
25	Tu	● ☺ *Christmas* · English quarter day	† Nativity of Our Lord
26	W	● ☺ *Boxing Day*	✠ St Stephen
27	Th		✠ St John the Evangelist
28	F		✠ Holy Innocents
29	Sa		✠ Thomas Becket
30	⑤		✠ Holy Family · 1st ⑤ after Christmas
31	M	☺ *Hogmanay*	🜚 Is 72 years; he dies at 77

♈ 365, the number of days in a year, $= 10^2 + 11^2 + 12^2 = 13^2 + 14^2$

2006

JANUARY	FEBRUARY	MARCH	APRIL

JANUARY
```
S  M  T  W  T  F  S
1  ●  3  4  5  6  7
8  9 10 11 12 13 14
15 16 17 18 19 20 21
22 23 24 25 26 27 28
29 30 31
```

FEBRUARY
```
S  M  T  W  T  F  S
         1  2  3  4
5  6  7  8  9 10 11
12 13 14 15 16 17 18
19 20 21 22 23 24 25
26 27 28
```

MARCH
```
S  M  T  W  T  F  S
   W  2  3  4
5  6  7  8  9 10 11
12 13 14 15 16  I 18
19  ☛ 21 22 23 24 25
26 27 28 29 30 31
```

APRIL
```
S  M  T  W  T  F  S
                  1
2  3  4  5  6  7  8
9 10 11 12 13  ● 15
★  ● 18 19 20 21 22
E 24 25 26 27 28 29
30
```

MAY
```
S  M  T  W  T  F  S
   ●  2  3  4  5  6
7  8  9 10 11 12 13
14 15 16 17 18 19 20
21 22 23 24 25 26 27
28  ● 30 31
```

JUNE
```
S  M  T  W  T  F  S
            1  2  3
4  5  6  7  8  9 10
11 12 13 14 15 16 17
18 19 20  ☛ 22 23 24
25 26 27 28 29 30
```

JULY
```
S  M  T  W  T  F  S
                  1
2  3  4  5  6  7  8
9 10 11 12 13 14 15
16 17 18 19 20 21 22
23 24 25 26 27 28 29
30 31
```

AUGUST
```
S  M  T  W  T  F  S
      1  2  3  4  5
6  7  8  9 10 11 12
13 14 15 16 17 18 19
20 21 22 23 24 25 26
27  ● 29 30 31
```

SEPTEMBER
```
S  M  T  W  T  F  S
               1  2
3  4  5  6  7  8  9
10 11 12 13 14 15 16
17 18 19 20 21 22  ☛
24 25 26 27 28 29 30
```

OCTOBER
```
S  M  T  W  T  F  S
1  2  3  4  5  6  7
8  9 10 11 12 13 14
15 16 17 18 19 20 21
22 23 24 25 26 27 28
29 30 31
```

NOVEMBER
```
S  M  T  W  T  F  S
         1  2  3  4
5  6  7  8  9 10 11
12 13 14 15 16 17 18
19 20 21 22 23 24 25
26 27 28 29  S
```

DECEMBER
```
S  M  T  W  T  F  S
               1  2
3  4  5  6  7  8  9
10 11 12 13 14 15 16
17 18 19 20 21  ☛ 23
24  ●  ● 27 28 29 30
31
```

2007

JANUARY
```
S  M  T  W  T  F  S
   ●  2  3  4  5  6
7  8  9 10 11 12 13
14 15 16 17 18 19 20
21 22 23 24 25 26 27
28 29 30 31
```

FEBRUARY
```
S  M  T  W  T  F  S
            1  2  3
4  5  6  7  8  9 10
11 12 13 14 15 16 17
18 19 20 21 22 23 24
25 26 27 28
```

MARCH
```
S  M  T  W  T  F  S
   W  2  3
4  5  6  7  8  9 10
11 12 13 14 15 16  I
18 19 20  ☛ 22 23 24
25 26 27 28 29 30 31
```

APRIL
```
S  M  T  W  T  F  S
1  2  3  4  5  ●  7
★  ● 10 11 12 13 14
15 16 17 18 19 20 21
22  E 24 25 26 27 28
29 30
```

MAY
```
S  M  T  W  T  F  S
      1  2  3  4  5
6  ●  8  9 10 11 12
13 14 15 16 17 18 19
20 21 22 23 24 25 26
27  ● 29 30 31
```

JUNE
```
S  M  T  W  T  F  S
               1  2
3  4  5  6  7  8  9
10 11 12 13 14 15 16
17 18 19 20  ☛ 22 23
24 25 26 27 28 29 30
```

JULY
```
S  M  T  W  T  F  S
1  2  3  4  5  6  7
8  9 10 11 12 13 14
15 16 17 18 19 20 21
22 23 24 25 26 27 28
29 30 31
```

AUGUST
```
S  M  T  W  T  F  S
         1  2  3  4
5  6  7  8  9 10 11
12 13 14 15 16 17 18
19 20 21 22 23 24 25
26  ● 28 29 30 31
```

SEPTEMBER
```
S  M  T  W  T  F  S
                  1
2  3  4  5  6  7  8
9 10 11 12 13 14 15
16 17 18 19 20 21 22
☛ 24 25 26 27 28 29
30
```

OCTOBER
```
S  M  T  W  T  F  S
1  2  3  4  5  6
7  8  9 10 11 12 13
14 15 16 17 18 19 20
21 22 23 24 25 26 27
28 29 30 31
```

NOVEMBER
```
S  M  T  W  T  F  S
            1  2  3
4  5  6  7  8  9 10
11 12 13 14 15 16 17
18 19 20 21 22 23 24
25 26 27 28 29  S
```

DECEMBER
```
S  M  T  W  T  F  S
                  1
2  3  4  5  6  7  8
9 10 11 12 13 14 15
16 17 18 19 20 21  ☛
23 24  ●  ● 27 28 29
30 31
```

★ Easter   ☛ New season begins   ● Bank holiday (England & Wales)
E St George's Day   **W** St David's Day   **S** St Andrew's Day   **I** St Patrick's Day

TOWN

❦ UMBRELLAS

Two types of umbrellas are carried by men: a short, collapsible umbrella; and a long (36 inch) one with a curved handle. Both are black. A short umbrella is stored away in a pocket or briefcase when not in use, whereas a long umbrella is swung.

The chief umbrella rhythm repeats every four steps. With the umbrella carried in the right hand, it touches the ground with the first left step, rises just before the first right, stays high on the second left, and begins to fall just after the second right. (A step is the instant when the foot is fully planted on the ground.) The curved handle slides through the hand on the way down. Ideal for getting around town.

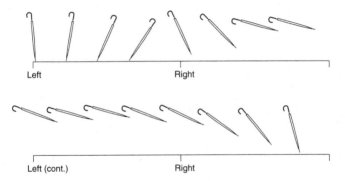

Less known is an umbrella rhythm which repeats with twice the frequency of the rhythm above. With the umbrella in the right hand, it follows the motions of the left leg but with a small delay. It is appropriate for slower strolls and walking over uneven ground, where the umbrella doubles as a walking stick.

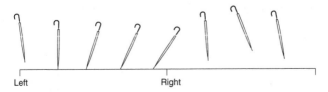

101

Whoever thinks of going to bed before twelve o'clock... is a scoundrel.
Samuel Johnson

A nightclub is any place that sells drinks and promotes dancing to music after midnight. This broad definition includes everything from basement bashes for hard-core ravers to exclusive glam in the West End. Nightclubs are a fickle business. A surprising number of clubs open and close each year, and few remain fashionable for long. The longest-standing nightclubs, interestingly, tend to be members-only establishments (marked * opposite).

The much-anticipated introduction of 24-hour licensing laws in late 2005 has, of course, had an effect on how clubbers club, but not in the way that everyone expected. Binge-drinking is less common than it once was, with the longer, moderate drinking seen on the Continent taking its place. At the same time, Spanish and Italian clubbers have influenced the way many clubs do business. The after-party—mellow merriment with the rising of the sun—has taken off. While these tend to be at private residences, an increasing number of clubs are hosting them on their premises. Some clubs, like Key and Turnmills, stretch Saturday night so far into Sunday that it is difficult to say when the night ends and the new day begins. Sunday-night clubbing is increasingly popular, which along with Thursday is the school night of choice for going to town. With increasing competition from late-night bars and restaurants, nightclubs are losing their monopoly on after-hours entertainment. Expect to see a shorter queues, less haughty staff and—but don't get your hopes up—cheaper drinks and tables.

The fashion for partner dancing—swing and rock-and-roll dancing to vintage jazz and pop favourites—continues unabated. *Time Out*'s prognostication for the 2006/7 dance scene: 'Fancy a bit of retro dancefloor action? Forget the cheesy 1980s chart trash, it's all about partying like it's 1929.'

Opposite are some of most popular and fashionable clubs in London, along with some dependable favourites.

24-HOUR RESTAURANTS

Despite being the preeminent capital of the world, central London has only a handful of restaurants open 24 hours a day. But when running on empty after a full night's clubbing, they can prove invaluable.

Bar Italia	22 Frith St, w1	0207 437 4520
Beigel Bake	159 Brick Lane, e1	0871 075 8778
Tinseltown	44–46 St John St, ec1	0207 689 2424
Vingt Quatre	325 Fulham Rd, sw10	0207 376 7224
Balans	60–62 Old Compton St, w1	0207 439 2183

Nightclub closing times can be flexible, depending on business, and the official hours below frequently change, especially for weekdays.

-1 = 11 p.m.; 0 = midnight; 1 = 1 a.m.; etc.   L = late, no set closing hour.
. = half past the hour: 1. = 1:30; 2. = 2:30; etc.   Blank = closed.

Club, address (London)	☎ (0207)	S	M	T	W	T	F	S
151, *151, King's Rd, SW3*	351 6826		3	3	3	3	3	3
333, *333 Old St, EC1*	739 1800	4	3	3	3	4	4	4
*Annabel's, *44 Berkeley Square, W1*	629 1096		3.	3.	3.	3.	3.	3.
Aquarium, *256–260 Old St, EC1*	251 6136	3	3	3	3	4	4	4
Attica, *24 Kingly St, W1*	287 5882					3	3	3
Bar Rumba, *36 Shaftesbury Ave, W1*	287 6933	2	3	3	3	3	3.	3.
Bethnal Green Working Men's Club, *42 Pollards Row, E2*	739 2727	0	-1	-1	-1	2	2	2
Boujis, *43 Thurloe St, SW7*	584 2000	3	3	3	3	3	3	3
Cargo, *83 Rivington St, EC2*	739 3440	0	1	1	1	1	3	3
Chinawhite, *6 Air St, W1*	343 0040		3	3	3	3	3	3
Crazy Larry's, *533 King's Rd, SW10*	376 5555					3	3	3
Cross, *Arches, 27–31 King's Cross Goods Yd, N1*	837 0828						5	6
Cuckoo Club, *Swallow St, W1*	287 4300				3.	3.	3.	3.
EGG, *200 York Way, N7*	609 8364	3					6	6
End, *18 West Central St, WC1*	419 9199		3	3	3	4	5.	7
Fabric, *77A Charterhouse St, EC1*	336 8898	L					5	7
Fridge, *1 Town Hall Parade, Brixton Hill, SW2*	326 5100						6	6
Heaven, *Under the Arches, Villiers St, WC2*	930 2020		6		6		6	6
Karabet's Prophecy, *16–18 Beak St, W1*	439 2229		3	3	3	3	3	3
Key, *King's Cross Freight Depot, N1*	837 1027						5	13
L'Equipe Anglaise, *21–23 Duke St, W1*	486 8281					5.	5.	5.
Mass, *St Matthew's Church, Brixton Hill, SW2*	738 7875	3			2	3	6	6
Ministry of Sound, *103 Gaunt St, SE1*	740 8600						5	7
Movida, *8-9 Argyll St, W1*	734 5776					3	3	3
Neighbourhood, *12 Acklam Rd, W10*	524 7979	-1				2.	2.	2.
Pacha, *Terminus Place, SW1*	833 3139						5	6
Pangaea, *85 Piccadilly, W1*	495 2595				3	3	4	4
Penthouse, *1 Leicester Square, WC2*	734 0900				3	3	3	3
Plan B, *418 Brixton Rd, SW9*	733 0926	3	3	3	3	3	5	5
Plastic People, *147–149 Curtain Rd, EC2*	739 6471	0				2	3.	3.
Scala, *275 Pentonville Rd, N1*	833 2022						5	6
Tantra, *62 Kingly St, W1*	434 0888	4	4	4	4	4	5.	5.
*Tramp, *40 Jermyn St, SW1*	734 0565		3	3	3	3	3	
Turnmills, *63B Clerkenwell Rd, EC1*	250 3409	4				3	7.	12
Umbaba, *15–21 Ganton St, W1*	734 6696	3				3	3	3

*Members-only. Tramp is the less strict in enforcing this.

It is an undisputed truth that the best collection of gentlemen's clubs in the world is to be found in London, perhaps because 'the English are the only clubbable people on the face of the earth', suggested George Augustus Sala. A gentlemen's club should be like a second home—that comfortable and that familiar. For those who live outside the city, London's clubs provide an ideal base within it.

Women: ┊ = full use   ┊ = limited use   – = no women members

GENTLEMEN'S CLUBS

Club	Address (London)	☎ (0207)	Since	┊
Army & Navy	36 Pall Mall, sw1	930 9721	1837	┊
Arts	40 Dover St, w1	499 8581	1863	┊
Athenaeum	107 Pall Mall, sw1	930 4843	1824	┊
Authors'	40 Dover St, w1	499 8581	1891	┊
Beefsteak	9 Irving St, wc2	930 5722	1876	┊
Boodle's	28 St James's St, sw1	930 7166	1762	–
Brooks's	St James's St, sw1	493 4411	1764	┊
Buck's	18 Clifford St, w1	734 2337	1919	┊
Caledonian	9 Halkin St, sw1	235 5162	1891	┊
Canning	4 St James's Sq., sw1	827 5757	1910	┊
Carlton	69 St James's St, sw1	493 1164	1832	┊
Cavalry & Guards	127 Piccadilly, w1	499 1261	1893	┊
East India	16 St James's Sq., sw1	930 1000	1849	┊
Garrick	15 Garrick St, wc2	379 6478	1831	–
Junior Carlton	69 St James's St, sw1	493 1164	1832	┊
Lansdowne	9 Fitzmaurice Place, w1	629 7200	1935	┊
National Liberal	Whitehall Place, sw1	930 9871	1883	┊
Naval	38 Hill St, w1	493 7672	1919	┊
Naval & Military	4 St James's Sq., sw1	827 5757	1862	┊
Oriental	11 Stratford Place, w1	629 5126	1824	┊
Oxford & Cambridge	71–77 Pall Mall, sw1	930 5151	1821	┊
Pratt's	14 Park Place, sw1	493 0397	1857	┊
Reform	104 Pall Mall, sw1	930 9374	1841	┊
RAC	89 Pall Mall, sw1	930 2345	1897	┊
RAF	128 Piccadilly, w1	499 3456	1922	┊
St James's	728 Park Place, sw1	629 7688	1857	┊
St Stephen's	34 Queen Anne's Gate, sw1	222 1382	1870	┊
Savage	1 Whitehall Place, sw1	930 8118	1857	–
Savile	69 Brook St, w1	629 5462	1868	┊
Travellers'	106 Pall Mall, sw1	930 8688	1819	–
Turf	5 Carlton House Terrace, sw1	930 8555	1861	┊
White's	37 St James's St, sw1	493 6671	1693	–

OTHER CLUBS

Club	Address (London)	☎ (0207)	Since	
Alpine	55 Charlotte Rd, EC2	613 0755	1857	❦
Anglo-Belgian	60 Knightsbridge, SW1	235 2121	1909/1942	❦
City of London	19 Old Broad St, EC2	588 7991	1832	❦
City University	50 Cornhill, EC3	626 8571	1895	❦
Groucho	45 Dean St, W1	439 4685	1984	❦
Hurlingham	Ranelagh Gardens, SW6	736 8411	1869	❦
MCC	St John's Wood Rd, NW8	289 1611	1787	❦
New Cavendish	44 Great Cumberland Place, W1	723 0391	1909	❦
Portland	69 Brook St, W1	499 1523	1816	❦
Roehampton	Roehampton Lane, SW15	8480 4205	1901	❦
Royal Thames Yacht	60 Knightsbridge, SW1	235 2121	1775	❦

SELECTED NOTES

Athenaeum More a club for dons than wits, but many people think the intellectual climate is less impressive than it once was. Little club atmosphere, but food and wine have greatly improved in recent years.

Beefsteak Terrible food at a single table where members sit where they are placed, but the best company and conversation. 'The Beefsteak is a pleasant little club. The only qualification is that you have to be a peer who has learned to read and write or a journalist who has learned table manners.' *The Earl of Kintore*

Boodle's Churchill was a member, as was Ian Fleming, who preferred it to White's because 'they gas too much'. In Fleming's James Bond novels, M.'s club, Blades, is modelled after Boodle's. 'M. looked like any member of any of the clubs in St James's Street. Dark grey suit, stiff white collar, the favourite dark blue bow-tie with white spots, rather loosely tied... the keen sailor's face, with the clear, sharp sailor's eyes.' *Ian Fleming, Moonraker*

Brooks's The most handsome of the remaining Regency clubs, in its early days it was a Whig outpost. Trevelyan described it as 'the most famous political club that will ever have existed in London'.

Buck's By his own account, the closest thing to P. G. Wodehouse's idea of the Drones Club. It invented the drink Buck's Fizz: 1 part orange juice and 1 part champagne.

Carlton Once a virtual Conservative Central Office, it remains deeply Tory. In *The Gentlemen's Clubs of London*, Anthony Lejeune writes that it is 'certainly the most famous political club of modern times, and for a while was perhaps even more directly influential than Brooks's had been in the politics of an earlier period'.

Garrick Once known for theatrical talent, now stuffed full of lawyers, the Garrick has lively conversation and a questionable club tie, of which some members are unaccountably proud. The waiting list is presently over five years. 'In 1861 I became a member of the Garrick Club. Having up to that time lived very little among men, having hitherto known nothing of clubs, having even as a boy been banished from social gatherings, I enjoyed infinitely at first the gaiety of the Garrick. It was a festival for me to dine there—which I did indeed but seldom.' *Anthony Trollope*

Groucho Founded as an antidote to the traditional club, it is consciously non-grand but has excellent food and drink. Mainly media members.

Hurlingham More an American country club than anything else, it helped introduce polo to the Western world. Very much in demand, largely for its spacious grounds and fine sports facilities.

Lansdowne Here women have long been on an equal footing with men. The club welcomes families and married couples, and has, as a result, less club atmosphere than others. A swimming pool and gym are on the premises, and lately well-attended balls for young people have been regularly organized there.

Oxford & Cambridge Housed in a fine building, it has a nondescript membership but remains a convenient first club to join. In 1996 it voted to admit women as full members.

Pratt's An intimate club which, like the Beefsteak, has a single dining table. One can dine late on straightforward, hearty fare. Until recently it had the longest waiting list of any club.

RAC Sir John Betjeman said that the great thing about the RAC is that one could sit there the whole afternoon and never see a single gentleman. Superb Turkish bath and swimming pool.

Reform Originally a hotbed of progressives, it now houses Old Turks, fabled liberals and civil servants. Phileas Fogg used the magnificent building to launch his 80-day trip around the world.

Savage Founded by the Victorian journalist George Augustus Sala and his literary circle, the Savage is a mix of gentility and Bohemia, one of the more warm-hearted clubs in London.

Travellers' Graced for years by permanent resident Monsignor Alfred Gilbey, who converted a cupboard into a tiny chapel, which still remains. Many young fogeys, some of indeterminate sex. 'There is a fine library... an excellent fire, billiards, cards, coffee, a thousand ways of dining badly for twelve francs, etc. I do not eat there... but I arrive with a serious expression [and] take off my hat in the English manner—that is to say with a bad grace as if someone is dragging it off me.' *Louis de Vignet*

White's From the days when Beau Brummell passed judgement from its famous bow window to the present, White's has remained the grandest club in the world, an 'oasis of civilisation in a desert of democracy'. 'I knew I could not be a knight of the garter, or a member of White's—the only two things an Englishman cannot command.' *Benjamin Disraeli*

As a whole, British men take shirts more seriously than those of any other country, and competition is severe. Nowhere else can you find as fine a cut in as many checks, stripes and colours for the price of two bottles of champagne. The shirtmakers' Mecca is Jermyn Street (p. 109), which has the highest concentration of shops selling shirts, ties and general men's kit in the world. It is named after Henry Jermyn, Earl of St Albans, who leased the surrounding land from Charles II. Isaac Newton lived at what is now number 87, Hackett. Note that the prices below do not take into account constant sales and reductions; year round, a Jermyn Street shirt can be had for as little as £30. Finer shirts will, of course, be dearer. Many companies have multiple branches, in which case the flagship store is listed.

R = ready made; ✂ = bespoke

Shirtmaker	Address (London)	☎ (0207)	Since	R (£)	✂ (£)
Brooks Brothers	1 Old Broad St, EC2	256 6013	1818	59	139
Budd	1A Piccadilly Arcade, SW1	493 0139	1910	65	135
Charles Tyrwhitt	92 Jermyn St, SW1	839 6060	1986	55	–
Coles	101 Jermyn St, SW1	383 7879	1878	50	110
Cordings	19–20 Piccadilly, W1	734 0830	1839	55	–
Frank Foster	40 Pall Mall, SW1	930 6420	1959	–	135
Duchamp	75 Ledbury Rd, W11	243 3970	1988	105	–
Emma Willis	66 Jermyn St, SW1	930 9980	1987	120	190
Ede & Ravenscroft	8 Burlington Gardens, W1	734 5450	1689	95	175
Emmett Shirts	380 King's Rd, SW3	351 7529	1992	79	125
Ermenegildo Zegna	37–38 New Bond St, W1	493 4471	1910	125	–
Gieves & Hawkes	1 Savile Row, W1	434 2001	*c.* 1785	80	–
Hackett	137–138 Sloane St, SW1	730 3331	1983	79	110
Hardy Amies	14 Savile Row, W1	734 2436	1946	89	149
Harvie & Hudson	77, 97 Jermyn St, SW1	839 3578	1946	40	165
Hawes & Curtis	23 Jermyn St, SW1	287 8111	1913	59	–
Hilditch & Key	37 & 73 Jermyn St, SW1	930 2329	1899	70	160
John Bray	78–79 Jermyn St, SW1	839 6375	1991	49	–
Marks & Spencer	458 Oxford St, W1	935 7954	1884	29	–
New & Lingwood	53 Jermyn St, SW1	499 5340	1865	80	165
Paul Smith	40–44 Floral St, WC2	379 7133	1970	120	200
Racing Green	193–197 Regent St, W1	437 4300	1990	40	–
Ralph Lauren	1 New Bond St, W1	535 4600	1967	65	–
Stephen Lachter	16 Savile Row, W1	734 1433	1986	–	130
Thomas Pink	85 Jermyn St, SW1	498 3882	1984	65	160
Thresher & Glenny	50 Gresham St, EC2	606 7451	*c.* 1780	60	115
T. M. Lewin	106 Jermyn St, SW1	839 3372	1898	75	–
Turnbull & Asser	71–72 Jermyn St, SW1	808 3000	1885	70	165
Van Heusen	Paddington Station, W2	402 2916	*c.* 1919	32	–

SELECTED NOTES

Brooks Brothers Once the definitive and most influential men's store in America, Brooks Brothers invented and popularized the button-down collar. Over the next five years they plan to open a dozen shops in the UK.

Budd These cramped quarters house one of the most traditional of the London shirtmakers. Budd also offers the most comprehensive range of shirts and accessories for black and white tie.

Charles Tyrwhitt A recent addition to Jermyn St, Tyrwhitt (pronounced 'territ') provides moderate shirts at bargain prices.

Emma Willis Smart, clean-cut shirts from 'one of the few women to be making waves in the traditionally male-dominated tailoring world' (*Time Out*).

Coles Once a familiar sight on Jermyn St, Coles packed up after 'more and more discount shirt businesses sought to establish shops in Jermyn Street hoping to gain credibility by association'. The company now operates largely online. Fine fit and cutaway collars, if limited breadth of patterns.

Ermenegildo Zegna 'British style is something the Americans have been stealing for years, the French have been nicking constantly, and the Italians just take and sell back to us,' observes designer Jeff Banks. One of the best of the Italian designers, Zegna makes fine shirts. But pound for pound, the only men's clothes the Italians do better than the English are trousers.

Hackett 'Hackett is the only London firm with the savvy and taste to revive the true classics of old England without making them appear either showy or retrospective,' writes Alan Flusser. They design some of the most handsome patterns, stripes and checks.

Harvie & Hudson Especially known for their colourful and bold stripes.

Hawes & Curtis Once shirtmakers to the Duke of Windsor, they have recently opened a second shop on Jermyn St.

Hilditch & Key Along with T. & A. and Budd, one of the top three traditonal UK shirtmakers. Their ready-made shirts were ranked best by *The Times*.

New & Lingwood Originally founded as outfitters to Eton College, their Jermyn St branch has been selling shirts to men of 'quiet good taste' since 1922.

Thomas Pink Pink must be lauded for contributing to the revival of interest in English shirtmaking. Despite their polished image, they are one of the trendier of the Jermyn St shirtmakers.

Turnbull & Asser This shirtmaker to the Prince of Wales is always listed among the world's best. Their array of colours, stripes and checks are enough to make Daisy cry stormily.

Paul Smith Unconventional and smart. Look under the double cuffs for pin-up girls and other surprises.

T. M. Lewin Despite its lengthy history, Lewin today operates in volume. With constant half-price bargains, they have contributed to the sometimes fierce price war amongst English shirtmakers. Good value even if their shirts do not compare to the best of Jermyn Street.

Van Heusen Since 2000 the number-one-selling shirtmaker in the world.

ST JAMES'S ST

Davidoff	Beretta	
Emma Willis	Franco's of St James	
Tricker's	Vincci	
Vincci	The Weiss Gallery	
Crockett & Jones	Dickenson	Waterford Wedgwood
Estate House	Victor Frances Gallery	Mark Stephen Marengo
Turnbull & Asser	Wiltons	Carlo Anichini
	Favourbrook	Jeffery-West
BURY ST	New & Lingwood	Favourbrook
Hilditch & Key		
Taylor of Old Bond St	PICCADILLY ARCADE	
Edward Green	New & Lingwood	Favourbrook
Trevor Philip & Sons		Armoury of St James
Harvie & Hudson		St James's Art Books
John Bray	Alfred Dunhill	Chocolaterie Casemir
		Neal & Palmer
DUKE ST ST JAMES'S		Benson & Clegg
S. Frances	Fortnum & Mason	Semlo Antiques
Cavendish Hotel	J	Iconastas
Hawes & Curtis	E	Budd
W. S. Foster	R	
Thomas Pink	M	Tramp	Celadon Art Gallery
Hackett		John English
John Lobb	Y	Czech & Speake	S. Conway
Floris	N		Andy & Tuly
Roderick Charles		Princes House	Eaton Gallery
Charles Tyrwhitt	S		Prestat
Paxton & Whitfield	T	Nigel Milne	Andy & Tuly
Links of London			Kitchen, La Francois
Russell & Bromley	PRINCES ARCADE	
Harvie & Hudson	Hilditch & Key	St Raphael Gallery
		Sage Brown
DUKE OF YORK ST	Caffè Nero	KLM
Crombie	St James's Church	Reuben Alexander
Von Posch		Perfect Presents
Daks	CHURCH PLACE	
T. M. Lewin	Hawes & Curtis	
T. M. Lewin	NatWest Bank	
Eagle House		
Church's	Waterstones	# JERMYN ST
		London SW1
BABMAES ST	EAGLE PLACE	
Jones	Hawes & Curtis	
	No. 22	
Emmett London	Bates	
	Herbie Frogg	
Rowley's	Geo. F. Trumper	
	Herbie Frogg	
	Jermyn Street Theatre	
	Getti	
Tesco Metro	Barclays Bank	
		PICCADILLY
REGENT ST		CIRCUS

TEXAS HOLD'EM RULES

The rules for poker are not complicated, but the game allows for considerable strategic and psychological play. Texas Hold'em poker is by far the most popular version. It is the most common form of poker in American casinos and is the main event at the World Series of Poker.

The game is played with a standard 52-card deck and aces high by two or more players. Eventually two private (called hole) cards and five public (called community) cards will have been dealt, and the object of the game is to form the highest hand using any combination of one's two hole cards and the five community cards.

The dealer (whether he actually deals or not) is marked by a disc. Before any cards are dealt, the person to the left of the dealer contributes to the pot the small blind (usually half the minimum bet) and the person to the left of him contributes to the pot the big blind (usually the minimum bet). Each person is dealt two hole cards, face down. The first round of betting begins with the player to the left of the two blinds, and rotates clockwise until it returns to the dealer. At his turn a player may do one of the following:

call: make a bet equal to the most recent bet in the round;
raise: bet more than the most recent bet in the round; or
fold: quit the game, forfeiting any chips he may have bet.

After the first round of betting, players have four options: in addition to call, raise and fold, a player can now *check*, which means to remain in the game but bet no money, so long as no one before him in the round has made a bet. Three more betting rounds follow (henceforth beginning with the player to the dealer's left), each after more community cards are dealt. These three dealings are known as the:

flop: first 3 community cards, dealt before the second round of betting;
turn: fourth community card, dealt before the third round of betting;
river: fifth community card, dealt before the fourth round of betting.

If during any round of betting all but one players have folded, the remaining player wins the pot but need not show his hole cards. If after the fourth and final round of betting two or more players remain, they enter a showdown. Here the players turn their two hole cards face up, and the player with the highest hand formed by any combination of his two hole and the five community cards wins the pot. If two players have the same hand, then the player with the highest hole card not forming part of his hand (the kicker) wins. If there are no kickers (both players' hole cards are part of their winning hands) or the kickers are the same, the pot is divided equally between them. The next round begins with the dealer disc passed clockwise by one player.

ORDER OF HANDS

Given a 52-card deck with no wild cards, there are 2,598,960 distinct 5-card hands possible. The order of hands (which are never broken by suit) is as follows:

Hand	Definition	Example	No.	Prob.(%)
Royal flush	10–A, same suit	10♦ J♦ Q♦ K♦ A♦	4	0.00015
Straight flush	seq. of five, same suit	4♠ 5♠ 6♠ 7♠ 8♠	40	0.0015
Four of a kind	four of same rank	8♠ 8♥ 8♣ 8♦	624	0.024
Full house	pair + three of a kind	5♣ 5♦ 9♥ 9♠ 9♦	3,744	0.14
Flush	five of same suit	3♠ 6♠ 7♠ J♠ A♠	5,108	0.20
Straight	sequence of five	7♥ 8♦ 9♠ 10♦ J♥	10,200	0.39
Three of a kind	three of same rank	9♠ 9♥ 9♣	54,912	2.1
Two pair	pair + pair	2♣ 2♦ 8♥ 8♦	123,552	4.7
One pair	two of same rank	10♠ 10♦	1,098,240	42
No pair	none of the above		1,302,540	50

ORDER OF PRE-FLOP HANDS

Before the flop, each player has the option of folding on the basis of his first two (pre-flop) cards, thereby avoiding any losses if his cards are poor. There are 1,326 distinct possible pre-flop hands, but these can be reduced to 169 by keeping in mind that in poker suits have no relative value. In *Hold'em Poker for Advanced Players*, David Sklansky and Mason Malmuth arranged the better hands into eight groups, where group 1 contains the most valuable hands, group 2 the next most valuable hands, and so on; hands are not ordered within a group. The letter 's' means same suit and 'T' means 10.

Group 1	AA	KK	QQ	JJ	AKs					
Group 2	TT	AQs	AJs	KQs	AK					
Group 3	99	JTs	QJs	KJs	ATs	AQ				
Group 4	T9s	KQ	88	QTs	98s	J9s	AJ	KTs		
Group 5	77	87s	Q9s	T8s	KJ	QJ	JT	76s	97s	Axs	65s
Group 6	66	AT	55	86s	KT	QT	54s	K9s	J8s	75s	
Group 7	44	J9	64s	T9	53s	33	98	43s	22	Kxs	T7s	Q8s
Group 8	87	A9	Q9	76	42s	32s	96s	85s	J8	J7s	65	54
	74s	K9	T8	43						

USUAL CHIP VALUES

Chip colour	white	red	blue	green	black	purple
Chip value	1	5	10	25	100	500

While regional variations of the game of darts were played in England during the 19th century, the game as we know it was created in 1896 when Brian Gamlin arranged the 20 numbers around the board as they appear below. After a long battle, the game of darts was finally recognized as an official sport in the UK in 2005.

RULES

In the standard game of darts, players take turns throwing three darts in an effort to reduce an initial score—usually 301 or 501 or 701 or 1001—to zero. Scoring is as follows. All wedges are face value, apart from the double and triple regions, which are two and three times face value. The bull is 50 and the outer bull (the 25) is 25. No points are awarded for darts landing outside the double ring or bouncing off the wire. The last dart thrown must land in the double ring or bull and bring the score to exactly zero; this is called checking out. How long a game lasts greatly depends on the skill of the players. In principle, 501 can be reached with 9 darts: seven triple-20s, triple-19 and double-12.

Checking out is one of the most strategic parts of the game. The maximum score with which the game can be won with three darts is 170: two triple-20s and a bull. It can be won with all scores below this except 159, 162, 163, 165, 166, 168 and 169. Sometimes it is more important when checking out to hit an even or odd wedge than a specific value. Note that the numbers around the board alternate between even and odd apart from 18-4; 6-10; 17-3-19-7; and 16-8.

Dartboard set-up is as follows. The centre of the bull should be 5 ft 8 in off the ground. The oche—a raised ridge beyond which a player cannot step but can lean—is parallel to the face of the board and is 7 ft 9¼ in from a plumb line dropped from it.

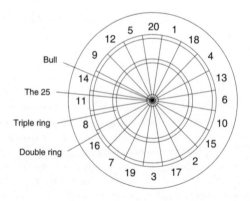

BEST PLACE TO AIM

The distribution of the numbers 1–20 around the board is far from random. They are strategically placed such that the advantage of high numbers is offset by low-number neighbours; this penalizes inaccurate throwing. One way of measuring the difficulty of an ordering is to add up the differences between consecutive numbers around the board. By this reckoning, the most difficult ordering of the numbers yields a total of 200. Gamlin's ordering is near perfect: the differences add up to 198.

While the very best players can always hit a given wedge, beginners' and amateurs' aim is less predictable. Therefore they should aim for the most points-rich regions on the board. The location of these regions depends on just how bad a player's aim is. The table below shows the average face value for darts thrown with increasingly large spreads. The bold numbers are the face values of the wedges. A spread of 0 means that you can hit a given wedge; a spread of 1 means that, if you aim for the wire between two numbers, you will hit one of them; a spread of 2 means that you can hit a wedge or one of its two nearest neighbours; and so on.

What are the best parts of the board to aim at? Overall, the left side is more generous than the right, with 19-7-16 and 11-14-9 especially valuable. Consult the table below for more detailed information.

Spread	Average score for a single dart – right half of board									
0	**20**	**1**	**18**	**4**	**13**	**6**	**10**	**15**	**2**	**17**
1		10.5	9.5	11.0	8.5	9.5	8.0	12.5	8.5	9.5	10.0
2	11.5	10.0	10.2	9.8	9.0	8.8	10.2	10.5	9.0	9.8
3		10.8	10.1	10.0	9.4	8.9	9.5	10.4	9.8	9.4	10.1
4	10.9	10.4	10.1	9.7	9.1	9.2	9.9	10.1	9.6	9.8

Spread	Average score for a single dart – left half of board									
0	**3**	**19**	**7**	**16**	**8**	**11**	**14**	**9**	**12**	**5**
1		11.0	13.0	11.5	12.0	9.5	12.5	11.5	10.5	8.5	12.5
2	10.5	12.0	12.2	11.8	10.8	11.0	12.0	11.0	9.5	10.5
3		11.2	12.1	12.0	11.2	10.9	11.5	11.5	10.2	10.0	11.0
4	10.7	11.7	12.1	11.6	11.1	11.2	11.5	10.9	10.1	10.5

♣ *For geeks* The expected point scores above are not uniform but weighted averages, biased towards the number or wire aimed for. For spread 1, the weights are $1/2$ and $1/2$; for spread 2, $1/4$, $2/4$ and $1/4$; for spread 3, $1/8$, $3/8$, $3/8$ and $1/8$. In general, if the spread is s, the denominator is 2^s and the numerators are the binomial coefficients $\binom{s}{i} = \frac{s!}{i!(s-i)!}$, where i ranges from 0 to s. In the limit of large s, the distribution of weights approaches a bell curve, or Gaussian.

Chilli is the archetypal male dish. It is simple to make, mostly red meat and served from a single pot—from which it can in principle be eaten. It is not necessary to have fine ingredients to prepare an excellent specimen. It frequently divides the sexes, men finding it addictive and women unremarkable.

The best definition of chilli con carne (spelt 'chili' in America) is a literal translation of its Spanish name: peppers with meat. These are the chief and essential ingredients. Chilli originated in the American south-west (but not what is now Mexico) as a simple and palatable preparation of staple foods. Early 19th-century recipes called for beef and suet and as much again chilli peppers, onions and garlic—alas, no tomatoes, which could not always be had. The inclusion of beans is particularly contentious. The International Chili Society defines chilli as any kind of meat or combination of meats, cooked with chilli peppers, spices and other ingredients, with the exception of beans and pasta, which are forbidden. This regulates its annual cook-off, the largest chilli, and indeed food, competition in the world.

JOE COOPER'S CHILLI, 1951

3 lb cubed lean beef	1 tbsp sugar
1 quart water	1 tsp ground cumin
6 tbsp chilli powder	1 tsp oregano or marjoram
10 cloves chopped garlic	1 tsp red pepper
4 tbsp olive oil	1/2 tsp black pepper
3 tbsp paprika	2 bay leaves
1 tbsp salt	flour or cornmeal

(As with most chilli recipes, 1 tsp = 1/3 tbsp; see p. 18.) Sear meat in oil over high heat. Add water and bay leaves and simmer. Remove bay leaves, add all but last ingredient and simmer again. Add flour or cornmeal to taste, previously mixed with cold water. Serves 6–8.

MAN'S CHILLI

1 lb cubed lean beef	2 tsp ground cumin
1 tin red kidney beans	1 tsp paprika
1/2 tin chopped tomatoes	1 tsp sugar
2 chopped chilli peppers	1/2 tsp salt
1 small chopped onion	1/2 tsp black pepper
4 cloves chopped garlic	1/2 tsp cayenne pepper
1 1/2 tbsp chilli powder	1/2 tsp oregano
3 tsp olive oil	1 beef stock cube

Fry beef in 1 tsp oil over high heat. Add salt and black pepper. Fry peppers, onion and garlic separately in 2 tsp oil. Combine with remaining ingredients except beans in saucepan and simmer for at least an hour, adding water to taste. Add beans 30 minutes before serving. Serves 2.

COUNTRY

❦ TOOLS

The number of tools necessary for most domestic repairs and building projects is not large. Below are the 50 most useful.

ESSENTIAL TOOLS

adjustable wrench Perhaps the most elegant tool of them all, it can fill in for countless wrenches and sockets.

chisels A small set of wood chisels (1/4, 1/2, 3/4 inch) is indispensable. Ideally hit with a carpenter's wooden mallet, not a hammer.

drill Whilst a hand-held drill may be convenient for small jobs, it cannot compete with the efficiency of a cordless electric drill.

hammer There are several kinds: claw, ball peen, tack. A 16 oz claw hammer with a hickory or fibreglass handle is the most versatile.

hand saw There are many kinds of saw, but for quick results and cutting long straight lines a hand saw is the best saw.

level Of the torpedo sort. Determines true horizontal, vertical and 45° angles, for jobs from hanging pictures to framing a house.

measuring tape, 25 ft At least 1 in wide and marked with imperial and metric units. Wider tapes remain extended at greater distances.

screwdriver Flathead and Phillips in a few sizes each. Keep similar bits for the cordless drill.

slip-joint pliers Of the many varieties of pliers available, these are the most versatile for everyday use.

utility knife Apart from cutting through cardboard, insulation and carpet, this sharp edge is useful for scoring wood. Best with breakable blades.

BASIC TOOLS

Allen keys
awl
bar-clamps
bench vice
bevel gauge
bullnose nippers
carpenter's pencil
carpenter's square
cat's-paw (prybar)
caulking gun
C-clamps
chalk line, 100 ft
channel-lock pliers
circular saw

cold chisel
compass
drill bit set
electrical tape
files (wood & metal)
glass cutter
hacksaw
hand plane
interchangeable tip
   screwdriver
locking pliers
nail set
needle-nose pliers
pipe wrench

plumb bob
random orbital sander
reciprocating saw
sandpaper, various
socket set (imperial
   & metric)
staple gun
surform
tin snips
tool belt
tool box
whetstone
wire-stripper
wooden mallet

FIRE STARTING

Primitive methods of starting a fire, such as the bow and drill or striking rocks, are attractive in principle but require considerable effort and optimization. Lighting tinder from sparks thrown off by striking flint requires literally weeks of practice and experimentation. Some more practicable and ingenious methods are described below.

Compact OED   One of the easiest ways of starting a fire is by using a magnifying glass. A well-suited specimen is conveniently included with the compact edition of the *Oxford English Dictionary*. Held a couple of inches above the ground, it focuses the parallel rays of the sun into a sharp focus capable of igniting most dark tinder (see FIREWOOD opposite).

Cling film   If the *OED* is not at hand, a simple but effective lens can be constructed from water and cling film. With the four corners gathered together, fill a 12-inch-square piece of film with water and twist the ends so as to create an approximate sphere. With some manipulation, the sun's rays can be concentrated into a point sufficiently tight to ignite tinder (see opposite).

Coke can   In principle the sun's rays can be concentrated by a number of hand mirrors, each reflecting the rays onto the same spot. The continuum limit of such a collection of small nearby mirrors is a parabolic mirror. True parabolic mirrors, sometimes found in telescopes, can be hard to come by. Much more common, and just as effective once modified, is the bottom of a Coke (or other aluminium) can. The concave can bottom already has the right shape, but its dull, machined outer surface must be polished. This is best done in steps, starting with an abrasive polish, such as kitchen cleaning powder or steel wool, then finishing with a finer paste like chocolate or toothpaste. Use a small cloth or toothbrush to apply the polish, and finish with just the cloth itself. The choice of polish is not crucial—some are simply faster than others. It is essential, however, that the final polish be fine.

Magnesium   This lightweight metal is extremely flammable (though not explosive) as a powder or in the form of shavings, but resistant to combustion in bulk. A small block of the metal, along with a flint for making sparks, can be bought as an extreme-weather fire starter. Form a pile of shavings, at least half an inch in diameter, by scraping the soft metal with a knife. Strike the back of the knife against the flint to cast sparks onto the shavings. Once ignited, the magnesium will burn with an intensely hot white flame. It should immediately be covered with tinder.

FIREWOOD

Easily combustible material for the purpose of starting a wood fire is called tinder—any dry paper or leaves, or finely prepared bark or wood, will work. When using concentrated light to start a fire, it is important that the tinder is dark, which absorbs light, rather than fair, which reflects it. In the case of the Coke-can mirror, the tinder must be suspended by a thin stick so as not to obstruct the sun's rays.

Once a fire is started, additional tinder and kindling should be added stage-wise to keep the fire going. After a base of coals has collected and the fire is robust, just about any wood can be used to keep it going indefinitely, even green or wet wood which, if placed close by, will quickly dry. Nevertheless, some species of tree make better firewood than others. The chief desired properties are high heat production and low smoke emissions and ash deposits. The energy output of firewood is measured in British thermal units (BTUS). A BTU is the amount of energy necessary to heat one pound of water one degree Fahrenheit; it will light a 60-watt lamp for 18 seconds. The energy output per cord in millions of BTUS for different North American and European trees is listed below. A good guide is the weight of the wood—energy output is almost directly proportional to density. In general, slow-growing trees, such as oak and most fruit trees, are the densest. A cord is the standard unit for measuring firewood: it is a stack of parallel logs 8ft by 4ft by 4ft, or the equivalent volume.

Species	MBtu/cord				
Oak, Live	35	Douglas Fir	25	Fir, White	20
Eucalyptus	33	Juniper, Western	25	Pine, Ponderosa	20
Locust, Black	30	Walnut, Black	25	Alder	19
Beech	29	Cherry	23	Cedar, Incense	19
Dogwood	29	Elm	23	Fir, Red	19
Birch	27	Hemlock, Western	23	Redwood, Coast	19
Oak, White	27	Magnolia	23	Pine, Sugar	18
Tanoak	27	Sycamore	23	Willow, Black	18
Ash	25	Maple, Big Leaf	22	Aspen	17
		Sweetgum	21	Cottonwood	16

In their broadest sense, knots comprise all practically useful or decorative complications in cordage, though not periodic ones, which are known as weaves. Most practical knots can be assorted into three categories: *bends*, used to join two lines; *hitches*, used to attach a line to an object; and *knots*, any conformation tied into a single line itself.

The simplest knot is the overhand, which is the first half of a reef knot. When tied around an object, it is called a half-hitch. While the reef is probably the most familiar of all knots, it is nevertheless often confused with the practically useless granny knot. The bowline, sometimes called the king of knots, offers a simple, strong fixed loop in the end of a line. A more foolproof and extremely dependable alternative is the figure-eight knot, used in rock climbing.

Some of the knots below are used in man's daily rituals. A half-hitch is used to tie a jumper around the waist. An Ascot is tied with a reef knot before pinning the overlapping ends. The usual four-in-hand necktie knot is the buntline hitch. The seemingly complicated bow tie knot is just the reef bow, which is also the knot used to tie shoelaces. When a bow tie or shoelace knot is offset by 90°, it has been tied with a granny bow rather than a reef bow. (For a discussion of necktie knots and bow tie knots, see pp. 65 and 68.)

KNOTS TO KNOW

Knots   *Any complication in a single rope*

Reef or square knot	Common knot for tying packages, bandages, etc.	A
Granny knot	Common, useless result of a mistied reef knot.	B
Reef bow	Easily untied knot used for shoelaces, gifts and bows.	C
Surgeon's knot	Less likely to slip whilst tying than the reef knot.	D
Bowline	Essential knot for a fixed loop at the end of a rope.	E
Figure-eight loop	Easily remembered fixed loop for critical situations.	F
Butterfly knot	A fixed loop along a rope. Useful as a handle.	G
Spanish bowline	Two adjustable fixed loops along a rope.	H
Sheepshank	Reduces excess length in a rope without using the ends.	P

Hitches   *Used to attach a rope to an object*

Timber hitch	Useful under constant tension, e.g., when hauling logs.	O
Clove hitch	Used for attaching line to round posts or sticks.	J
Constrictor hitch	A surprisingly secure knot around trees or posts.	I
Buntline hitch	A sturdy slip knot which will resist jerking.	K
Tautline hitch	Easily adjusted to keep line taut. Useful for tents.	L
Clinch or half-blood knot	Joins monofilament line to a hook or swivel.	Q

Bends   *Used to unite two ropes*

Sheet bend	If one rope is thicker, it should be the one on the right.	M
Carrick bend	For ropes of equal width, especially heavy ones.	N

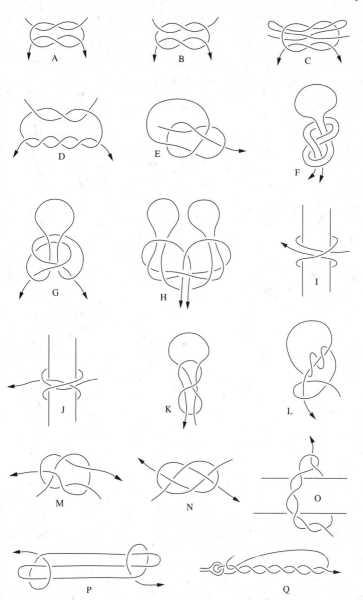

The still waters, rivers and seas of Britain possess such a diversity of fish, caught in so varied a manner, that 'angling may be said to be so like the mathematics that it can never be fully learned', wrote Izaak Walton. *The Compleat Angler*, Walton's guide to catching and eating different species of fish, was first published in 1653 during the English interregnum. It is the most printed book in the English language after the Holy Bible and *Pilgrim's Progress*. As fellow brothers of the angle know, fishing brings the purest form of contentment, enjoyed by 'such men as lived in those times when there were fewer lawyers'.

Commonly caught fish in the UK can be divided into three types. *Game fish* by tradition refers to members of the *Salmonidae* family and includes some of the most prized of fishes. Angling for game fish, especially by fly, is steeped in ceremony and tradition. *Coarse fish* include all other angled freshwater fish, although there is little that is coarse about them: many require considerable skill to tempt, are tenacious fighters and make fine fare. *Sea fish* include saltwater fish found offshore and in the mouths of rivers, caught from the coastline, piers or boats. Many of these are the largest fishes of all.

GAME FISH

Common name	Scientific name	British record (lb - oz)
Atlantic Salmon	*Salmo salar*	64
Brown Trout	*Salmo trutta*	25 - 05
Rainbow Trout	*Oncorhynchus mykiss*	24 - 02
Sea Trout	*Salmo trutta*	22 - 08
Grayling	*Thymallus thymallus*	4 - 03

COARSE FISH

Common name	Scientific name	British record (lb - oz)
Catfish	*Silurus glanis*	62 - 00
Carp	*Cyprinus carpio*	56 - 06
Pike	*Esox lucius*	46 - 13
Zander	*Stizostedion lucioperca*	19 - 05
Barbel	*Barbus barbus*	17 - 01
Bream	*Abramis brama*	16 - 09
Tench	*Tinca tinca*	14 - 03
Eel	*Anguilla anguilla*	11 - 02
Chub	*Leuciscus cephalus*	8 - 10
Perch	*Perca fluviatilis*	5 - 09
Rudd	*Scardinius erythrophthalmus*	4 - 08
Roach	*Rutilus rutilus*	4 - 03
Crucian Carp	*Carassius carassius*	4 - 02
Dace	*Leuciscus leuciscus*	1 - 04

While the most common names of fishes in the UK are listed below, other names are sometimes used in other English-speaking countries. In case of ambiguity, the scientific name should be consulted. British record weights are measured in pounds and ounces. These are maxima, most caught from a boat, and typical sizes range from 10% to 25% of these. Many of the records have been recently set, and there is a consensus that fish in the UK have become bigger in recent decades, partly owing to milder winters associated with global warming.

The best months for catching game fish and sea fish vary from species to species. In still water most of the coarse fish can be caught all year long. A number of rivers have specific legal restrictions on the time of year during which they can be fished, particularly for game fish.

For instructions on attaching a line to a hook, see ❦Knots (p. 118). An introduction to filleting a fish can be found in the *U.S. Army Survival Manual* ebook (p. 131).

SEA FISH

Common name	Scientific name	British record (lb - oz)
Common Skate	*Raja batis*	227
Blue Shark	*Prionace glauca*	218
Conger Eel	*Conger conger*	133 - 04
Tope	*Galeorhinus galeus*	82 - 08
Ling	*Molva molva*	59 - 08
Cod	*Gadus morrhua*	58 - 06
Coalfish	*Pollachius virens*	37 - 05
Turbot	*Scophthalmus maximus*	33 - 12
Thornback Ray	*Raja clavata*	31 - 07
Pollack	*Pollachius pollachius*	29 - 04
Spurdog	*Squalus acanthias*	21 - 03
Bass	*Dicentrarchus labrax*	19 - 09
Thick-Lipped Mullet	*Chelon labrosus*	14 - 02
Plaice	*Pleuronectes platessa*	10 - 03
Ballan Wrasse	*Labrus bergylta*	9 - 07
Black Bream	*Spondyliosoma cantharus*	6 - 14
Whiting	*Merlangius merlangus*	6 - 12
Dover Sole	*Solea solea*	6 - 08
Mackerel	*Scomber scombrus*	6 - 02
Flounder	*Platichthys flesus*	5 - 11
Pouting	*Gadus luscus*	5 - 08
Lesser-Spotted Dogfish	*Scyliorhinus canicula*	4 - 15
Garfish	*Belone belone*	3 - 09
Dab	*Pleuronectes limanda*	2 - 12

The legal shooting periods for game and deer, compiled by the British Association for Shooting and Conservation, are as follows:

GAME

Technically, game includes partridge, pheasant, grouse, heath and moor game, blackgame and hare. It is illegal to shoot game on Sundays, Christmas Day or at night, as well as out of season.

Species	England, Scotland & Wales	Northern Ireland
Blackgame	20 Aug–10 Dec	not found
Common Snipe	12 Aug–31 Jan	1 Sep–31 Jan
Coot/Moorhen	1 Sep–31 Jan	always closed
Duck & Geese (inland)	1 Sep–31 Jan	1 Sep–31 Jan
Duck & Geese (below high water-mark)	1 Sep–20 Feb	1 Sep–31 Jan
Golden Plover	1 Sep–31 Jan	1 Sep–31 Jan
Grouse	12 Aug–10 Dec	12 Aug–30 Nov
Hare (restrictions on whom)	always open	12 Aug–31 Jan
Partridge	1 Sep–1 Feb	1 Sep–31 Jan
Pheasant	1 Oct–1 Feb	1 Oct–31 Jan
Ptarmigan	12 Aug–10 Dec	not found
Woodcock	1 Oct[1]–31 Jan	1 Oct–31 Jan

DEER

Although no season applies to Chinese Water Deer, the customary close season is 1 Mar–31 Oct.

Species	Sex	England, Wales & Northern Ireland	Scotland
Fallow	Bucks	1 Aug–30 Apr	1 Aug–30 Apr
	Does	1 Nov–28 Feb[2]	21 Oct–15 Feb
Red	Stags	1 Aug–30 Apr	1 Jul–20 Oct
	Hinds	1 Nov–28 Feb[2]	21 Oct–15 Feb
Roe	Bucks	1 Apr–31 Oct	1 Apr–20 Oct
	Does	1 Nov–28 Feb[2]	21 Oct–31 Mar
Sika	Stags	1 Aug–30 Apr	1 Jul–20 Oct
	Hinds	1 Nov–28 Feb[2]	21 Oct–15 Feb
Chinese Water Deer	both	no season	not found
Muntjac	both	no season	no season

(1) 1 Sep in Scotland. (2) 29 Feb in a leap year.

FOXHUNTING

Along with rabbits and grey squirrels, foxes can be controlled all year round. The traditional foxhunting season is 1 November to 1 April. Opening meets are held on the Saturday closest to 1 November.

The year 2007 marks the 100th anniversary of the Boy Scouts, founded in England by Sir Robert Baden-Powell (B-P) in 1907. The Girl Guides was set up in 1910 with the assistance of B-P's sister, Agnes. Scouting can now be found in nearly every country, with a worldwide population of 25 million boys and young men. It is by far the largest youth organization in the world.

Scouting has its origins in Baden-Powell's military training manual, *Aids to Scouting for N.C.O.s and Men*, published in 1899. When B-P shot to fame with his legendary defence of the town of Mafeking during the Second Boer War, his manual was widely adopted by youth organizations throughout Britain. Encouraged to adapt it for a younger audience, Baden-Powell wrote *Scouting for Boys* (see p. 131), the basis of what is today called the *Boy Scout Handbook* in America. Baden-Powell put his ideas into practice at a camp he organized for 22 boys on Brownsea Island in 1907. Scouting was spontaneously taken up by adolescents throughout the country and the British Empire at an extraordinary rate. On the advice of the King, B-P retired from the army in 1910 to devote his energy to the organization, which 12 years later numbered one million worldwide.

Knowing his days were numbered, B-P wrote his Last Message to Scouts, found amongst his possessions after his death in 1941. It ended:

> I have had a most happy life and I want each one of you to have as happy a life too. I believe that God put us in this jolly world to be happy and enjoy life. Happiness doesn't come from being rich, nor merely from being successful in your career, nor by self-indulgence. One step towards happiness is to make yourself healthy and strong while you are a boy, so that you can be useful and so can enjoy life when you are a man.
>
> Nature study will show you how full of beautiful and wonderful things God has made the world for you to enjoy. Be contented with what you have got and make the best of it. Look on the bright side of things instead of the gloomy one.
>
> But the real way to get happiness is by giving out happiness to other people. Try and leave this world a little better than you found it and when your turn comes to die, you can die happy in feeling that at any rate you have not wasted your time but have done your best. 'Be Prepared' in this way, to live happy and to die happy—stick to your Scout promise always—even after you have ceased to be a boy—and God help you to do it.
>
> Your Friend Baden-Powell

The centenary of Scouting will be celebrated with the 21st World Scout Jamboree at Hylands Park in Chelmsford, Essex, from 27 July until 8 August, 2007. A total of 40,000 people are expected to attend.

SCOUT ESSENTIALS

Central to Scouting is the so-called Scout Method, a philosophy of education based on learning by doing, the formation of small groups and the stage-wise completion of activities. Considerable attention is given to Scoutcraft, a collection of skills for proficiency out of doors. They include such things as chivalry, edible wild plants, fire building, first aid, nature lore, patriotism, physical fitness, signalling, swimming, tracking, tying knots and using an axe. Advancement in these and related skills is marked by earning badges (listed opposite), a key aspect of day-to-day Scout activity.

The Scout Promise
On my honour, I promise that I will do my best
To do my duty to God and to the Queen,
To help other people
And to keep the Scout Law.

The Scout Law
A Scout is to be trusted.
A Scout is loyal.
A Scout is friendly and considerate.
A Scout belongs to the worldwide family
  of Scouts.
A Scout has courage in all difficulties.
A Scout makes good use of time and is careful
  of possessions and property.
A Scout has self-respect and respect for others.

The Scout Motto
Be Prepared.
(after B-P's initials)

10 Essentials
Canteen or water bottle
Extra clothing
First aid kit
Map and compass
Matches and fire starter
Pocket knife
Rain gear
Sun protection
Torch
Trail food

SCOUT SECTIONS AND BADGES

There are five Scout Sections, organized by age. It is not necessary to have been active in one section to join the next.

Section	Abb.	Ages	Meet in
Beaver Scouts	BS	6–8	Colonies
Cub Scouts	CS	8–10 1/2	Packs
Scouts	S	10 1/2–14	Troops
Explorer Scouts	ES	14–18	Units
Scout Network	SN	18–25	largely autonomous

In addition to the badges listed opposite, there are four *Staged Activity Badges* which apply throughout all of the Scout Sections and three *Group Awards* to be completed between Sections.

Staged Activity Badges   Information Tech., Musician, Nights Away, Swimming
Group Awards   International Award, Faith Award, Environment Award

Beaver Scouts

❧ *Badges*
BS Membership
  Award
Joining In Awards

Moving-On Award
Outdoor Challenge
Discovery Chal.
Friendship Chal.

Chief Scout's
  Bronze Award
❧ *Activity Badges*
Animal Friend

Creative
Experiment
Explore
Faith

Cub Scouts

❧ *Badges*
CS Membership Award
Joining In Awards
Moving-On Award
Outdoor Challenge
Creative Challenge
Fitness Challenge
Global Challenge
Caring Challenge
Chief Scout's
  Silver Award

❧ *Activity Badges*
Adventure
Air Activities
Animal Carer
Art
Athletics
Book Reader
Camper
Chef
Collector
Communicator

Cyclist
DIY
Emergency Aid
Entertainer
Equestrian
Global Conservation
Hobbies
Home Help
Home Safety
Local Knowledge
Martial Arts

My Faith
Naturalist
Navigator
Personal Safety
Physical Recreation
Road Safety
Scientist
Skater
Sports Enthusiast
Water Activities
World Faiths

Scouts

❧ *Badges*
S Membership
  Award
Participation Awards
Moving-On Award
Outdoor Challenge
Outdoor Plus Chal.
Creative Challenge
Fitness Challenge
Global Challenge
Community Chal.
Adventure Chal.
Expedition Chal.
Chief Scout's
  Gold Award
❧ *Activity Badges*
Administrator
Aeronautics
Air Researcher
Air Spotter
Basic Aviation Skills
Aviation Skills

Adv. Aviation Skills
Angler
Artist
Art Enthusiast
Astronomer
Athletics
Camp Cook
Camper
Campsite Service
Canoeist
Caver
Chef
Circus Skills
Climber
Community
Craft
Cyclist
Dinghy Sailor
DIY
Dragon Boating
Electronics
Emergency Aid

Entertainer
Equestrian
Fire Safety
Forester
Global Conservation
Guide
Heritage
Hiker
Hill Walker
Hobbies
Interpreter
Librarian
Life Saver
Martial Arts
Master at Arms
Mechanic
Meteorologist
Model Maker
My Faith
Naturalist
Basic Nautical Skills
Nautical Skills

Adv. Nautical Skills
Navigator
Orienteer
Photographer
Physical Recreation
Pioneer
Power Coxswain
Public Relations
Pulling
Quartermaster
Racing Helm
Radio Communicator
Skater
Smallholder
Snowsports
Sports Enthusiast
Survival Skills
Water Sports
World Faiths
Writer

Explorer Scouts

❧ *Badges*
ES Membership Award
Moving-On Award
Chief Scout's
  Platinum Award
Chief Scout's

Diamond Award
Queen's Scout Award
Explorer Belt
❧ *Activity Badges*
Air Activities
Aviation Skills

Adv. Aviation Skills
Community
Creative
Emergency Aid
Lifesaver
Mountain Activities

Recreation
Science and Tech.
Scouting Skills
Nautical Skills
Adv. Nautical Skills
Water Activities

Despite the fascination with treehouses innate in all men, few understand the principles of constructing a stable, comfortable platform in a
tree. The secret to treehouses, in a word, is bolts—of which, more later.
We begin with some planning considerations.

Obstacles There are two potential external obstacles to keep in mind:
planning permission and neighbours. Planning permission is not required if (i) a treehouse does not overlook an adjoining property and
(ii) it can be classified as a temporary structure. For the sake of the latter, electricity and plumbing are not advised—an electrical lead to the
tree can serve most power requirements. Second, by its very nature,
a treehouse will most likely be visible from a distance, and unhappy
neighbours are likely to complain. The best approach is to involve potentially difficult neighbours from the start—it is harder to complain
about something you have long known about. Moreover, it is wise to
make the treehouse as handsome as possible. Anything other than natural wood finishes, such as paint or plywood, looks conspicuous in a
tree and should not be used.

Foundation Building a treehouse is little different from building any
other outdoor shelter apart from the foundation, which poses three
concerns. First, a tree is a living thing, and the points of treehouse
support must be strong but not injurious. Second, the foundation must
rest on a limited number of contact points. Contrary to intuition, it is
best to keep the number of support points as small as possible, usually
three or four. Third, trees move, mostly owing to swaying in the wind
rather than growth, so the contact points must not be vulnerable to a
relative shift in the trunks or branches. Once the foundation has been
built, further work on the walls and roof can be done in a conventional
fashion. Many of the grandest treehouses have stairs or a bridge leading to them, but this seems to go against their spirit, which is one of
elevation and exclusion of the outside world. A rope ladder is the best
way to access the house. Once in, you can pull up the ladder behind
you.

Bolts To understand how best to attach the treehouse to the tree, a
cursory knowledge of tree biology is helpful. The living part of a tree
is the bark and outermost layers (the outer $1/2$–2 inches, depending on
species and size) which carry resources to the branches and foliage.
The interior, called heartwood, is dead but remains strong. Accordingly, the most damaging injury is one which disrupts a significant
fraction of the bark along a circumference; the least harmful is a hole
perpendicular to the surface, such as a bolt. A cable tied around a tree
will eventually cut off its supply line, literally strangling it. Screws and
nails, whilst individually safe, are not appropriate for treehouse con-

struction for two reasons. They do not penetrate deep enough to hold fast; and too many minor wounds in a cluster can lead to compartmentalization, in which the tree blocks off the damaged region and let's it decay. Heavy bolts are the best solution, at least 3/4 inch diameter. These are threaded and screwed into a pre-drilled hole. Purpose-built bolts, called Garnier Limbs and available online, are 1 1/4 inch in diameter and are rated at 8,000 pounds.

Movement The distance that a tree sways increases with height, while the force it can exert decreases with height. In other words, a tree acts as a lever, with small but powerful motions near the base. Relative movement of an inch during a storm can snap the strongest bolt. Tree growth, on the other hand, is not normally a concern. Growth in height takes place at the tips of the branches, not in the trunk or branches themselves. Growth in girth, which occurs throughout and gives rise to annual rings in the wood, is a much slower process. There are three approaches to minimizing the effects of tree motion. The first is to build on a single trunk (bottom left). The second is to build close enough to the ground for the amount of motion between trees or branches to be negligible. The third, and preferable, method is to incorporate floating contacts on the bolts, described below.

Contacts Choosing which trees or limbs to build on is something of an art. Coniferous (needle-bearing) trees tend to have long, vertical trunks with few sturdy or accessible branches, and treehouses built on them use either a single trunk or multiple trunks close together. Deciduous (leaf-bearing) trees allow more imaginative possibilities. A forked branch can act as a convenient floating support point. The three foundation configurations below make use of one, three and four trunks or branches. Note that the first requires four bolts and diagonal supports. The frames are made of 2"×6" beams. The regions of the beams where they rest on the bolts should be covered with steel brackets or sheet metal. If the bolt ends do not already protrude, nuts can be welded to them to keep the supports from sliding off.

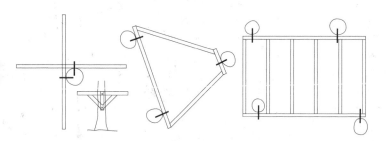

The traditional game of conkers is played using the nuts of the common horse-chestnut tree (*Aesculus hippocastanum*). A hole is drilled through the centre of the conker and a thick string or shoelace is threaded through it with a stopping knot tied at the end to retain the nut. Conkers left to dry for a year are harder than freshly fallen ones, though the latter can be hardened by baking them in the oven for several hours.

Players take turns swiping each other's conker, and continue until one of the conkers is sufficiently wrecked to fall off the string. The score associated with a conker is reckoned as follows: Every conker starts off with a score of zero. A conker gains a point for every win, plus the score of every conker it defeats. For instance, if a conker with a score of 2 beats a conker with a score of 4, the winning conker's new score is 7, 1 for winning and 4 for inheriting the points of the defeated. Thus if 100 new conkers were fought until only one remained, it would have a score of 99, a point for every defeated conker. A conker with a score of n is called an n-er, apart from $n = 0$, in which case the conker is called a none-er.

WORLD CONKER CHAMPIONSHIPS RULES

The World Conker Championships are held in Ashton, England, on the second Sunday in October. The official rules (edited for clarity) are as follows:

The game begins with a toss of a coin; the winner of the toss may elect to strike or receive.

The length of string between knuckle and nut must be at least 8 inches.

Each player is allowed 3 attempted strikes before swapping positions.

An attempted strike must be clearly aimed at the nut; deliberate mis-hits are not allowed.

The game continues until one of the conkers is smashed.

A small piece of nut or skin shall be judged out. To remain in competition, a conker must be substantial enough to mount an attack.

If both nuts smash at the same time then the match shall be replayed with new conkers.

Any nut knocked from the lace but not smashed may be rethreaded and the game continued.

A player causing a knotting of the laces (a snag) will be noted. Three snags will lead to disqualification.

If a game lasts for more than five minutes, then play is halted and the 'five-minute rule' comes into effect. Each player is allowed nine further attempted strikes at the opponent's nut, again alternating three strikes each. If neither conker has been smashed by the end, then the player with the most strikes during this period is judged the winner.

N-ER STATISTICS

Unlike in most sports, all conkers are undefeated. To lose is to be destroyed. A conker's score tells us something about its strength, although it also leaves room for surprises. Lurking behind a none-er could be a future champion. Alternatively, a 10-er could be a weak nut in disguise, having defeated a series of easy competitors. In general, conkers with higher scores will be stronger and rarer. But just how strong is an n-er, and how many of them are about?

Below is a table of statistics for n-ers. The proportion is the percentage of conkers with a given score at any one time: half of all conkers are none-ers, an eighth are 1-ers, $1/16$th are 2-ers, and so on. The median strength measures the hardness of a conker, where 0 is the weakest and 1 the hardest. It is the fraction of random conkers (none-ers) that the median n-er could beat. The life expectancy indicates, on average, the score that the median n-er will go on to achieve before being beaten assuming it only plays none-ers. It is about $2.44 \times n$.

Score	Proportion	Strength	Life expect.	Score	Proportion	Strength	Life expect.
none-er	50%	0.500	1.0-er	10-er	0.80%	0.939	25.4-er
1-er	12.5%	0.707	3.4-er	20-er	0.30%	0.968	49.8-er
2-er	6.25%	0.794	5.8-er	30-er	0.16%	0.978	74.2-er
3-er	3.91%	0.841	8.3-er	40-er	0.11%	0.983	98.6-er
4-er	2.73%	0.870	10.7-er	50-er	0.08%	0.986	123-er
5-er	2.05%	0.891	13.2-er	60-er	0.06%	0.989	148-er
6-er	1.61%	0.906	15.6-er	70-er	0.05%	0.990	172-er
7-er	1.31%	0.917	18.0-er	80-er	0.04%	0.991	196-er
8-er	1.09%	0.926	20.5-er	90-er	0.03%	0.992	221-er
9-er	0.93%	0.933	22.9-er	100-er	0.03%	0.993	245-er

☢ *For geeks* The n-er statistics above can be derived or simulated by considering an imaginary playground of some large number M of conkers. All conkers are assigned a random strength between 0 and 1 and start as none-ers. Two randomly chosen conkers are played against each other and the harder conker wins; we do not take into account here differences in skill. The winner's score increases in the usual way and the loser is replaced by a new none-er. Thus the total number of conkers is always M.

After a long time, the following conker theorems hold: The proportion of n-ers is $C_n / 2^{(2n+1)}$, where $C_n = \frac{1}{n+1}\binom{2n}{n}$ is the nth Catalan number; this gives the proportions $1/2$, $1/8$, $2/32$, $5/128$, and so on. The strength of the median n-er is $s_n = 1/\sqrt[n+1]{2}$. The life expectancy of the median n-er is $n + s_n/(1 - s_n)$ (here we have assumed it will only play none-ers); in the limit of large n the life expectancy is $(1 + 1/\ln 2)\, n$.

SCIENCE & LETTERS

❦ BOOKS

Below is a collection of classic books for men, most of which are the definitive work in their field. In general the earliest date of publication is listed. Some of the books have remained continuously in print, others have been reissued after a dormant period. Those which are out of print can often be found second-hand on abebooks.co.uk or bibliofind.com; alternatively, many of those out of copyright can be found free online at digital.library.upenn.edu/books or gutenberg.org.

Men

Manners for Men	Mrs Humphry	1897
Manful Assertions: Masculinities in Britain Since 1800		
	Michael Roper & John Tosh	1991
Gentleman	Bernhard Roetzel	1999
London Man	Francis Chichester	2000
The Chap Manifesto	Gustav Temple & Vic Darkwood	2001
The Modern Gentleman	Phineas Mollod & Jason Tesauro	2002
The Man Manual	Ian Banks	2002
Manliness	Harvey Mansfield	2006
The Alphabet of Manliness	Maddox	2006
The Dangerous Book for Boys	Conn Iggulden, Hal Iggulden	2006

Consumption

The Stag Cook Book	C. Mac Sheridan	1922
The Pipe Book	Alfred Dunhill	1924
The Gentleman's Companion, vols 1 & 2	Charles Baker, Jr	1939
The Fine Art of Mixing Drinks	David A. Embury	1948
With or Without Beans, Being a compendium…of chile	Joe Cooper	1952
Spirits and Liqueurs	Peter Hallgarten	1979
The Ultimate Pipe Book	Richard Carlton Hacker	1984
The Rituals of Dinner	Margaret Visser	1991
Beer Companion	Michael Jackson	1993
'A classification of pure malt Scotch whiskies', *Applied Statistics* **43**, 237		
	F.-J. Lapointe and P. Legendre	1994
Malt Whisky Companion	Peter Jackson	1999
The Faber Book of Smoking	James Walton	2000
Sauce Guide to Drink & Drinking; Sauce Guide to Cocktails		
	Simon Difford	2002; 2003
Mr Boston Official Bartender's and Party Guide	Chris Morris (ed.)	1935–2005

Pursuits

Style

The Year

Best account of conquest   Lermontov, 'Princess Mary', *A Hero of Our Time* [1]
Best American fashion influence   Blue jeans (p. 58); penny loafer [2]
Best Bond novel (film)   *From Russia with Love* (*Goldfinger*)
Best book on men's clothes   Hardy Amies, *The Englishman's Suit*
Best bottle to take to a drinks party   Whisky and a candle [3]
Most popular boys' names (England and Wales, 2005)
                                    Jack, Joshua, Thomas, James, Oliver
Best British designer   Sir Paul Smith [4]
Best buttonhole flower   Carnation [5]
Best casual clothes   Hackett
Best cigar   Trinidad Fundadore [6]
Best cigarettes to be seen smoking   Silk Cut; Marlboro Red
Best cloth   Vicuña, from the coat of the wild South American camelid
Best cocktail today   Caipirinha (p. 35)
Hottest curry   Phal, generally available though not always on the menu
Second-best dandy   Count d'Orsay [7]
Least-documented common male ailment   Blue balls (p. 11)
Best (domestic) beer   (Fuller's London Porter) Westvleteren 12
Best drinking accessory   Curved metal hip flask for the breast pocket
Worst drink to order in a pub   Half-pint [8]
Best endurance sport   Tour de France; Iditarod Sled Dog Race
Best guns   Holland & Holland (shotguns); Purdey (rifles)
Best hat(ter)   Boater; Bowler (James Lock & Co.)
Best jeans for men   Levi's; Diesel
Best liqueur   Green Chartreuse (p. 28)
Best male fashion eras   The late Plantagenet, Regency and
                            1950s Edwardian revival periods [9]
Most naff fashion item (accessory)   sleeveless T-shirt (white silk scarf)
Most prolific known textonum   22737, with 12 words [10]
Best public (private) London nightclub   The Cuckoo Club (Annabel's)
Best regiment   22nd SAS Regiment [11]
Best second club   The Garrick [12]
Best shirtmakers   Turnbull and Asser; Charvet (France)
Best shoemakers   Lobb; G. J. Cleverley
Best smoking accessory   Parabolic mirror solar cigarette lighter
Strongest spirit (commercially available)   Everclear [13]
Best tailors   Anderson & Sheppard; Huntsman & Sons;
                Henry Poole & Co.; Kilgour, French & Stanbury
Best tie   Seven-fold tie, made from a single piece of silk with no lining
Best tie knot   Nicky ($L_\odot C_\otimes R_\odot L_\otimes C_\odot T$, p. 66) [14]
Best umbrellas   Swaine Adeney Brigg & Sons
Best way to give up smoking   Take up snuff (p. 39)
Best overall whisky distillery   Highland Park (p. 31)

1 Free online from gutenberg.org/etext/913.

2 Soon after loafers became fashionable in the 1930s and 40s, copper pennies were inserted into the strap across the vamp. Swells prefer to use 1943 wartime steel pennies, issued when copper was scarce.

3 Between refills force the lighted candle into the bottle. No one expects a vessel with a candle in it to contain anything drinkable.

4 With several hundred shops in the UK and abroad, his clothes combine traditional English tailoring and cut with eclectic fabrics and patterns.

5 'Best', argues fashion writer John Taylor, 'because its *calyx* (the cup beneath the bloom from which the petals grow out) is bulky enough to be held firmly in place by the best buttonhole—which should be between one inch and one and an eighth inches long.'

6 Although the Trinidad has been privately produced by the El Laguito factory in Havana, Cuba, for many years to provide gifts of state, it became commercially available in limited quantities in 1998. It was made in a single size only, the Fundadore at $7^1/2$ inches × ring gauge 39, until 2003 when the Reyes, Coloniales and Robusto Extra sizes were introduced.

7 The best, of course, was Brummell, who turned men's dress away from finery and extravagance to understatement, restraint and studied indifference, now so ingrained in masculine costume.

8 Despite being standard issue in France, in Britain ordering a half-pint is suspect. Order a pint or go home.

9 Not, as many argue, the 1930s, during which men's and women's fashion de-emphasized sex. The eras opposite 'idealized the "natural" but virile shape—emphasizing masculinity with shoulder focus and hose, breeches or trousers which revealed the shape of the leg', writes John Taylor.

10 Entered in a mobile phone with predictive text, 22737 can give *acres, bards, barer, bares, baser, bases, caper, capes, cards, carer, cares,* and *cases.* The total is 14 if *caser* and *barfs* are also allowed as words.

11 Generally considered the most elite special force in the world. The now famous sas mission to find Iraqi Scud missile launchers in 1991 was recounted in Andy McNab's addictive book *Bravo Two Zero.*

12 Not the same as the second-best club. A man's second club, given that he belongs to one of the smart Regency gentlemen's clubs (and the best club is indisputably White's), should be spirited, garrulous and collegiate, and the best of these is the Garrick.

13 Everclear is nearly pure grain alcohol, or ethanol, which comes in two strengths: 151 proof (75.5% ABV) and 190 proof (95% ABV). The latter is very flammable.

14 A symmetric knot, in between the four-in-hand and half-Windsor in size. The earliest known description of the Nicky is by Italian tie-shop owner Ernesto Curami. It was rediscovered by David Kelsall as an improvement on the Pratt knot and reported in the *Sunday Telegraph* in 1991.

Below is a summary of most of the units of measurement that a man is likely to need. The *Système International d'Unités*, or SI units, is a coherent system of base 10 (metric) units. With the exception of imperial units, it is the customary system of units throughout the world. Imperial units are the traditional English units of measurement; their use persists in the UK and, with some differences, the US.

SI UNITS

Base units

metre (m)	length
kilogram (kg)	mass
second (s)	time
ampere (A)	electric current
kelvin (K)	temperature
mole (mol)	amount of substance
candela (cd)	luminous intensity

Associated units

are (a) = 100 m^2	unit of area
litre (l) = <u>0.001</u> m^3	unit of volume

Note: 1 l of water weighs 1 kg

Prefixes (base ten)

deca (da)	$\times 10$	deci (d)	$\times 10^{-1}$
hecto (h)	$\times 10^2$	centi (c)	$\times 10^{-2}$
kilo (k)	$\times 10^3$	milli (m)	$\times 10^{-3}$
mega (M)	$\times 10^6$	micro (μ)	$\times 10^{-6}$
giga (G)	$\times 10^9$	nano (n)	$\times 10^{-9}$
tera (T)	$\times 10^{12}$	pico (p)	$\times 10^{-12}$
peta (P)	$\times 10^{15}$	femto (f)	$\times 10^{-15}$
exa (E)	$\times 10^{18}$	atto (a)	$\times 10^{-18}$
zetta (Z)	$\times 10^{21}$	zepto (z)	$\times 10^{-21}$
yotta (Y)	$\times 10^{24}$	yocto (y)	$\times 10^{-24}$

IMPERIAL UNITS

Apothecaries' capacity

pint	20 fluid ounces
fl. ounce	8 drachms
drachm	3 scruples
scruple	20 minims

Apothecaries' weight

pound	12 ounces
ounce	8 drams
dram	3 scruples
scruple	20 grains

Area

square mile	640 acres
acre	4 roods
rood	1210 sq. yards
sq. yard	9 sq. feet
sq. foot	144 sq. inches

Avoirdupois (common) weight

ton	20 hundredweight
hundredweight	4 quarters
quarter	2 stones
stone	14 pounds
pound (lb)	16 ounces
ounce (oz)	16 drams

Capacity (UK)

bushel	4 pecks
peck	2 gallons
gallon	4 quarts
quart	2 pints
pint	4 gills
gill	5 fl. ounces

Length

league	3 miles
mile	1760 yards
yard (yd)	3 feet
foot (ft)	12 inches
inch (in)	3 barleycorns

Surveyors' length

mile	8 furlongs
furlong	10 chains
chain	4 rods
rod	25 links
link	<u>0.66</u> feet

Troy weight (precious metal)

pound	12 ounces
ounce	20 pennyweights
pennyweight	24 grains

OTHER UNITS

Alcoholic strength
See p. 19.

Angular measure

circle	360 degrees
degree	60 minutes
minute	60 seconds
circle	2π radians

Astronomical distance

parsec	3.08×10^{13} km
light year	9.46×10^{12} km
astronomical unit	1.50×10^8 km

Beauty

Helen	25.6 Helenas
10 Helenas	beauty to die for

Cooking & drinks capacity
See p. 18.

Folded paper

folio	folded in half once
quarto	' ' twice
octavo	' ' 3 times
sextodecimo	' ' 4 times

Gem weight

gram	5 carats
carat	100 points

Gym (typical)

workout	8 exercises
exercise	3 sets
set	10 repetitions

Memory

terabyte (TB)	2^{40} bytes
gigabyte (GB)	2^{30} bytes
megabyte (MB)	2^{20} bytes
kilobyte (kB)	$1024 = 2^{10}$ bytes

byte (B)	8 bits

Microscopic length

micron (μ)	10^{-6} m
angstrom (Å)	10^{-10} m

Nautical measures

cable	100 fathoms
fathom	6 feet
league (at sea)	3 nautical miles
nautical mile (intl)	1852 m
knot	1 nautical mile/hour

Paper sheets

bale	10 reams
ream	20 quires
quire	25 sheets

Paper size

letter	8.5 in × 11 in
legal	8.5 in × 14 in
A4	210 mm × 297 mm
A0	841 mm × 1189 mm
B0	1000 mm × 1414 mm
C0	917 mm × 1297 mm

A0 = 2 A1 = 4 A2 = 8 A3, etc.
Same for B0 and C0.

Pre-decimal coinage

pound	20 shillings
shilling	12 pence
penny	2 halfpennies
halfpenny	2 farthings

Shoe size
See p. 55.

Typography

0.9961 inches	6 picas
pica	12 points

CONVERSION BETWEEN UNITS

inch	2.54 centimetres
foot	0.3048 metres
mile	1.609344 kilometres
acre	0.4047 hectares
ounce (avoirdupois)	28.35 grams
ounce (apoth., troy)	31.10 grams

pound	0.4536 kilograms
fluid ounce (UK, apoth.)	28.41 ml
quart	1.136 litres
temp (°C)	temp (K) − 273.15
temp (°F)	9/5 × temp (°C) + 32

Integers and underlined decimal numbers are exact.

Since ancient times, mathematically derived relations between lengths have been considered more attractive than arbitrary ones: the square and double square, of course, but also the Golden ratio and ISO standard. A number of fundamental relations are found in the proportions of man, captured in da Vinci's Vitruvian Man and Le Corbusier's Modulor (see p. 4). They also feature in design and architecture.

Proportion can be considered in two ways: arithmetically, in terms of simple integer ratios; and geometrically, derived from the regular polygons and circle (see opposite). Some proportions have special properties. For instance, if one removes a square from a rectangle in the proportion of the Golden ratio, the resulting rectangle is again in the same proportion (see p. 5). If the ISO standard is cut in half, the resulting two rectangles have the same proportion as the original. Below are the most important proportions and their constructions.

	Name	Ratio	Exact ratio	Examples
A	Octave (double sq.)	1:2	1:2	trad. man's visiting card; Modulor
B	Major seventh	1:1.875	8:15	
C	Tall hexagon	1:1.866	$1:1 + \sqrt{3}/2$	
D	Minor seventh	1:1.778	9:16	HDTV screen
E	Hexagon	1:1.732	$1:\sqrt{3}$	
F	Tall pentagon	1:1.701	$1:\sqrt{2 + 2/\sqrt{5}}$	
G	Major sixth	1:1.667	3:5	
H	Golden section	1:1.618	$1:(1 + \sqrt{5})/2$	this text block;
			Western architecture; Modulor (p. 4); stages of man (p. 5)	
I	Minor sixth	1:1.6	5:8	
J	Pentagon	1:1.539	$1:\sqrt{5 + 2\sqrt{5}}/2$	
K	Fifth	1:1.5	2:3	35 mm still film; medieval books
L	ISO standard	1:1.414	$1:\sqrt{2}$	A3, A4, A5, etc. paper;
				Islamic architecture; passports
M	Short pentagon	1:1.376	$1:\sqrt{1 + 2/\sqrt{5}}$	35 mm motion picture film
N	Fourth	1:1.333	3:4	TV screen; medieval books
O	Tall half-octagon	1:1.307	$1:\sqrt{1 + \sqrt{2}/2}$	
P	Major third	1:1.25	4:5	
Q	Half-octagon	1:1.207	$1 : (1 + \sqrt{2})/2$	
R	Minor third	1:1.2	5:6	
S	Turned hexagon	1:1.155	$1:2/\sqrt{3}$	
T	Major second	1:1.125	8:9	
U	Tall cross octagon	1:1.082	$1:2\sqrt{1 - \sqrt{2}/2}$	
V	Minor second	1:1.067	15:16	
W	Turned pentagon	1:1.051	$1:\sqrt{2 - 2/\sqrt{5}}$	
X	Unison (square)	1:1	1:1	Vitruvian Man (p. 4)

HARMONIC PROPORTIONS

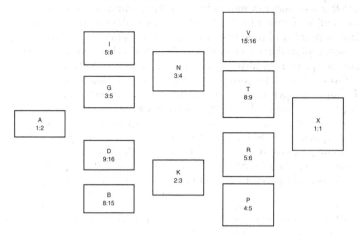

Proportions derived from the Pythagorean scale. If one associates the square (X) with unison and the double square (A) with its octave, one finds a parallel between harmonious proportions and the harmonic interval.

GEOMETRIC PROPORTIONS

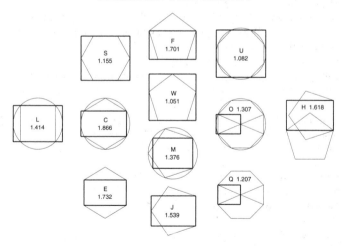

Proportions derived from the square, pentagon, hexagon, octagon and circle. All ratios of height to width are irrational—that is, they cannot be expressed as a ratio of two integers.

In essence, the closing of letters, email and text messages indicates how *I* relate to *you*, with the basic formulae being

I [verb] *your* [noun phrase]   or   *I* [verb] *yours* [modifier].

The verb is usually *am* or *remain*; the noun phrase might be *humble subject* or *friend* or *affectionate brother*; the modifier can be an adverb, like *sincerely*, or an adverbial clause, usually *with...*, as in *with best wishes*. Today these formulae are usually not written out in full but implied, and we are left with such familiar artefacts as *Yours sincerely* or *With best wishes*. (Note that only the first word is capitalized.) Which variations mean what, and which parts are made explicit, is a subject of some subtlety, conveying as much about the sender as about his relationship with the recipient.

In English there is a broad range of customary closings, particularly for men, who do not end very much of their correspondence with *Love* or a string of *x*s. Some are more appropriate on paper; others are best suited to digital communication. For racier ways of signing off, see p. 43. Closings range from chav to non-chav as follows:

Chav	C	c	~	N	N	*Non-Chav*

I have the honour to remain, Madam, Your Majesty's most humble and obedient
    servant   N When addressing the Queen.

I remain, Sir, your obedient servant
                    N Once widely used, now rare.

Yours   c *I am* or *I remain* is implied. Informal, if somewhat cool.

Yours aye   N *Aye* means always, ever. Used in the military and by Scots
                       between close acquaintances.

Yours ever   N Between friends. The variation *As ever*, short for *Yours as
                       ever*, suggests frequent correspondence.

Yours truly   c Earnest or American.

Yours in haste   N A handy construction for short notes. Note the change of
                       adverbial clause from the usual *with....*

Yours cordially   C Meant to be somewhere between *Yours sincerely* and *Yours
                       affectionately*, but is self-conscious and pretentious.

Yours in Christ   N Apart from by clerics, indiscriminate use can be awkward.
                       Yours in Jesus (c) suggests a Protestant sender.

Yours sincerely   ~ *Sincerely* means honestly, without pretence. Used when a
                       letter begins *Dear Mr Simpson*. Americans frequently use
                       Sincerely yours.

Yours faithfully N When a letter begins *Dear Sir*.

Yours respectfully N To Catholic clergy. In letters to the pope, brother
                       bishops close with *Yours devotedly in Christ*.

Yours affectionately N Sometimes used between family members or friends.

Best	C	Short for *With best wishes* or *With best regards*. OK for short emails, clumsy when written.
Best wishes	~	*With best wishes* is more intimate.
All the best	C	Naff, although *All best* is not. The latter is frequently used by thespians and those in the literary business.
All good wishes	N	Curiously warmer than *Best wishes*.
Regards	~	Literally, affection and good wishes. Cool if unqualified.
Best regards	~	One of the most common closings. More familiar than *Best wishes*, but unoriginal.
Kind regards	N	Often cool. But *Kindest regards* (N) is meant to be warm.
Fond regards	N	*Fond* once suggested doting, but now means affectionate, loving. It can imply mild romantic interest.
Warm regards	N	Hearty. Used both with friends and acquaintances.
Cheers	C	Mostly used in writing by the French and Americans, thinking it is colloquial amongst the British. Not to be confused with *Cheers, mate* (C), mostly used in speech.
Cheerio	~	'A parting exclamation of encouragement', according to the OED. Mostly used in speech.
Thanks	C	Expressions of thanks are correctly part of the letter. A separate closing should be added.
Love	N	Apart from romantic contexts, indiscriminate use can have camp associations.
Luv	C	Attempt to deflate the meaning by a parody of spelling.
Lots of love	C	From women. Less intimate than *Love*, it is an example of a phrop—a phrase which means the opposite of what it says. Sometimes abbreviated LOL.
All my love	N	For romantic or familial contexts. Simple but effectual.
xxx	~	From women. See SMS paralanguage, p. 143.
See you later	C	This and its derivatives (*See you soon, Speak later*) are part of the letter proper, not closings.
See you later, alligator	~	This, on the other hand, is a closing, and invites the response *In a while, crocodile*.
Take care	C	From women or metrosexuals. Less grating when spoken.
Farewell	N	In correspondence it suggests finality.
TTYL, TTFN	C, N	Initialisms for *Talk to you later* (text speak) and *Ta ta for now* (twee). TTFN was popularized during WWII and was since adopted by the animated Tigger.
—John or *—J*	~	A simple dash. Cool when hand-written, neutral when digital. An initial only suggests familiarity.
Adieu	N	Literally, *to God* (see you in Heaven). Used when the next meeting is distant or uncertain.
Ciao	~	From the Italian *schiavo* (servant), it now means *hello* or *goodbye*. In English it first appeared in Hemingway's *A Farewell to Arms*. Today it can come across as Eurotrash.

TEXT MESSAGE THEORY

Texting (also known as short message system, or SMS) is for many people the main form of non-verbal communication, exceeding letters and even emails. The Mobile Data Association has estimated that 100 million text messages are sent per day in the UK in 2006. Part of the attraction of texting is its immediacy—messages are usually read by the recipient within seconds of sending. Unlike postal or electronic mail, a message is often neither essential nor interrogative, placing no responsibility on the recipient to respond. But because composing a text is a lot slower than typing or writing, it is in the interests of the sender to make it brief. Over the years a unique form of expression has evolved with a haiku-like economy. It includes a number of conventions for the concise expression of English (p. 142). Punctuation is kept to a minimum, apart from the use of paralanguage (p. 143). It is now common to compose texts without regard to capitalization.

The principal hurdle in entering text into a small device is the difficulty of incorporating a full-size keyboard. The solution has been to reduce the number of keys and take advantage of the limited range of words: not every arrangement of letters forms a word. The number of letter combinations grows with the number of characters N as 26^N: there are 26 possible 1-letter combinations, 676 2-letter combinations, and so on. The number of English words, as found in the official Scrabble word list, grows much more slowly: there are 3 1-letter words, 96 2-letter words, etc. Roughly in between is the number of possible SMS numbers, which grows as 8^N: 8 1-digit numbers, 64 2-digit numbers, and so on (only the digits 2–9 are used). As the graph below suggests, apart from between 2 and 4 characters, most SMS numbers correspond to one or no words, and the chance for ambiguous input (textonyms, see opposite) is low.

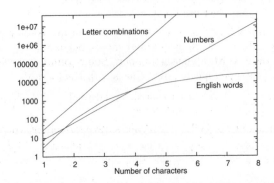

TEXT MESSAGE INPUT

The numeric keys on a mobile phone produce the following letters, digits and punctuation (the output for 1 varies):

0 ␣	1 .,?!'" 1	2 abc2	3 def3	4 ghi4
5 jkl5	6 mno6	7 pqrs7	8 tuv8	9 wxyz9

But not all keys are used equally. In English the distribution is:

		12.4% abc	19.2% def	15.1% ghi
4.9% jkl	16.7% mno	14.3% pqrs	12.8% tuv	4.6% wxyz

The original form of input is so-called multitap, in which the number of times a key is pressed is the rank of the letter on that key. Thus

55523 = lad	2224427 = chap	225556665533 = bloke

Most phones offer a more efficient method of input, called predictive text, in which the keys are pressed once. This reduces the above to

523 = lad	2427 = chap	25653 = bloke

But more than one word can correspond to a number; 2427 also yields agar, bias, bibs and char. Words with the same number are called textonyms, e.g., 5477 = kiss, lips, lisp; the number itself is called a textonum. Textonyms require the user to manually scroll through the possibilities. Without scrolling, typing 'Ask the cool barmaid for nine pints of beer' produces 'Ask the book carnage for mind shots of adds'. Some notable textonyms include

63 = me, of	627 = map, mar, nap, oar
46 = go, im, in	269 = any, bow, box, boy, cow, cox, coy
7468 = pint, riot, shot	2263 = acme, acne, band, bane, came, cane
27766 = apron, arson	7673 = pope, pore, pose, rope, rose, sore
22743 = acrid, barge	746637 = phones, simmer, sinner
33284 = death, debug	7425464 = picking, shaking, sibling
4663 = gone, good, goof, home, hone, hood, hoof	

(See p. 132 for the longest set known.)

The probability that a word is a textonym decreases rapidly with word length, as the opposite graph shows: beyond 5 characters, there are far fewer words than SMS numbers. Some common words are composed of a single repeated digit (marked ⁻). There are 18:

$\bar{2}$ = cab	$\bar{3}$ = eff, fed, fee; deed, feed; deeded	$\bar{4}$ = hi; gig; high
$\bar{6}$ = no, on; mom, moo; moon, noon		$\bar{8}$ = tv; tutu

Even rarer are words that form consecutive sequences. There are ten:

23(4) = be(g)	2345 = ceil	3456(7) = film(s)	56(7) = lo(p)
5678 = lost		678 = opt	789 = sty

TEXT MESSAGE ENGLISH

Text messages are condensed in a variety of ways, the principles of which are outlined here. Many common words can be abbreviated (full stops are omitted), for example,

& and	cd could	cuz because	gf girlfriend	msg message
pls please	spk speak	t the	thx thanks	tmr tomorrow
v very	w with	wd would	wk week	wt what

Common phrases can also be abbreviated, such as

bbl be back later	btw by the way	fyi for your info.
lol laugh out loud	omg oh my god	ttyl talk to you later

Some words can be replaced by single letters:

b be, bee	c see, sea	g gee	i eye	j jay
o oh, owe	p pea, pee	q cue, queue	r are	t tea
u you	y why			

Similarly, some words can be replaced by punctuation marks or digits:

@ at	1 one, won	2 to, too	4 for	8 ate

Compound examples include iball, jwalk, qball, tbag, any1 and 4taste. There are a few conventions for abbreviating groups of letters:

$ ss	% oo	oz orr... ,

whereby bo$ = boss, c%l = cool, soz = sorry and tomoz = tomorrow
Some characters can replace groups of phonemes:

@ at	2 tū	4 fôr	8 āt	b bē
n en	r ar	s es	u yū	x eks

Examples include:

@empt	attempt	m8	mate	rt		art
ch@	chat	l8r	later	gs		guess
2nite	tonight	b4	before	ls		less
2moro	tomorrow	bleve	believe	urope		europe
a4d	afford	bn	been	ur		your, you're
4mer	former	nter	enter	chx		cheques
4ward	forward	br	bar	xlnt		excellent

Several digits are contained in their product with 10:

4ty forty	6ty sixty	7ty seventy	8ty eighty	9ty ninety

Sometimes it is easier to write Roman numerals than Arabic numerals:

I 1	V 5	X 10	L 50	C 100	D 500	M 1000

Digits can be abbreviated by the first letters of their names:

0 z	1 o	2 t	3 T	4 f	5 F	6 s	7 S	8 e	9 n

TEXT MESSAGE PARALANGUAGE

Machine-printed and digital communication, with its cool and unchanging letter forms, brings with it an ambiguity of meaning and tone. This has led to an explosion in the use of digital paralanguage— ASCII characters on a single line for non-verbal communication—to prevent misunderstandings. These are also known as emoticons (from emotion and console, not icon), and should not to be confused with ASCII art, which occupies multiple lines. The most familiar examples are the question and exclamation marks, ? and !. More recent is the use of x and :-) to denote a kiss and a smiley. (The first documented use of the smiley was on 19 September 1982 by Scott Fahlman.) Emoticons fall into several classes, each containing variations on a theme. Examples, which are easily extended, are shown below.

The emoticon x is mostly used by women at the end of text and other messages. Affection grows with the number of xs, but only up to a point; after, say, four, the intended intimacy *decreases*. One x is often considered a minimum civilized closing, but there is no set convention, and it is only the relative increase of xs that is significant. (See *Love* and *Lots of love*, p. 139.)

x	friendship	xxx	eros?	xxxxx	friendship

Smileys are read sideways, usually from left to right.

:-)	smiley	:-D	big smile	:-P	tongue out
;-)	winking	:-]	polite smile	:-Q	smoking
:-#	with braces	:-(	frown	:-*	kissing
8-)	with glasses	:'-(	crying	:-v	lying

Head and hands are read vertically.

\o/	joy	o\	scratching head	\o_/ _o/	fencing
/o\	despair	<o>	covering ears	~~\o/~~	drowning
o/	waving	o7	saluting	>-<o	jumping off

Kaomoji, literally face characters, is a style of emoticons originating in Japan. Read vertically, they can take advantage of the horizontal line space to form a much richer variety of expression than smileys.

(ˆ_ˆ)	smiley	m(_ _)m	bowing	@ˆ_ˆ@	blushing
(ˆ_˜)	winking	(*_*)	dazed	(ˆ_ˆ;	sweating

Orz, or bowing emoticons, show a prostrated man where o is the head, r the arms and z the legs. A curious subculture in East Asia, it connotes despair or rejection by a girl for being a 'nice guy'. Variations include

orz	on_	Sto	OTZ	OTL	O72	O7Z

On the occasion of the first Bond year it is appropriate to consider the eponymous British spy—code-named 007—in some detail. James Bond is the central character of Fleming's 14 books and the inspiration for 21 official films and countless other publications. The 3,000 pages penned by Fleming, however, remain the authoritative record of Bond, and in them can be found a coherent picture of the man.

James Bond was (likely) born in 1924, the son of Andrew Bond of Glencoe, Scotland, and Monique Delacroix of Switzerland. His family motto is *Orbis non sufficit* (The world is not enough). Bond's father was an arms dealer for Vickers, what is now part of BAE Systems Land and Armaments, and as a consequence Bond's childhood was spent abroad. When Bond was 11 his parents died climbing in the Aiguilles Rouges and he was taken in by his aunt Charmian Bond in Pett Bottom, Kent, a stone's throw from what is now the Duck Inn restaurant. A year later Bond entered Eton College, following his father's instructions, but had to be removed after two halves due to 'alleged trouble with one of the boys' maids'. He transferred to his father's old school, Fettes, where by comparison he prospered: he was an avid judo wrestler and light-weight boxer and spoke French and German, of which he had had early exposure abroad, with ease.

At 17 Bond finished school and began study at the University of Geneva; this was interrupted when he joined the Royal Navy Volunteer Reserve in 1941. By the end of the war he had achieved the rank of Commander and his service record soon drew the attention of M (Miles), the director of the UK's Secret Intelligence Service (MI6). It was at this stage that Bond became 'associated with certain aspects of the Ministry's work'. After his second assassination, Bond was awarded a double-0 number, indicating a licence to kill, and it is from this point that a number of his missions have been documented. In 1954 Bond was made a Companion of the Order of St Michael and St George (CMG). He was later offered a knighthood for his services to MI6 but refused for the sake of professional anonymity.

At the end of *On Her Majesty's Secret Service*, Bond married Contessa Teresa di Vicenzo (Tracy), daughter of Marc-Ange Draco; she was killed shortly after the wedding by Ernst Stavro Blofeld, Bond's longstanding enemy. Nonetheless Bond is known to have at least one (illegitimate) child, through the Japanese agent Kissy Suzuki whom he met in *You Only Live Twice*.

At six feet and 165 pounds, Bond is slim, almost wiry (body mass index = 22.4). He has blue-grey eyes, a rather cruel mouth, a long vertical scar on his left cheek and short, dark hair which falls to his forehead in a wandering comma. On the back of his hand is a scar in the shape of the Russian character Ш, carved by a SMERSH agent in *Casino Royale*. His dress is simple but elegant: single-breasted blue serge or houndstooth check suits (probably from a tailor just off the Row; certainly not Italian) with a white shirt and and slip-on shoes. His tie is black knit silk, evidently tied in a four-in-hand or half-Windsor (Bond thought the Windsor knot was 'the mark of a cad'; see p. 67). Alas, his bow tie is black satin rather than barathea.

Bond is an able amateur sportsman, particularly at skiing, golf and hand-to-hand combat, the last being the subject of his book-in-progress, *Stand Firm*. He rode the Cresta Run from Top. He has few possessions but they are fine: a wide, flat gun-metal cigarette case; a black oxidized Ronson lighter; and a Rolex Oyster Perpetual watch. Contrary to the films, Bond prefers Bentleys; in order, he drives a 1930 (or 1933) Mark IV convertible, a 1953 Mark VI and a Mark II Continental, all of them grey with navy or black interior. He occasionally dines at the London club Blades (modelled after Boodle's).

Bond dislikes tea but frequently drinks coffee, brewed in an American Chemex. His taste in food is refined if unadventurous, with a preference for traditional English fare. His favourite meal is breakfast, for which we are given his recipe in the short story '007 in New York':

> He would have one more dry martini at the table, then smoked salmon and the particular scrambled eggs he had once (Felix Leiter knew the head-waiter) instructed them how to make:
>
> For four individualists: 12 fresh eggs   Salt and pepper   5–6 oz. of fresh butter. Break the eggs into a bowl. Beat thoroughly with a fork and season well. In a small copper (or heavy bottomed saucepan) melt four oz. of the butter. When melted, pour in the eggs and cook over a very low heat, whisking continuously with a small egg whisk. While the eggs are slightly more moist than you would wish for eating, remove the pan from heat, add rest of butter and continue whisking for half a minute, adding the while finely chopped chives or *fines herbes*. Serve on hot buttered toast in individual copper dishes (for appearance only) with pink champagne (Taittinger) and low music.

Bond smokes approximately 60 cigarettes a day, usually a mix of Turkish and Balkan tobaccos, with three gold bands on the filter, indicative of his naval rank. He is a heavy drinker. Despite his cinematic preference for vodka martinis, Fleming's Bond prefers whisky. Throughout the books his most common drinks are 25% whisky or bourbon, 11% sake, 10% champagne and 6% vodka martini.

Bond's secretary, Mary Goodnight, suggested for Bond this simple if simplistic epitaph: 'I shall not waste my days in trying to prolong them. I shall use my time.'

BOOKS

Ian Fleming wrote 12 novels and two collections of short stories about Bond, published once a year between 1953 and 1966. The last two volumes were published posthumously after Fleming's death in 1964.

Casino Royale	1953	*For Your Eyes Only*	1960
Live and Let Die	1954	*Thunderball*	1961
Moonraker	1955	*The Spy Who Loved Me*	1962
Diamonds are Forever	1956	*On Her Majesty's Secret Service*	1963
From Russia with Love	1957	*You Only Live Twice*	1964
Dr. No	1958	*The Man with the Golden Gun*	1965
Goldfinger	1959	*Octopussy and The Living Daylights*	1966

The Bond series was extended by Kingsley Amis, who wrote *Colonel Sun* in 1968 under the pseudonym Robert Markham. Between 1981 and 1996 John Gardner wrote 14 novels and two film novelizations. He was followed by Raymond Benson, who wrote six novels and three novelizations between 1997 and 2002. Of the many nonfiction books on Bond, three can be considered classics:

The James Bond Dossier	Kingsley Amis	1965
James Bond: The Authorised Biography of 007	John Pearson	1973
The James Bond Bedside Companion	Raymond Benson	1984

FILMS

There are 21 official Bond films, with the 21st, *Casino Royale*, scheduled for release in November 2006. Bond has been played by six actors, though Fleming saw only Sean Connery (SC). According to Vesper Lynd in *Casino Royale*, we know that Bond resembled singer Hoagy Carmichael, and on this basis Timothy Dalton (TD) looks most like the spy. The other actors are George Lazenby (GL), Roger Moore (RM), Pierce Brosnan (PB) and Daniel Craig (DC).

Dr. No	SC	1962	*Moonraker*	RM	1979
From Russia with Love	SC	1963	*For Your Eyes Only*	RM	1981
Goldfinger	SC	1964	*Octopussy*	RM	1983
Thunderball	SC	1965	*A View to a Kill*	RM	1985
You Only Live Twice	SC	1967	*The Living Daylights*	TD	1987
On Her Majesty's Secret Service	GL	1969	*Licence to Kill*	TD	1989
			GoldenEye	PB	1995
Diamonds Are Forever	SC	1971	*Tomorrow Never Dies*	PB	1997
Live and Let Die	RM	1973	*The World Is Not Enough*	PB	1999
The Man with the Golden Gun	RM	1974	*Die Another Day*	PB	2002
The Spy Who Loved Me	RM	1977	*Casino Royale*	DC	2006

Unlike books (p. 130), websites are free and never go out of print—just down. Here are some essential and eccentric sites for men, with a bias towards depth over breadth.

abebooks.co.uk	World's largest marketplace for secondhand books.
askmen.com	Essays and forum on all men's questions.
barbecue-online.co.uk	Tips, tales and techniques for cooking over fire.
britishsnoring.co.uk	Win the snore war.
http://chemex.125west.com	Bond's classic, elegant coffee maker.
coffeegeek.com	Coffee, espresso, cafés and coffee culture.
curryhouse.co.uk	Recipes, restaurants and web magazine for curry fans.
dandyism.net	Insufferably bored since 1828.
dcs.ed.ac.uk/home/jhb/whisky/	Comprehensive single malt whisky tour.
diydoctor.org.uk	Self-build and DIY tricks, tips and projects.
drinkinggadgets.com	Essential kit for drinking at home.
englishcut.com	Savile Row tailor's blog, reviewed in *New York Times*.
equipped.com/fm21-76.htm	Pdf of *U.S. Army Survival Manual FM 21-76*.
explorersweb.com	Discover the most extreme parts of the world.
fieggen.com/shoelace/	Comprehensive shoelace theory and practice.
fishing.co.uk	Over one and a half million words of UK angling.
howstuffworks.com	For the engineering geek inside every man.
kiltmen.com	Bravehearts in kilts against trouser tyranny.
littleplasticmen.co.uk	About the classic table-top football game Subbuteo.
malehealth.co.uk	Free, independent information from Men's Health Forum.
mame.com	Multiple Arcade Machine Emulator for long-lost arcade games.
mathworld.com	The web's most extensive mathematics resource.
members.garbersoft.net/spartacus/home.htm (Men's Tribune)	Men's rights.
motorcyclebuzz.com	Guide and web roadmap for the motorcycle community.
nomarriage.com	Why men shouldn't marry, at least not their girlfriends.
pubs.com	Traditional English pubs and inns online.
ratebeer.com	Most accurate and most-visited source for beer information.
repairclinic.com	Don't throw it out, now you can fix it.
research.att.com/~njas/sequences/	Guess the pattern: 0, 0, 0, 0, 10, 36, 322.
scouts.org.uk	Official website of the Scout Association in the UK.
stagweb.co.uk	Stag night suggestions and best man advice.
tanyakhovanova.com/Numbers/numbers.html	Properties of your fav. number.
textonyms.com	Find the complete list of textonyms (p. 141) for any word.
thegenuineman.com	Helping guys become men.
themetroguy.com	For men who appreciate sophistication (and a chest wax).
wackyuses.com	Hundreds of little-known uses for well-known products.
webtender.com	Over 6,000 drinks recipes and bartender's handbook.
wildwoodsurvival.com	Wilderness survival skills, tracking and nature.
wordsmith.org/anagram/	Internet anagram server = I, rearrangement servant.

TIME

NAMES, CYCLES AND ERAS

1	Roman numerals	MMVII	13	Julian Period		6720
2	Athenian numerals	XXΠΙΙΙ	14	Age of Earth (creationist)		7206
3	Binary (base 2)	11111010111	15	Liturgical cycles (e. 1 Dec)		C/1
4	Octal (base 8)	3727	16	Chinese year (b. 18 Feb)		Pig
5	Hexadecimal (base 16)	7D7	17	Grecian (Seleucidae) year		2319
6	Prime factorization	3 3 223	18	French Rep. yr (b. Sep 23)		CCXVI
7	Phinary	1010001010101010	19	Saka (Indian) yr (b. 22 Mar)		1929
		.0000000000100001	20	Japanese Era year		Heisei 19
8	Dominical Letter	G	21	Muslim year (b. 20 Jan)		1428
9	Epact	11	22	Jewish year (AM, b. 13 Sep)		5768
10	Golden Number	XIII	23	Masonic year (AL)		6007
11	Solar Cycle	28	24	Regnal year (b. 6 Feb)		56
12	Roman Indiction	15	25	Roman year (AUC)		2760

(1) Described on p. 142. (2) The Athenian number system uses I for 1, Π for 5, Δ for 10, H for 100, X for 1,000 and M for 10,000. Writing a symbol inside Π indicates five times its value. (3) In other words, 2007 = 1024 + 512 + 256 + 128 + 64 + 16 + 4 + 2 + 1. (5) The letters A–F represent the numbers 10–15. (6) The smallest positive numbers which when multiplied give 2007. (7) Expressed in base ϕ (the Golden ratio, see p. 5), where, for example, $.1 = \phi^{-1}$ and $.11 = \phi^{-1} + \phi^{-2}$. Remarkably, all integers can be so expressed with a finite number of digits. (8) The letter corresponding to the date in January on which the first Sunday of the year falls: A=1, B=2, and so on. (9) The age of the ecclesiastical moon in days on 1 January, minus one. (10) The place in the 19-year Metonic cycle after which the phases of the moon return to the same days of the month (19 solar years equals 235 lunar cycles). (11) The place in the 28-year cycle after which the calendar (days and dates) repeats itself. (12) The place in the 15-year cycle initiated in the late Roman Empire for the organization of tax, used until medieval times in written records alongside the year. (13) The number of years since 4713 BC, now used only by astronomers. (14) Amongst strict creationists, the most accepted year for the creation of the world is 5199 BC. (15) Readings at Masses cycle over three years for Sundays (A, B, C) and two for weekdays (1, 2). (24) The number of whole years the current monarch has reigned plus one, starting from the day of accession.

PROGNOSTICATIONS

The year 2007 promises some major shake-ups, both at home and abroad: a freak snowstorm; trouble for the NHS; collapse of the European Union; and a sad day for mathmos everywhere.

	Anagrams of
	two thousand seven
Freak winter weather strikes England:	?th Nov: snow due east.
World community responds:	UN vows to send heat.
Surprise reshuffle of world economies:	USA down to seventh.
Europe responds to superpower loss:	vast EU shown to end.
Geeks distraught as Caltech's days numbered:	US to end swot haven.
At home, a botched budget:	NHS won't evade oust.
Meanwhile, Basque separatists	shun ETA vows to end.

CURIOUS PROPERTIES

♠ *For geeks* The number 2007 itself has a number of unusual mathematical properties.

2007 is *odd* because it is not divisible by two.

2007 is *composite* (not prime), having divisors 3, 3 and 223. These constituent numbers are themselves of interest.

3, apart from its frequent mythological and biblical use, was thought by the Pythagoreans to be the first male number.

223, despite being lucky (part of the series 1, 3, 7, 9, 13, 15,...), ominously is a textonum (a sequence of keystrokes on a mobile phone) for 'bad', see p. 141.

2007 is *odious* because it has an odd number of 1s in its binary expansion (11111010111).

2007 is *deficient*: the sum of its divisors apart from itself is less than itself.

2007 is a *hexadecimal palindrome*, meaning it reads the same in both directions in base 16: 7D7.

2007 is an *apocalyptic power*, meaning that 2^{2007} contains three consecutive 6s in its decimal expansion.

2007 is a *self number*: it is not equal to a number plus the sum of that number's digits.

$2^{2007} + 2007^2$ is prime; the next smallest number with this property is 33.

The sum of its digits in base 10 (2007) equals the sum of its digits in base 2 (11111010111).

2007 is divisible by the sum of its digits, and the sum of the digits of $2^{2007} \times 2007!$ is divisible by 2007.

$(1 + 1/2007)^{2007} \simeq e$, the base of the natural logarithm (this is a joke).

SUN, EARTH AND MOON IN 2007

(All times GMT.) The solstices mark the points in the Earth's orbit where its axis is maximally tilted towards the sun; the equinoxes, where its axis is perpendicular to the sun. Because the Earth's orbit is slightly elliptical, its distance from the sun varies throughout the year, although this has only a nominal effect on the seasons. The point of shortest distance is called perihelion; the point of longest, aphelion.

Vernal equinox	00:09	21 Mar		Perihelion	20 o'clock	3 Jan
Summer solstice	18:07	21 Jun		Aphelion	0 o'clock	7 Jul
Autumnal equinox	09:52	23 Sep				
Winter solstice	06:09	22 Dec				

Only three objects move across the face of the sun that are visible from Earth. The moon eclipses the sun about twice a year, Mercury 13 times a century and Venus 13 times per millennium. There will be no planetary transits in 2007, nor in any year after until 2012. However, on 8–9 November 2006 there will be a transit of Mercury, starting at 19:12 and finishing at 00:10. The entire transit will be visible from eastern Australia, New Zealand and western North America. Mercury will appear as a point which can only be seen with a telescope.

An eclipse occurs when one object moves into the shadow of another. When the Earth casts its shadow on the moon, it is called a lunar eclipse; and when the moon casts its shadow on the Earth, it is called a solar eclipse (technically an occultation—a true eclipse only for an observer on the moon). Both occur in 2007 as follows:

	First contact	Max. coverage	Last contact	
Partial solar eclipse	0:38	2:32	4:25	19 Mar
Partial solar eclipse	10:26	12:31	14:37	11 Sep

	First contact	Enters totality	Leaves totality	Last contact	
Total lunar eclipse	21:30	22:44	23:58	1:12	3–4 Mar
Total lunar eclipse	8:51	9:52	11:23	12:24	28 Aug

PLANETS

Conjunction between a planet and the sun occurs when the two appear nearby in the sky; when the two are on opposite sides of the Earth, the event is called opposition. The planets Mercury and Venus cannot enter into opposition because their orbits are smaller than Earth's, but they can enter into two kinds of conjunction: inferior, when one of the planets lies in a line with Earth on the same side of the sun; and superior, when in a line on the opposite side of the sun. See the left-hand pages of the Almanack (pp. 73–100) for dates of planetary ephemerae.

METEOR SHOWERS

Because meteor showers result from the Earth's passage through trails of dust left by comets, they tend to be annual events. The major annual showers, listed below, can vary in intensity from year to year, depending on how recently the parent comet passed. The showers last several days, sometimes weeks; the dates below are the peak days, although these can vary by a day or two. Viewing is optimal with a dim moon; see the Almanack for daily moon phases.

Name	Meteors/hr	Parent comet	
Quadrantids	30–50	minor planet 2003 EH$_1$	3–4 Jan
Lyrids	10–20	Thatcher	21–22 Apr
Eta Aquarids	10–20	Halley	4–6 May
Delta Aquarids	20–30		28–29 Jul
Alpha Capricornids	0–10		29–30 Jul
Perseids	50–100	Swift-Tuttle	12–13 Aug
Draconids	0–10	Giacobini-Zinner	8–9 Oct
Orionids	10–20	Halley	21–22 Oct
Taurids	0–10	Encke	1–10 Nov
Leonids	20–30	Temple-Tuttle	17–18 Nov
Geminids	50–100	3200 Phaethon	13–14 Dec
Ursids	10–20	Tuttle	19–22 Dec

ZODIAC

The Zodiac is the imaginary band in the heavens marked out by the path of the sun and 8° to either side. It is broken into 12 segments, each of which is associated with a star-sign (*zodia*, little beasts). These have by convention taken on fixed periods within the year.

Aquarius	water bearer	♒	*b*. 20 Jan	Leo	lion	♌	*b*. 23 Jul
Pisces	fish	♓	*b*. 20 Feb	Virgo	virgin	♍	*b*. 23 Aug
Aries	ram	♈	*b*. 21 Mar	Libra	scales	♎	*b*. 23 Sep
Taurus	bull	♉	*b*. 21 Apr	Scorpio	scorpion	♏	*b*. 23 Oct
Gemini	twins	♊	*b*. 21 May	Sagittarius	archer	♐	*b*. 23 Nov
Cancer	crab	♋	*b*. 21 Jun	Capricorn	sea-goat	♑	*b*. 22 Dec

SUMMER TIME

British Summer Time (BST), also known as Daylight Saving, is the practice of moving the clocks forward by one hour during the lighter months, hence the mnemonic 'spring forward, fall back'. It was introduced in Britain during the First World War.

		in 2007
British Summer Time begins	1:00 a.m., last Sun of Mar	25 Mar
British Summer Time ends	1:00 a.m., last Sun of Oct	28 Oct

SEASONS

Although ancient, the division of the year into four parts, or seasons, is not universal. At the equator, the association of seasons with hot and cold breaks down: the length of the day is 12 hours all year round. Here two seasons, rainy and dry, provide a more useful division. Subtropical regions sometimes assume three: hot, rainy and cool. Even today there is no broad agreement about when one season ends and another begins. The most commonly used starting points are the equinoxes and solstices (p. 150): thus winter, for example, begins on the shortest day of the year and continues until the days and nights are of equal length. More sensible is the Elder Pliny's division, with winter approximately centred on the winter solstice, and so on. The Irish calendar and meteorological convention associate seasons with months, winter beginning with 1 November and 1 December respectively.

	Irish calendar	*Elder Pliny*	*Met. office*	*Astronomical*	*(in 2007)*
Spring begins	1 Feb	8 Feb	1 Mar	Vernal equinox	(21 Mar)
Summer begins	1 May	10 May	1 Jun	Summer solstice	(21 Jun)
Autumn begins	1 Aug	11 Aug	1 Sep	Autumnal equinox	(23 Sep)
Winter begins	1 Nov	11 Nov	1 Dec	Winter solstice	(22 Dec)

Part of the confusion rests with the fact that the shortest and longest days do not correspond with the coldest and hottest. Because it takes weeks for the surface of the earth to warm and cool, the temperature of the earth lags behind the period of greatest sunshine by about 40 days, depending on location.

	in 2007		*on average*
Shortest day (7h 50m)	22 Dec	Coldest day	1 Feb
Longest day (16h 38m)	21 Jun	Hottest day	1 Aug

QUARTER DAYS AND TERM DAYS

In England the quarterly payment of rent and other fees, as well as the hiring of domestic staff, occurs by tradition on set quarter days. In Scotland the analogous days are called term days, which in 1990 were moved from their respective festivals to the 28th day of the month, nevertheless keeping their old names.

English quarter days		*Scottish term days*	
Lady Day	25 Mar	Candlemas	28 Feb
Midsummer Day	24 Jun	Whitsunday	28 May
Michaelmas	29 Sep	Lammas	28 Aug
Christmas	25 Dec	Martinmas	28 Nov

LAW TERMS

Since the end of the 12th century the year has been divided into four distinct periods, or terms, for determining questions of law. These remained about three weeks long until the 19th century, when they were abolished and replaced with longer sessions. In England and Wales the Court of Appeal and the High Court are presently active during the following periods, technically called sittings but commonly referred to as terms.

		in 2006/7
Michaelmas	1 Oct to 21 Dec	1 Oct – 21 Dec
Hilary	11 Jan to Wed before Easter	11 Jan – 4 Apr
Easter	2nd Tue after Easter to 7th Fri after Easter	17 Apr – 25 May
Trinity	9th Tue after Easter to 31 July	5 Jun – 31 Jul

UNIVERSITY TERMS

At Oxford and Cambridge the active period of the universities is divided into three terms, within which the shorter period of instruction is called Full Term. The dates for Full Term are not formulaic but are set by the universities several years in advance. In Oxford all Full Terms last eight weeks, beginning on Sunday and ending on Saturday. In Cambridge, Full Terms last 60, 60, and 53 days, beginning on Tuesday and ending on Friday.

Oxford Terms, all years		*Cambridge Terms, all years*	
Michaelmas	1 Oct–17 Dec	Michaelmas	1 Oct–19 Dec
Hilary	7 Jan–25 Mar[1]	Lent	5 Jan–25 Mar[3]
Trinity	20 Apr[2]–6 Jul	Easter	17 Apr–25 Jun[4]

Oxford Full Terms 2006/7		*Cambridge Full Terms 2006/7*	
Michaelmas	8 Oct–2 Dec	Michaelmas	3 Oct–1 Dec
Hilary	14 Jan–10 Mar	Lent	16 Jan–16 Mar
Trinity	22 Apr–16 Jun	Easter	24 Apr–15 Jun

Durham Terms 2006/7		*St Andrews Semesters 2006/7*	
Michaelmas	4 Oct–13 Dec	Martinmas	25 Sep–19 Jan
Epiphany	15 Jan–16 Mar	Candlemas	5 Feb–25 May
Easter	23 Apr–22 Jun		

[1] Or 2nd Sun before Easter, whichever is earlier.
[2] Or Wed after Easter, whichever is later.
[3] 24 Mar in a leap year.
[4] But if Full Easter Term begins before 22 Apr, 10 Apr–18 Jun.

The association of certain days with saints and martyrs has been customary since the early Church. Alongside days marking the events of Christ's life, these have been formalized as follows. (Any movable dates are shown for 2007.)

CHURCH OF ENGLAND

The Church of England observes the feast days set out in *The Book of Common Prayer*.

All Sundays in the year		St Barnabas	11 Jun
Circumcision of Our Lord	1 Jan	St John the Baptist	24 Jun
Epiphany	6 Jan	St Peter	29 Jun
Conversion of St Paul	25 Jan	St James	25 Jul
Purification of the		St Bartholomew	24 Aug
Blessed Virgin	2 Feb	St Matthew	21 Sep
St Matthias	24 Feb	St Michael & All Angels	29 Sep
Annunciation	25 Mar	St Luke	18 Oct
Monday after Easter	9 Apr	SS Simon & Jude	28 Oct
Tuesday after Easter	10 Apr	All Saints	1 Nov
St Mark	25 Apr	St Andrew	30 Nov
SS Philip & James	1 May	St Thomas	21 Dec
Ascension		Nativity of Our Lord	25 Dec
(6th Thu after Easter)	17 May	St Stephen	26 Dec
Monday after Whit Sunday	28 May	St John the Evangelist	27 Dec
Tuesday after Whit Sunday	29 May	Holy Innocents	28 Dec

ROMAN CATHOLIC CHURCH

In the Catholic Church, saints' days are divided into three kinds: Solemnities, Feasts and Memorials. While most are universal, some vary from country to country; those not observed throughout the UK are marked E (England), W (Wales), S (Scotland) and I (Ireland). Memorials, which are of the least significance, are not listed here.

Solemnities		(9th Thu after Easter)	7 Jun
All Sundays in the year		Sacred Heart	
Solemnity of Mary	1 Jan	(10th Sat after Easter)	16 Jun
Epiphany	6 Jan	Birth of St John the Baptist	24 Jun
St David (w)	1 Mar	SS Peter & Paul	29 Jun
St Patrick (I)	17 Mar	Assumption	15 Aug
St Joseph	19 Mar	All Saints	1 Nov
Annunciation	25 Mar	Christ the King	
Ascension		(Sun nearest to 23 Nov)	25 Nov
(6th Thu after Easter)	17 May	St Andrew (s)	30 Nov
Holy Trinity		Immaculate Conception	8 Dec
(8th Sun after Easter)	3 Jun	Nativity of Our Lord	25 Dec
Corpus Christi			

Feasts

Baptism of the Lord (Sun after 6 Jan)	7 Jan
Conversion of St Paul	25 Jan
St Brigid (I)	1 Feb
Presentation of the Lord	2 Feb
Chair of St Peter	22 Feb
St David (E)	1 Mar
St John Ogilvie (S)	10 Mar
St Patrick (not I)	17 Mar
St George (E & W)	23 Apr
St Mark	25 Apr
SS Philip & James	3 May
Beatified Martyrs of England & Wales (E)	4 May
St Matthias	14 May
St Augustine of Canterbury (E)	27 May
Visitation of the BVM	31 May
St Columba (I)	9 Jun
SS John Fisher & Thomas More (E)	22 Jun
St Oliver Plunkett (I)	1 Jul
St Thomas	3 Jul
St James	25 Jul
Transfiguration of the Lord	6 Aug
St Lawrence	10 Aug
St Bartholomew	24 Aug
St Gregory the Great (E)	3 Sep
Birthday of the BVM	8 Sep
Triumph of the Cross	14 Sep
St Matthew	21 Sep
SS Michael, Gabriel & Raphael	29 Sep
St Luke	18 Oct
40 Martyrs of England & Wales (E)	25 Oct
6 Welsh Martyrs & Companions (W)	25 Oct
SS Simon & Jude	28 Oct
All Saints of Ireland (I)	6 Nov
All Saints of Wales (W)	8 Nov
Dedication of Lateran Basilica	9 Nov
St Margaret of Scotland (S)	16 Nov
St Columban (I)	23 Nov
St Andrew	30 Nov
St Stephen	26 Dec
St John	27 Dec
Holy Innocents	28 Dec
Thomas Becket (E)	29 Dec
Holy Family (Sun after 25 Dec & bef. 1 Jan; if none, 30 Dec)	30 Dec

HOLY DAYS OF OBLIGATION

In addition to all Sundays, Roman Catholics are obliged to attend Mass on up to ten days throughout the year, all of which are Solemnities. To these may be added the feast day of each country's patron saint. Some days may be transferred to the nearest Sunday.

Holy Day	*Day in 2007*	*Date*	E & W	I*	US
Solemnity of Mary	Mon	1 Jan			○
Epiphany	Sat	6 Jan	○	○	
St Joseph	Mon	19 Mar			
Ascension	Thu	17 May	○		○
Corpus Christi	Thu	7 Jun	○		
SS Peter & Paul	Fri	29 Jun	○		
Assumption	Wed	15 Aug	○	○	○
All Saints	Thu	1 Nov	○	○	○
Immaculate Conception	Sat	8 Dec		○	○
Nativity of Our Lord	Tue	25 Dec	○	○	○

*Also St Patrick's Day.

The two principal days of Christian significance are Christmas, set by the solar cycle, and Easter, set by the lunar cycle. From the date of Easter all movable holy days and fasts are fixed by their separation in number of days, apart from Advent Sunday, which is always the Sunday nearest to 30 November, and Christ the King.

HOLY DAYS

		in 2007
Epiphany	6 Jan	6 Jan
Presentation of the Lord	2 Feb	2 Feb
Ash Wednesday	7th Wed before Easter	21 Feb
Annunciation (Lady Day)	25 Mar	25 Mar
Palm Sunday	Sun before Easter	1 Apr
Maundy Thursday	Thu before Easter	5 Apr
Good Friday	Fri before Easter	6 Apr
Easter	see below	8 Apr
Rogation Sunday	5th Sun after Easter	13 May
Ascension Day	6th Thu after Easter	17 May
Whit Sunday (Pentecost)	7th Sun after Easter	27 May
Trinity Sunday	8th Sun after Easter	3 Jun
Corpus Christi	9th Thu after Easter	7 Jun
All Saints' Day	1 Nov	1 Nov
All Souls' Day	2 Nov	2 Nov
Christ the King	Sun before Advent Sunday	25 Nov
Advent Sunday	Sun nearest to 30 Nov	2 Dec
Christmas Day	25 Dec	25 Dec

EASTER DAY

Easter is the first Sunday after the first full ecclesiastical moon falling on or after the vernal equinox; if the full moon falls on a Sunday, Easter is the following Sunday. The ecclesiastical moon is not the astronomical moon but a tabulated theoretical moon which closely approximates it, deemed full on its 14th day. The equinox is defined to be 21 March. The earliest and latest dates of Easter are 22 March and 25 April, and the most likely date 19 April.

The Book of Common Prayer gives a prescription for determining the date of Easter. The problem is somewhat complicated, and the 1662 instructions fill three pages. Devising an elegant and concise prescription has attracted the attention of amateur and professional mathematicians alike. The following algorithm (P. Kenneth Seidelmann, ed., *Explanatory Supplement to the Astronomical Almanac*) is a refined version of Oudin's 1940 algorithm. It gives the month and day of Easter for any Gregorian calendar year.

✦ *For geeks* Let 'year' be the Christian year AD, 'month' the number 3 (March) or 4 (April) and 'day' a number between 1 and 31. In all divisions the integer is kept and the remainder discarded. The operation 'mod' is the opposite: the remainder is kept and the integer discarded. For example, $23/5 = 4$ and $23 \bmod 5 = 3$. In the case of year = 2007, we find from below that $A = 20$, $B = 12$, $C = 12$, $D = 12$, $E = 1$. This gives month = 4 (April) and day = 8.

$$A = \tfrac{\text{year}}{100} \qquad B = \text{year} \bmod 19 \qquad C = \left(A - \tfrac{A}{4} - \tfrac{8A+13}{25} + 19B + 15\right) \bmod 30$$

$$D = C - \tfrac{C}{28}\left(1 - \tfrac{29}{C+1}\,\tfrac{21-B}{11}\right) \qquad\qquad E = \left(\text{year} + \tfrac{\text{year}}{4} + D + 2 - A + \tfrac{A}{4}\right) \bmod 7$$

$$\text{month} = 3 + \tfrac{D-E+40}{44} \qquad\qquad \text{day} = D - E + 28 - 31 \times \tfrac{\text{month}}{4}$$

The algorithm is guaranteed to repeat only after 5,700,000 years, which means (for the curious) that Easter in AD 5,702,007 will also be 8 April.

FASTS

In order to correspond in length to the forty days which it commemorates, it is customary to omit from the Lenten fast the six Sundays preceding Easter, Sundays always being feast days. Fasting, which originally meant avoiding all food, now indicates that only one meal should be had; it should not be confused with abstinence, avoiding only meat.

		in 2007
Lent	Ash Wednesday to Sat before Easter, inclusive	21 Feb–7 Apr
Advent	Advent Sunday to 24 Dec, inclusive	2–24 Dec

	Wed, Fri & Sat on or after	
Spring Embertide (Ember days)	1st Sunday of Lent	28 Feb, 2, 3 Mar
Summer Embertide	Whit Sunday (Pentecost)	30 May, 1, 2 Jun
Autumn Embertide	Triumph of the Cross (14 Sep)	19, 21, 22 Sep
Winter Embertide	St Lucy's Day (13 Dec)	19, 21, 22 Dec

	Mon, Tue & Wed after	
Rogation Days	Rogation Sunday	14, 15, 16 May

The two principal periods of abstinence or fasting, Advent and Lent, are customarily preceded by celebrations and feasts. The days before Lent are called Shrovetide, which culminates on Shrove Tuesday, also known as *Mardi Gras* (Fat Tuesday). On the Sunday before Advent Sunday, popularly known as Stir-Up Sunday, wives are encouraged to begin preparations for Christmas. The day's collect from *The Book of Common Prayer*, which reads: 'Stir up, we beseech thee, O Lord, the wills of thy faithful people,' is commonly taken to be an indication to begin the Christmas puddings.

Holiday, while derived from, and once synonymous with, 'holy day', now refers to any day of national festivity, which may or may not have religious significance. The Reformation diminished their number in England, particularly the popular saints' days and their religious and secular customs. Today the UK has conspicuously fewer days of festivity than its Catholic neighbours. Only America has fewer still, as one New Yorker notes:

> Our Protestant Faith affords no religious holiday & processions like the Catholics. From the period of the Jews & Heathens down thro the Greeks & Romans, the Celts, Druids, even our Indians all had & have their religious Festivals. England retains numerous red letter days as they are called which afford intervals of rest, together with the Christmas, Easter & Whitsun holidays, for all the public offices Banks &c., but with us, we have only Independence, Christmas & New Year, 3 solitary days, not enough & which causes so much breach of the Sabbath in this city…
>
> John Pintard, 1823

MOVABLE HOLIDAYS

		in 2007
Handsel Monday	1st Mon in the New Year	1 Jan
Plough Monday	1st Mon after 6 Jan (Epiphany)	8 Jan
Shrove Tuesday	7th Tue before Easter	20 Feb
Commonwealth Day	2nd Mon in Mar	12 Mar
Mothering Sunday	3rd Sun before Easter	18 Mar
Easter	see p. 156	8 Apr
Father's Day	3rd Sun in Jun	17 Jun
Harvest Festival	Sun closest to the Autumnal equinox	23 Sep
Remembrance Sunday	Sun closest to 11 Nov	11 Nov
Stir-Up Sunday	Sun before Advent Sun	25 Nov

FIXED HOLIDAYS

New Year's Day	1 Jan	Orangemen's Day (I)	12 Jul
Twelfth Day	6 Jan	Trafalgar Day	21 Oct
Burns Night	25 Jan	All Saints' Day	1 Nov
Candlemas Day	2 Feb	All Souls' Day	2 Nov
St Valentine's Day	14 Feb	Guy Fawkes Day	5 Nov
St David's Day (w)	1 Mar	Armistice Day	11 Nov
St Patrick's Day	17 Mar	St Andrew's Day (s)	30 Nov
All Fools' Day	1 Apr	Christmas	25 Dec
St George's Day (E)	23 Apr	Boxing Day	26 Dec
May Day	1 May	Hogmanay (s)	31 Dec
Oak Apple Day	29 May		

For bank holidays, see p. 161; for civil holidays, see p. 162.

NOTABLE AMERICAN DAYS

While the United States does not technically have any national holidays, it observes nationwide ten annual days and one day every four years. These are called federal holidays, during which government employees do not normally work.

Federal holidays		*in 2007*
New Year's Day	1 Jan	1 Jan
Martin Luther King's Birthday	3rd Mon in Jan	15 Jan
Inauguration Day[1]	20 Jan, but if Sun, 21 Jan	n/a
Washington's Birthday	3rd Mon in Feb	19 Feb
Memorial Day	last Mon in May	28 May
Independence Day	4 Jul	4 Jul
Labor Day	1st Mon in Sep	3 Sep
Columbus Day	2nd Mon in Oct	8 Oct
Veterans Day	11 Nov	11 Nov
Thanksgiving	4th Thu in Nov	22 Nov
Christmas	25 Dec	25 Dec

[1]Only in years following a presidential election.

Other holidays (not listed elsewhere)		*in 2007*
Groundhog Day	2 Feb	2 Feb
Mardi Gras	7th Tue before Easter	20 Feb
Arbor Day	last Fri in Apr	27 Apr
Mother's Day	2nd Sun in May	13 May
Flag Day	14 Jun	14 Jun
Halloween	31 Oct	31 Oct
Sadie Hawkins Day	Sat closest to 9 Nov	10 Nov
Election Day	Tue after 1st Mon in Nov	6 Nov

Sadie Hawkins, known as 'the homeliest gal in the hills', is a comic strip character who takes romantic matters into her own hands. On Sadie Hawkins Day women are meant to put aside custom and invite a man out, a refreshing variation but in direct conflict with *The Rules'* first prescription: *Don't talk to a man first (and don't ask him to dance)* (p. 46). The only other prescribed day of feminine initiative is leap day: February 29 in years divisible by 4. On this day women so inclined are meant to propose to men, though the man invariably has to pay for her ring.

Jamestown, the first permanent English settlement in what is now the United States, was founded on 14 May, 1607. A total of 104 men and boys arrived on the three ships *Susan Constant*, *Godspeed* and *Discovery*. The 400th anniversary will be marked in 2007 by a visit of Queen Elizabeth II, who was also present as Queen for the 350th anniversary in 1957.

NATIONAL DAYS

Wales

- *Motto Cymru am byth* (Wales for ever)
- *Flag* Red dragon on a green and white field
- *National day* 1 March, St David's Day, Flag day in Wales, Red-Letter day, RC Solemnity in Wales and RC Feast day in England
- *Patron* St David (Dewi in Welsh), Bishop in Mynyw, is 'perhaps the most celebrated of British saints', according to *Butler's Lives*. He died around 600, but his principal biographer, not writing until 1090, combined much fiction with fact. David founded, amongst others, an abbey in Menevia, Wales, known for its severe asceticism. An old custom, mentioned in Shakespeare's *Henry V*, is the wearing of leeks in hats on St David's feast day.

Northern Ireland

- *Motto* No consensus, but arguably *Quis separabit?* (Who shall separate?)
- *Flag* Until 1972, Cross of St George with crown, red hand and white star
- *National day* 17 March, St Patrick's Day, RC Solemnity in Ireland and RC Feast in England, Wales and Scotland
- *Patron* St Patrick, Archbishop of Armagh, Apostle of Ireland, was born around 389 of Romano-British origin. In his adolescence he was captured and sent to Ireland as a slave, but escaped after six years to return to his family. It is at this time that he determined to return to the island to evangelize, which he later did, setting up see at Armagh in 444. He died around 461, having converted, in 30 years, the whole of Ireland to Christianity.

England

- *Motto Dieu et mon droit* (God and my right)
- *Flag* Cross of St George (red cross on a white field)
- *National day* 23 April, St George's Day, Flag day in England and RC Feast day in England and Wales
- *Patron* St George, Martyr, Protector of the Kingdom of England. All that can be said with confidence about this saint is that he died a martyr's death in Palestine around 300. Although it is unlikely that St George set foot in England, his cult in that country precedes the Norman Conquest. He gradually came to replace St Edward the Confessor as the patron saint of England after being promoted by Edward III. The last few years have seen a revival of St George's Day celebrations. On the day men wear red roses (see p. 71).

Scotland

- *Motto Nemo me impune lacessit* (No one provokes me with impunity)
- *Flag* Cross of St Andrew (white X-shaped cross on a blue field)
- *National day* 30 November, St Andrew's Day, Flag day in Scotland, Red-Letter day, CofE feast day, RC Solemnity in Scotland and RC Feast day
- *Patron* St Andrew, Apostle, was from Bethsaida in Galilee, the brother of Simon Peter. The first of Christ's disciples, he is sometimes called the Protoclete, or First-called. Little is known about his later life, though he is said to have been crucified on an X-shaped cross, hence St Andrew's Cross.

PUBLIC (BANK) HOLIDAYS

Holy days and holidays not falling on a Sunday are sometimes marked with the cessation of work. In the United Kingdom these are called public holidays, of which there are two kinds: common law (by custom and habit) and statutory. In England and Wales and Northern Ireland, Christmas and Good Friday are common-law holidays. Statutory holidays, also known as bank holidays, took the place of holy days and feast days during the 19th century. The Bank of England closed on over 40 saints' days and festivals before 1830; by 1834 the number had been reduced to four. Today most public holidays are observed on days of no religious nor cultural significance.

England and Wales		*in 2007*
New Year's Day	1 Jan*	1 Jan
Good Friday	Fri before Easter	6 Apr
Easter Monday	Mon after Easter	9 Apr
Early May Bank Holiday	1st Mon in May	7 May
Spring Bank Holiday	last Mon in May	28 May
Summer Bank Holiday	last Mon in Aug	27 Aug
Christmas	25 Dec*	25 Dec
Boxing Day	26 Dec*	26 Dec

Scotland Same as England and Wales apart from

2 January	2 Jan*	2 Jan
Not Easter Monday		
Summer Bank Holiday	1st Mon in Aug	6 Aug

Thus the 2007 days for Scotland are
1, 2 Jan, 6 Apr, 7, 28 May, 6 Aug, 25, 26 Dec.

Ireland (Northern) Same as England and Wales apart from

St Patrick's Day	17 Mar*	19 Mar
Battle of the Boyne (Orangemen's Day)	12 Jul*	12 Jul

Thus the 2007 days for Northern Ireland are
1 Jan, 19 Mar, 6, 9 Apr, 7, 28 May, 12 Jul, 27 Aug, 25, 26 Dec.

*If Sun, the Mon after is a bank holiday; if Sat, the Mon may be a bank holiday. If 25 and 26 Dec are Sat and Sun, the Mon and Tue after are bank holidays.

With eight public holidays per year, Britain has the second-fewest of all European countries; only the Netherlands has fewer with seven. Not far off was the Soviet Union after Lenin's calendar reform in 1929, which likewise made no reference to days of religious significance. The year was composed of twelve months of 30 days each, with the five remaining days national holidays: two Workers' days, two Industry Days and Lenin Day. The week was reduced to five days by removing the weekend, with one-fifth of the workforce resting on any given day.

(Any movable dates are shown for 2007.)

RED-LETTER DAYS

The more important saints' days, holy days and days associated with the royal family are called Red-Letter days, originally printed in red ink in early church calendars. On these days the High Court Queen's Division judges wear, when sitting, scarlet robes.

Conversion of St Paul	25 Jan	Official BD of HM the Queen	
Purification	2 Feb	(a Sat in Jun, appointed annually)	
Accession of HM the Queen	6 Feb	St John the Baptist	24 Jun
Ash Wednesday (see p. 156)	21 Feb	St Peter	29 Jun
St David's Day	1 Mar	St Thomas	3 Jul
Annunciation	25 Mar	St James	25 Jul
BD of HM the Queen	21 Apr	St Luke	18 Oct
St Mark	25 Apr	SS Simon & Jude	28 Oct
SS Philip & James	1 May	All Saints	1 Nov
St Matthias	14 May	Lord Mayor's Day	
Ascension Day (see p. 156)	17 May	(2nd Sat in Nov)	10 Nov
Coronation Day	2 Jun	BD of HRH Prince of Wales	14 Nov
BD of HM Duke of Edinburgh	10 Jun	St Andrew's Day	30 Nov
St Barnabas	11 Jun		

FLAG DAYS

The Union flag derives from the superposition of three heraldic crosses: the cross of St George, and the saltires (X-shaped crosses) of St Andrew and St Patrick. These are the respective flags of England, Scotland and, until 1922, Ireland (see p. 160). The first two were combined in 1606, with the third added in 1801. (Wales was legally part of the Kingdom of England when the first Union flag was created.) Government buildings fly the Union flag on the days below throughout the UK, apart from the three saints' days, when the flag is flown nationally.

BD of Countess of Wessex	20 Jan	Official BD of HM the Queen	
Accession of HM the Queen	6 Feb	(a Sat in Jun, appointed annually)	
BD of Duke of York	19 Feb	BD of Duchess of Cornwall	17 Jul
St David's Day (W)	1 Mar	BD of Princess Royal	15 Aug
BD of Earl of Wessex	10 Mar	Remembrance Sunday	
Commonwealth Day		(Sun closest to 11 Nov)	11 Nov
(2nd Mon in Mar)	12 Mar	BD of HRH Prince of Wales	14 Nov
BD of HM the Queen	21 Apr	Wedding Day of HM Queen	20 Nov
St George's Day (E)	23 Apr	St Andrew's Day (S)	30 Nov
Europe Day	9 May	Opening of a session of Parliament	
Coronation Day	2 Jun	Prorogation of a session of Parliament	
BD of HM Duke of Edinburgh	10 Jun	(both Greater London area only)	

UN DAYS

The United Nations comprises 191 member states, the only notable exceptions being Vatican City, which has not sought membership but is an observer state, and Palestine, also an observer state. The United Nations officially recognizes a number of days, listed below, to be observed internationally throughout all its member countries. Notably, there are days for women, youth and children, but not for men.

Victims of the Holocaust	27 Jan
Mother language	21 Feb
Women's rights	
& international peace	8 Mar
Elimination of	
racial discrimination	21 Mar
Peoples struggling against racism &	
racial discrimination (week)	21–27 Mar
Water	22 Mar
Meteorological	23 Mar
Road safety (week)	during Apr
Mine awareness & assistance	
in mine action	4 Apr
Health	7 Apr
Book & copyright	23 Apr
Press freedom	3 May
Those who lost their lives	
during WWII	8–9 May
Families	15 May
Telecommunication	17 May
Cultural diversity for	
dialogue & development	21 May
Biological diversity	22 May
Peoples of non-self-governing	
territories (week)	25–31 May
United Nations peacekeepers	29 May
No-tobacco	31 May
Innocent children victims	
of aggression	4 Jun
Environment	5 Jun
Combat desertification & drought	17 Jun
Refugee	20 Jun
Public service	23 Jun
Against drug abuse &	
illicit trafficking	26 Jun
Support of victims of torture	26 Jun
Cooperatives (1st Sat in Jul)	7 Jul
Population	11 Jul
Indigenous people	9 Aug
Youth	12 Aug

Slave trade & its abolition	23 Aug
Literacy	8 Sep
Preservation of the ozone layer	16 Sep
Peace	21 Sep
Maritime	during last week in Sep
Older persons	1 Oct
Habitat (1st Mon in Oct)	1 Oct
Space (week)	4–10 Oct
Teachers	5 Oct
Post	9 Oct
Mental health	10 Oct
Natural disaster reduction	
(2nd Wed in Oct)	10 Oct
Food	16 Oct
Eradication of poverty	17 Oct
United Nations	24 Oct
Development information	24 Oct
Disarmament (week)	24–30 Oct
Preventing the exploitation of the envi-	
ronment in war & armed conflict	6 Nov
Tolerance	16 Nov
Road traffic victims	
(3rd Sun in Nov)	18 Nov
Africa industrialization	20 Nov
Children	20 Nov
Television	21 Nov
Elimination of violence	
against women	25 Nov
Palestinian people	29 Nov
AIDS	1 Dec
Abolition of slavery	2 Dec
Disabled persons	3 Dec
Volunteer day for economic	
& social development	5 Dec
Civil aviation	7 Dec
Human rights	10 Dec
Mountain	11 Dec
Migrants	18 Dec
South–South cooperation	19 Dec
Human solidarity	20 Dec

DISMAL DAYS

From medieval times certain days, collectively called *dies mali*, or 'evil days', were held to be unwise for starting any enterprise. Thus the word dismal was originally a noun referring to these unlucky days, only later taking on its descriptive sense of causing gloom. The most common accounts list two days per month:

January	1	25	April	10	20	July		13	22	October		3	22
February	4	26	May		3	25	August		1	30	November	5	28
March	1	28	June	10	16	September		3	21	December	7	22

FRIDAY THE 13TH

Friday the 13th is the coincidence of two events in themselves associated with ill fortune. Friday, the day on which Adam fell and Christ was crucified, is thought to be the least lucky of the weekdays: 'Sneeze on a Friday, sneeze for sorrow'; 'Cut your nails on a Friday, cut them for woe.' The number 13 is prime, and is the number of men who sat at the Last Supper. According to *The Da Vinci Code*, the decimation of the Knights Templar under King Philip IV of France occurred on Friday, 13 October 1307.

Friday the 13ths occur on average once every 213 days, but they are not evenly distributed; some years have one, some two and some three. The table below repeats every 28 years from 1901 to 2099. The 13th is (marginally) more likely to be a Friday than any other day of the week.

	Years			*Fri 13th in*				*Years*			*Fri 13th in*		
2001	2007	2018		Apr	Jul		2009	2015	2026	Feb	Mar	Nov
2002	2013	2019	2024	Sep	Dec		2010	2021	2027	Aug		
2003	2008	2014	2025	Jun			2012			Jan	Apr	Jul
2004				Feb	Aug		2020			Mar	Nov	
2005	2011	2016	2022	May			2028			Oct		
2006	2017	2023		Jan	Oct							

MONDAYS

While all Mondays are associated with questionable fortune, the first Mondays in April and August and the last in December (in 2007, 2 Apr, 6 Aug and 31 Dec) are particularly inauspicious:

> Anyone who lets blood of man or beast on them will not last the week, anyone who accepts a drink, or eats goose, will die within the fortnight, and any child, male or female, born on them will come to a bad end.
>
> B. Blackburn & L. Holford-Strevens (see p. 131)

DOG DAYS

Dog days, generally accepted to be from 3 July to 11 August, correspond to the hottest days of the year (though not the longest, see p. 152). In ancient times they were thought to result from the coincidence of the rising and setting of the sun and the star Sirius, the major star of the constellation Canis Major (Big Dog). Sirius is the brightest of the stars seen from Earth, and the combined heat of it and the sun was thought to be the cause of this sweltering period. It is traditional to avoid blood-letting and medical treatment and to abstain from women. As *Poor Robin* (1675) indicates, not everyone agrees with the latter:

> Husband give me my due, the woman saies;
> The man replies, 'Tis naught Wife these Dog daies;
> But she rejoins, Let women have their rights,
> Though there be Dog daies, there are no Dog nights.

12:34 5-6-7 AND 7-7-7

The time and date form the consecutive sequence $1, 2, \ldots, 7$ at 12:34 a.m. on 5 June 2007. The sequence $1, 2, \ldots, 8$ will appear in 2078, and $1, 2, \ldots, 9$ 711 years after that. ❧ The date 7 July 2007 is as auspicious as 6 June 2006 is inauspicious. The latter date, written in shorthand, gives the Number of the Beast described in the Book of Revelation, 6-6-6. It is the first such number occurring after the prophecy of the creation of Israel was fulfilled in 1948. The date 7-7-7, on the other hand, is composed wholly of the sacred number 7. Seven is the day on which God rests after creating the world in Genesis, and it is the number of sacraments in the Catholic Church. Furthermore, the number 777 is a Harshad number, which means that it is divisible by the sum of its digits: $777 / (7 + 7 + 7) = 37$.

BERRY DAY

❧ *For geeks* The date 27-1-2007 is paradoxical in the following way. Any date can be expressed in words by a fixed number of syllables. For instance, 6-03-2002 requires eight: 'sixth of March, two thousand and two'. Similarly, 15-07-04 requires ten syllables. Restricting ourselves to the third millennium, we find that 27-1-2007 is the 'first date not nameable in under fifteen syllables' (it requires fifteen). But we have just defined it, in fourteen syllables. Known as Berry's paradox, it also applies to the integer 111,777, which is the 'least positive number not nameable in under nineteen syllables'. These are not the only examples, but the implications for mathematics have been serious, and the paradox is key to George Boolos's alternate proof of the Gödel Incompleteness Theorem.

Below are sports highlights for 2007. Events which were not scheduled by July 2006 are not included. Keep in mind that the dates below are subject to change, especially those set far in advance. For Cricket and Rugby World Cup details, see pp. 170–171.

tba = to be announced   tbc = to be confirmed

American football	*in 2007*
American Football Conference Championship Game, *tba, US*	21 Jan
National Football Conference Championship Game, *tba, US*	21 Jan
Super Bowl XLI (AFC *v.* NFC champions), *Miami Gardens, FL, US*	4 Feb
Athletics	
European Athletics Indoor Championships, *Birmingham*	2–4 Mar
World Cross Country Championships, *Mombasa, Kenya*	24 Mar
European Athletics Cup, *Munich, Germany*	23–24 Jun
World Championships in Athletics, *Osaka, Japan*	24 Aug–2 Sep
European Cross Country Championships, *Toro, Spain*	9 Dec
Badminton	
All England Badminton Championships, *Birmingham*	6–11 Mar
Sudirman Cup, *Glasgow*	10–17 Jun
Basketball	
NBA All-Star Game, *Las Vegas, NV, US*	16–18 Feb
NCAA Basketball Final Four, *Atlanta, GA, US*	31 Mar–2 Apr
Euroleague Basketball Final Four, *Athens, Greece*	4–6 May
Cricket	
The Ashes (England *v.* Australia), *Australia*	23 Nov 2006–6 Jan
1st Test Match, *Brisbane*	23–27 Nov 2006
2nd Test Match, *Adelaide*	1–5 Dec 2006
3rd Test Match, *Perth*	14–18 Dec 2006
4th Test Match, *Melbourne*	26–30 Dec 2006
5th Test Match, *Sydney*	2–6 Jan
Twenty20 Match (Australia *v.* England), *Sydney, Australia*	9 Jan
Triangular One Day International Series (Australia, England, New Zealand), *Australia*	12 Jan–13 Feb
Cricket World Cup, *West Indies* (see p. 170)	11 Mar–28 Apr
Cycling	
Track World Cup, 3rd round, *Los Angeles, CA, US*	19–21 Jan
Track World Cup, 4th round, *Manchester*	23–25 Feb
Track World Championships, *Palma de Mallorca, Spain*	29 Mar–1 Apr
Tour de France, *Grand Départ in London; France*	7–29 Jul
Mountain Bike World Championships, *Fort William, Inverness-shire*	3–9 Sep
Road World Championships, *Stuttgart, Germany*	26–30 Sep
Field hockey	
European Nations Championship, *Manchester*	18–26 Aug
Champions Trophy, *Lahore, Pakistan*	1–9 Dec

Flat racing

2000 Guineas, *Newmarket, Suffolk*	5 May
1000 Guineas, *Newmarket, Suffolk*	6 May
The Oaks, *Epsom Downs, Surrey*	1 Jun
The Derby, *Epsom Downs, Surrey*	2 Jun
Gold Cup, *Ascot, Berkshire*	21 Jun
Eclipse, *Sandown Park, Surrey*	7 Jul
King George VI and Queen Elizabeth Diamond, *Ascot, Berkshire*	28 Jul
St Leger, *Doncaster, Yorkshire*	15 Sep
Champion, *Newmarket, Suffolk*	20 Oct

Football

UEFA Cup Final, *Glasgow*	16 May
FA Cup Final, *London*	19 May
European Champions' League Final, *Athens, Greece*	23 May
FIFA U-20 World Cup, *Canada*	30 Jun–22 Jul

Games

XXIII Winter Universiade, *Torino, Italy* — 17–27 Jan
  Biannual competition for university athletes (World University Games).
XV Pan American Games, *Rio de Janeiro, Brazil* — 13–29 Jul
  Quadrennial competition for nations of the Americas.
XXIV Summer Universiade, *Bangkok, Thailand* — 8-18 Aug
  15 Summer sports categories; 11 Winter sports categories (above).
Special Olympics World Summer Games, *Shanghai, China* — 2–11 Oct
  Quadrennial competition for people with learning disabilities.

Golf

US Masters, *Augusta, GA, US*	2–8 Apr
US Open, *Oakmont, PA, US*	14–17 Jun
British Open, *Carnoustie, Angus*	19–22 Jul
US PGA Championship, *Tulsa, OK, US*	9–12 Aug
Presidents Cup, *Montreal, Canada*	24–30 Sep

Ice hockey

NHL All-Star Game, *Dallas, TX, US*	24 Jan
Men's World Championship, *Moscow, Russia*	Apr 27–May 13

Marathons

Boston Marathon, *Boston, MA, US*	16 Apr
London Marathon, *London*	22 Apr
Berlin Marathon, *Berlin, Germany*	30 Sep
Chicago Marathon, *Chicago, IL, US*	7 Oct
New York City Marathon, *New York City, NY, US*	4 Nov

Motor racing

Indianapolis 500, *Speedway, IN, US*	27 May
British Grand Prix, *Silverstone Circuit, Northamptonshire*	tba Jun
Goodwood Festival of Speed, *Goodwood House, West Sussex*	tbc 6–8 Jul
London to Brighton Veteran Car Run, *Hyde Park, London*	4 Nov

National hunt

Champion Hurdle, *Cheltenham, Gloucestershire*	13 Mar
Queen Mother Champion, *Cheltenham, Gloucestershire*	14 Mar
Cheltenham Gold Cup, *Cheltenham, Gloucestershire*	16 Mar
Grand National, *Aintree, Liverpool*	14 Apr
Hennessy Gold Cup, *Newbury, Berkshire*	1 Dec
King George VI, *Kempton Park, Surrey*	26 Dec

Rowing

Head of the River Race (eights), *Mortlake to Putney, River Thames*	31 Mar
The Boat Race, *Putney to Mortlake, River Thames*	7 Apr
Rowing World Cup	
Stage I, *Linz, Austria*	1–3 Jun
Stage II, *Amsterdam, Netherlands*	22–24 Jun
Stage III, *Lucerne, Switzerland*	13–15 Jul
Henley Royal Regatta, *Henley-on-Thames, Oxfordshire*	4–8 Jul
World Rowing Championships, *Munich, Germany*	26 Aug–2 Sep
Head of the River Fours, *Mortlake to Putney, River Thames*	3 Nov

Rugby union

The Varsity Match, *Twickenham, Middlesex*	12 Dec 2006
Six Nations Championship	3 Feb–17 Mar

E=England F=France IR=Ireland IT=Italy S=Scotland W=Wales

IT *v.* F, *Stadio Flaminio, IT*	3 Feb	F *v.* W, *Stade de France, F*	24 Feb
E *v.* S, *Twickenham, E*	3 Feb	S *v.* IR, *Murrayfield, S*	10 Mar
W *v.* IR, *Millen. Stadium, W*	4 Feb	IT *v.* W, *Stadio Flaminio, IT*	10 Mar
E *v.* IT, *Twickenham, E*	10 Feb	E *v.* F, *Twickenham, E*	11 Mar
S *v.* W, *Murrayfield, S*	10 Feb	IT *v.* IR, *Stadio Flaminio, IT*	17 Mar
IR *v.* F, *Croke Park, IR*	11 Feb	F *v.* S, *Stade de France, F*	17 Mar
S *v.* IT, *Murrayfield, S*	24 Feb	W *v.* E, *Millen. Stadium, W*	17 Mar
IR *v.* E, *Croke Park, IR*	24 Feb		

Guinness Premiership Final, *Twickenham, Middlesex*	12/13 May
Heineken Cup Final, *Twickenham, Middlesex*	19/20 May
World Cup, *France; Edinburgh; Cardiff* (see p. 171)	7 Sep–20 Oct

Sailing

America's Cup, *Valencia, Spain*	23 Jun–7 Jul
World Championships, *Cascais, Portugal*	27 Jun–12 Jul
Cowes Week, *Cowes, Isle of Wight*	4–11 Aug
World Team Championships, *Truro, Cornwall*	20–25 Aug

Snooker

The Masters, *tba*	tbc 14–21 Jan
Malta Cup, *Portomaso, Malta*	29 Jan–4 Feb
Welsh Open, *tba*	11–18 Feb
China Open, *Beijing, China*	25 Mar–1 Apr
World Championship, *Sheffield*	21 Apr–7 May

Squash

National Championships, *Manchester* — 11–18 Feb

Men's World Open Championship, *Bermuda* — 27 Nov–8 Dec

Swimming

12th FINA World Championships, *Melbourne, Australia* — 17 Mar–1 Apr

    Synchronised Swimming — 17–24 Mar

    Diving — 18–25 Mar

    Open Water Swimming — 18–25 Mar

    Water Polo — 19 Mar–1 Apr

    Swimming — 25 Mar–1 Apr

Table tennis

World Championships, *Zagreb, Croatia* — 21–27 May

Men's World Cup, *Barcelona, Spain* — 12–14 Oct

Tennis

Australian Open, *Melbourne, Australia* — 15–28 Jan

French Open, *Paris, France* — 27 May–10 Jun

Queen's Club Championships, *London* — 11–17 Jun

Marsh Classic, *London* — 19–23 Jun

Wimbledon Championships, *Wimbledon, London* — 25 Jun–8 Jul

US Open, *New York City, NY, US* — tbc 27 Aug–9 Sep

Winter sports

Cresta Run University Week, *St Moritz, Switzerland* — 2–4 Jan

Alpine World Ski Championships, *Åre, Sweden* — 3–18 Feb

Iditarod Trail Sled Dog Race, *AK, US* — 3–18 March

World Men's Curling Championship, *Edmonton, Canada* — 31 Mar–8 Apr

Other

World Professional Darts Championship, *Frimley Green, Surrey* — 7–14 Jan

Bowls World Indoor Championship, *Norfolk* — 8–28 Jan

Arnold Classic (bodybuilding), *Columbus, OH, US* — 2–4 Mar

WWE WrestleMania 23, *Ford Field, Detroit, MI, US* — 1 Apr

World Amateur Boxing Championships, *Moscow, Russia* — tba Jul

Archery World Outdoor Championships, *Leipzig, Germany* — 5–15 Jul

World Netball Championships, *Suva, Fiji* — 8–21 Jul

Major League Baseball All-Star Game, *San Francisco, CA, US* — 10 Jul

National Rifle Association Imperial Meeting, *Bisley, Surrey* — 14–28 Jul

Triathlon World Championships, *Hamburg, Germany* — 29 Aug–2 Sep

Sports customs

Olney Pancake Race, *Olney, Milton Keynes* — 20 Feb

Scoring the Hales (Shrovetide Football), *Alnwick, Northumberland* — 20 Feb

Cheese Rolling, *Cooper's Hill, Gloucestershire* — 28 May

World Conker Championships, *Ashton, Northamptonshire* — 14 Oct

Tar Barrel Rolling, *Ottery St Mary, Devon* — 5 Nov

Peter Pan Cup Swimming Race, *Serpentine, Hyde Park, London* — 25 Dec

2007 CRICKET WORLD CUP

The Cricket World Cup is the international championship for one-day cricket and takes place every four years. The 9th World Cup runs from 11 March to 28 April and is hosted by the West Indies. Previous Cups have been won by Australia (thrice) and the West Indies (twice) but never by any of the home nations. The opening ceremony will be in Jamaica on 11 March. After each match is a reserve day, to be used in the case of inclement weather. This year the contest is between 16 nations:

Australia	England	New Zealand	Sri Lanka
Bangladesh	India	Pakistan	The Netherlands
Bermuda	Ireland	Scotland	West Indies
Canada	Kenya	South Africa	Zimbabwe

Group stage

Group A (St Kitts)	Mar	Group C (St Lucia)	Mar
Australia *v.* Scotland	14	Kenya *v.* Canada	14
South Africa *v.* The Netherlands	16	England *v.* New Zealand	16
Australia *v.* The Netherlands	18	England *v.* Canada	18
South Africa *v.* Scotland	20	New Zealand *v.* Kenya	20
Scotland *v.* The Netherlands	22	New Zealand *v.* Canada	22
Australia *v.* South Africa	24	England *v.* Kenya	24

Group B (Trinidad and Tobago)	Mar	Group D (Jamaica)	Mar
Sri Lanka *v.* Bermuda	15	West Indies *v.* Pakistan	13
India *v.* Bangladesh	17	Zimbabwe *v.* Ireland	15
India *v.* Bermuda	19	Pakistan *v.* Ireland	17
Sri Lanka *v.* Bangladesh	21	West Indies *v.* Zimbabwe	19
India *v.* Sri Lanka	23	Zimbabwe *v.* Pakistan	21
Bermuda *v.* Bangladesh	25	West Indies *v.* Ireland	23

Super Eight

Antigua & Barbuda		Guyana		Grenada		Barbados	
D2 *v.* A1	27 Mar	A2 *v.* B1	28 Mar	D2 *v.* A2	10 Apr	C2 *v.* B2	11 Apr
D2 *v.* C1	29 Mar	D1 *v.* C2	30 Mar	B1 *v.* C1	12 Apr	A1 *v.* D1	13 Apr
A1 *v.* B2	31 Mar	D2 *v.* B1	1 Apr	A2 *v.* C1	14 Apr	B2 *v.* D1	15 Apr
B2 *v.* C1	2 Apr	D1 *v.* A2	3 Apr	A1 *v.* B1	16 Apr	A2 *v.* C2	17 Apr
C2 *v.* B1	4 Apr	B2 *v.* A2	7 Apr	D1 *v.* B1	18 Apr	D2 *v.* B2	19 Apr
A1 *v.* C2	8 Apr	D1 *v.* C1	9 Apr	A1 *v.* C1	20 Apr	D2 *v.* C2	21 Apr

Semi-finals			Final	
Jamaica,	2nd *v.* 3rd	24 Apr	Barbados	28 Apr
St Lucia,	1st *v.* 4th	25 Apr		

2007 RUGBY UNION WORLD CUP

The Rugby World Cup is the premier international rugby championship. It takes place every four years; the 6th Cup will be in France from 7 September to 20 October. It consists of 20 nations: the eight quarter-finalists of the 2003 World Cup and 12 nations selected from qualifying series. (In July 2006, these included Samoa and Fiji and 10 teams restricted to the regions below.) Of the 48 matches, four will be in Cardiff and two in Edinburgh. The participating nations are:

Australia	New Zealand	Africa	Europe1
England	Samoa	Americas1	Europe2
Fiji	Scotland	Americas2	Europe3
France	South Africa	Americas3	Repechage1 (Rep1)
Ireland	Wales	Asia	Repechage2 (Rep2)

Group stage

Group A	Sep	Group C	Sep
England v. Americas3 (*Lens*)	8	N. Zealand v. Europe1 (*Marseille*)	8
S. Africa v. Samoa (*Paris*)	9	Scotland v. Rep1 (*St Etienne*)	9
Americas3 v. Rep2 (*Montpellier*)	12	Europe1 v. Europe2 (*Marseille*)	12
England v. S. Africa (*St Denis*)	14	N. Zealand v. Rep1 (*Lyon*)	15
Samoa v. Rep2 (*Montpellier*)	16	Scotland v. Europe2 (*Edinburgh*)	18
S. Africa v. Rep2 (*Lens*)	22	Europe1 v. Rep1 (*Paris*)	19
England v. Samoa (*Nantes*)	22	Scotland v. N. Zealand (*Edinburgh*)	23
Samoa v. Americas3 (*St Etienne*)	26	Europe2 v. Rep1 (*Toulouse*)	25
England v. Rep2 (*Paris*)	28	Scotland v. Europe1 (*St Etienne*)	29
S. Africa v. Americas3 (*Montpellier*)	30	N. Zealand v. Europe2 (*Toulouse*)	29

Group B	Sep	Group D	Sep
Australia v. Asia (*Lyon*)	8	France v. Americas1 (*St Denis*)	7
Wales v. Americas2 (*Nantes*)	9	Ireland v. Africa (*Bordeaux*)	9
Asia v. Fiji (*Toulouse*)	12	Americas1 v. Europe3 (*Lyon*)	11
Wales v. Australia (*Cardiff*)	15	Ireland v. Europe3 (*Bordeaux*)	15
Fiji v. Americas2 (*Cardiff*)	16	France v. Africa (*Toulouse*)	16
Wales v. Asia (*Cardiff*)	20	France v. Ireland (*St Denis*)	21
Australia v. Fiji (*Montpellier*)	23	Americas1 v. Africa (*Marseille*)	22
Americas2 v. Asia (*Bordeaux*)	25	Europe3 v. Africa (*Lens*)	26
Australia v. Americas2 (*Bordeaux*)	29	France v. Europe3 (*Marseille*)	30
Wales v. Fiji (*Nantes*)	29	Ireland v. Americas1 (*Paris*)	30

Quarter-finals

Q1: 1st B v. 2nd A (*Marseille*)	6 Oct	Q3: 1st A v. 2nd B (*Marseille*)	7 Oct
Q2: 1st C v. 2nd D (*Cardiff*)	6 Oct	Q4: 1st D v. 2nd C (*St Denis*)	7 Oct

Semi-finals · Finals

Semi-finals		Finals	
S1: 1st Q1 v. 1st Q2 (*St Denis*)	13 Oct	F1: 2nd S1 v. 2nd S2 (*Paris*)	19 Oct
S2: 1st Q3 v. 1st Q4 (*St Denis*)	14 Oct	F2: 1st S1 v. 1st S2 (*St Denis*)	20 Oct

INDEX

COLOPHON

This book was designed and typeset by the author in LaTeX, the typesetting program created by Donald Knuth. Figures were made with xfig and gnuplot.

Proportion of text block	1.618:1	Characters per line	70
Typeface	Palatino	Number of fonts (inc. sizes)	107
Principal text size	8.5 pt	Number of chapters	9
Displayed text size	7.1 pt	Number of sections (❦)	89
Lines per page	42	Number of index entries	755

Palatino was designed by Hermann Zapf in 1948. Based on the fonts of the Italian Renaissance, it is one of the most admired of the neo-humanist typefaces. The proportion of the text block is ϕ:1, where the Golden ratio $\phi = (\sqrt{5} + 1)/2$ (p. 5). It can be derived from the square and circle (p. 137) as well as the regular pentagon.

The author thanks Sebastian Ahnert, Jocelyn Baines, Thomas Hodgkinson, Jean Meiring, Julia Rafflenbeul, Margaret Strinati and Katherine Williams.